DATE DUE

D1405391

INDULGENCE

Also by Paul Richardson

Not Part of the Package: A Year in Ibiza
Our Lady of the Sewers and Other Adventures in Deep Spain
Cornucopia: A Gastronomic Tour of Britain

INDULGENCE:
AROUND THE WORLD IN SEARCH OF CHOCOLATE

Paul Richardson

LITTLE, BROWN

A *Little, Brown* Book

First published in Great Britain in 2003 by Little, Brown

Copyright © 2003 Paul Richardson

Illustrations copyright © Flying Fish

The moral right of the author has been asserted.

A CIP catalogue record for this book
is available from the British Library.

ISBN 0 316 86095 6

Typeset in Berling by M Rules
Printed and bound in Great Britain
by Clays Ltd, St Ives plc

Little, Brown
An imprint of
Time Warner Books UK
Brettenham House
Lancaster Place
London WC2E 7EN

www.TimeWarnerBooks.co.uk

CONTENTS

INDULGENCE

DEPARTURES

Proust's grandmother gave him sponge cakes and lime-scented tea. My grandmother was much more generous. Once a week I would cycle up to her house and spend the afternoon weeding her lawn. When I had finished she would give me a proper tea, then send me home with my favourite thing in the world: a box of Lindt Milk Chocolate Animals.

I was not to eat them right away, she enjoined, but, in true Protestant fashion, to 'make them last'. This was an easy promise to keep, since it was one I had already made to myself. I knew that the animals were too special to be scoffed all at once. Their packaging, each bear and squirrel and puppy accommodated in its own moulded plastic compartment, strongly intimated as much. But when its moment came, this was an experience I came to value for its multiple sensory excitements: the secret woodland rustle of the plastic as I carefully removed the cardboard outer sheath; the curves and angles of the animals' anthropomorphoid bodies against my lips and palate; the velvet creaminess of the chocolate and its

dark heart of indefinable flavours, a mixture of caramel, but-
termilk and smoke.

For me as a child, as for many children of the modern age,
food and eating were problematic issues. There was a ruthless
intolerance about my tastes. I disliked fish with bones and skin,
unless its true nature was concealed in orange crumbs, and
loathed anything that had come into contact, however briefly,
with garlic. Jelly-like textures, from aspic to tapioca, made me
physically ill – except for fruit jellies, oddly, which I lusted
after. Green vegetables were the work of the devil. Bitterness in
anything was repugnant; sweetness made almost anything
acceptable.

It's a curious fact that the act of eating does not bring pleasure to children as much or as often as it does to adults. Yet in
milk chocolate I found an endless source of satisfaction. It was
everything I wanted food to be, yet I had a thrilling sense that
in some way this was not really food at all. It was neither associated with mealtimes nor the moral structures imposed by
family life. The pleasures it offered took place in a separate
social space, unconditioned by routine or obligation. It was a
private ritual, a communion at which I was both celebrant and
high priest.

Familiarity breeds, if not contempt, then a much diminished
sense of significance – and, as we shall see, this is the history of
chocolate in a nutshell. With the years, my relationship with
chocolate lost its ceremonial importance and settled into the
comfortable intimacy of the day-to-day. In my shared kitchen at
university the fridge door was permanently stocked with bars of
milk chocolate, to be snapped off cold in place of dessert or
passed round among friends as we smoked and drank late into
a Saturday night. As an idealistic, romanticising teenager, I
wanted to like dark chocolate but was secretly bothered by its
bitterness and astringency. Perhaps I didn't want flavours that
drew attention to themselves, when they ought to have been

selflessly caressing my senses. My main indulgence as I grew into manhood, in any case, was the opposite of minimalist bitter black chocolate – a chunky choc bar crammed with nuts and caramel and toffee and puffed rice, baroque in its artificial complexity, that I would peel and devour on the train from work, or stretched out on the sofa when I got home. These giant lumps of confectionery were initially glorious to eat, wholly substantial in a grotesque kind of way, but left me contaminated by feelings of nausea and guilt.

For most of my life I failed to think very deeply about the nature or provenance of the chocolate I ate, except occasionally to worry about whether it might aggravate my adolescent acne or (much later) accelerate the growth of a nascent paunch. Chocolate would always be there when you wanted it. Unlike other luxuries, this one was always within reach, whatever the place or hour. Always available; the cheapest of cheap thrills.

That was until a winter's day in early 2000, when something happened that set me thinking afresh. As Februarys in London go, it was one of the bleakest I could remember. The city was bereft of colour; the tree trunks in the parks were as slick and black as liquorice sticks. One dark and somnolent Sunday, I wrapped myself up in a big sheepskin coat and took the Underground to the Royal Botanic Gardens at Kew. It was a caprice I often permitted myself on a Sunday morning. In some vague and indefinable way I felt it to be a substitute for church – a chance to mingle with the spirits of the forest, to reestablish for a short while some kind of contact with Mother Nature, or simply to ponder the mysteries of existence while wandering aimlessly among the plants.

From the station I walked the chilly avenues of suburban south-west London. Planes screamed ceaselessly overhead, queuing up on the Heathrow flight path. I was the first visitor through the turnstile that morning, and for an hour or two had the exhilarating privilege of having the Gardens practically to myself. I made, as usual, for the glass cathedral of the Palm House, feeling myself drawn as if by a magnet, and pushed through a side door into a parallel universe, a world apart not only from the storm and stress of the metropolis, but from the monochrome misery of the English winter. For me it was not only a place for silent contemplation but for feelings of primitive awe and wonder. By its very existence and grandeur, it seemed to be offering a salutary reminder of mankind's incalculable debt to the plant kingdom.

The atmosphere was dripping and heavy with steam, charged with the energy of exuberant vegetal life, the combination of heat and moisture making the glass run with streams of condensation. Leaves and branches, fronds and filaments of a hundred shades of intense, shiny, deep and delicate green, brushed past me with faint whispers as I walked. The air smelt of wet turf and quietly rotting undergrowth.

I tiptoed among the towering behemoths. All were forest trees from the remaining jungles of the tropical belt. Their architecture of soaring columns and overarching canopies, their curious and eccentric habits, were the end results of a million years of continuous adaptation. The fishtail palm *Carysta rumpliana* of Papua New Guinea, its fanning leaves now clawing at the uppermost roof of the greenhouse, spends twenty-five years growing, then suddenly decides to flower, then dies, but takes its final revenge on the world with a fruit whose red juice itches and burns the flesh of any animal it touches. It is said of the sacred Bo tree (*Ficus religiosa*) that devout Hindus refuse to chop it down even if its roots are undermining the foundations of their house.

'All life depends on plants', a kind of motto for Kew Gardens, was the rubric on the label attached to every species. This is incontestably true. Yet there are plants we depend on absolutely, and plants we appreciate for the curious luxuries they bring, the unnecessary joys of human life. The tropical forest is especially rich in these bearers of gifts. Within a few yards of each other in the Palm House were banana, ebony, pawpaw and starfruit. In a far corner of the greenhouse an example of *Macadamia tetraphylla*, the macadamia nut tree, and another of *Canangium odoratum*, otherwise known as ylang-ylang, familiar from the florid language of high-class perfume advertisements, stood side by side.

But another species, of much greater consequence for the human species, had caught my attention. It was not among the tallest trees in the Palm House; there was nothing superficially eye-catching about it, no garish or evil-scented flowers, no trailing fronds, no poison-bearing prickles. It stood modestly in its miniature tropical forest, dwarfed by a gigantic palm tree *Attalea speciosa* which seemed determined to prevent as much light as possible from reaching its diminutive neighbour. It seemed to emanate an aura of tranquillity.

The leaves of this tree were large and glossy, elegantly narrow like those of the avocado or the chestnut, and hung heavily from the tips of the slender branches. These branches, in turn, jutted out at intervals from the trunk as if the tree had grown in phases: first a length of bare wood, then a fanning out of branches, and so on, level after level. The tree leaned out gracefully over the paved walkway that ran between the beds of plants. ('Unsuitable for narrow heels.') I gently touched the nearest leaf: it had a plasticky, delicately papery feel, like the pages of a glossy magazine.

My curiosity aroused, I peered more closely at the trunk with its smooth bark splotched with pale green and yellow lichen. All the way up it were tiny flowers, each a complex, infinitely delicate arrangement of petals and sepals and pistils, curling and interlaced and spiky, coloured white and pink and purple and the faintest yellow hue. These flowerlets emerged either singly, or in clumps of two or three, like miniature crocuses, from a series of blackish warty excrescences on the otherwise unruffled surface.

The tree had a striking scientific name: *Theobroma cacao*. *Theo* being Greek for god and *broma* for food, its family name meant literally 'god-food'. But it was more commonly known by a nickname which vividly expressed its significance to mankind. 'The chocolate tree' once grew wild in the depths of the Amazon rainforest, whence it was hauled out and put to work. It still flourishes only in a strip of territory running like a belt around the belly of the globe, between 18 degrees north and 15 degrees south of the Equator, and steadfastly refuses to grow anywhere else, unless in the 'virtual tropics' of a botanical garden like the one at Kew. In its natural state *Theobroma* depends for the pollination of its diminutive flowers on the services of a midge so small that it is almost invisible to the naked eye. Only 1 to 5 per cent of all flowers eventually produce fruit. And yet somehow the tree in front of me had managed to produce two miniature cacao pods. They hung from the trunk like two unripe lemons, coloured a delicate peppermint green.

I could only imagine the look of the ripened pods and their interior cargo of pips or seeds from which is conjured, by a deliriously complex industrial process, the substance we call chocolate. But I felt as I gazed at the tree an inexplicable sense of mild exhilaration, a buzz beneath the skin like the passing of a light electric charge. Close to the roots of this tree lay the roots of my childhood consolations, my adult cravings, and the peculiarly intense relationship millions of people around the world claim to have with *cioccolato*, *Schokolade*, *zsekolada*, *chocolaad* . . . I had never really considered the links between cacao and chocolate, between plant and product. All at once, however, the connection had been made for me. My appetite was whetted; my eyes had been opened.

For the next few months I haunted London's libraries, scouring them for every conceivable reference to chocolate, historical, agricultural, industrial, scientific, artistic, culinary or gastronomical. I pored over Aztec codices that clearly showed, though in hieroglyphic form, the crucial role that chocolate had played in the religion and economy of ancient Mexico. I compared colonial accounts of Mayan rituals in which cacao played its part, with contemporary anthropological reports suggesting that similar rituals may still take place in the remaining Maya tribes of Mexico's deep south. Despite its various manifestations, I came to see chocolate use as a continuum in which many of the same elements are present from one historical moment to another.

Curious patterns, and parallels and resonances, began to emerge. The methods of cacao production described by De Chélus, published in English in 1724, are reproduced almost exactly in Cadbury's 1989 research findings on the post-harvest process – the point being that very little about this process has changed in the interim. 'The Kernels thus laid in a heap, and cover'd close on all sides, do not fail to grow warm, by the Fermentation of their insensible Particles; and this is what they call Sweating in those Parts. They cover the Kernels Morning and Evening, and send the Negroes among them; who with their Feet and Hands turn them topsy turvy . . . They continue to do this for five Days at the end of which they have commonly sweat enough, which is discovered by their Colour, which grows a great deal deeper, and very ruddy. The more the Kernels sweat, the more they lose their Weight and Bitterness . . .'

The prehistory of *Theobroma cacao* has been mired in controversy for years; botanists have fired off endless rival theories illustrated with charts with arrows pointing this way and that, with shadings and colourings-in and family trees as graceful and strange as the cacao tree itself. Adding it all together and weighing it up, however, I began to see some measure of agreement emerging from all the confusion.

The species had its evolutionary birthplace in South America, and its new life as a cultivated crop in Central America and Mexico. In fact the entire history of cacao and of its major derivative, chocolate, could be seen in terms of a gradual movement from south to north, as more and more 'northerly' societies in progressively colder climates fell under the spell of the plant and product. One branch of the species, that which subsequently became known as *forastero*, grew as a wild tree in the jungles of the Amazon and upper Orinoco River. The other, the rare and highly prized *criollo* type, seems to have existed (also in a wild state) in the upper Andes, on the coast of what is now Ecuador, and, above all, in the area just south of Lake Maracaibo in present-day Venezuela, where its descendants are still cultivated in tiny quantities. From here, the theory goes, it was taken north by successive waves of tribal peoples and finally brought to the peak of its possibilities as a crop in Soconusco, southern Mexico, whence it was taken back south to the Caribbean coast by Spanish Capuchin friars in the seventeenth century.

From what we know of wild populations still existing in the tropical rainforests of Central and South America, 'prehistoric' cacao would have grown four or five times the size of its domesticated cousin. The wild fruit would have been more bitter and astringent to taste even than the cultivated kind, which is almost inedible to modern palates without adding at least a little sugar. And there would have been very much less fruit on the tree, for, as Allen Young explains in his natural history of the species, *The Chocolate Tree* (1994), in its wild state cacao puts less energy into sexual reproduction (flowers, pods, seeds) and more into vegetative asexual reproduction between clumps, with young shoots becoming new trees. Evidently *Theobroma cacao* has inherited something of this primitive sexual reluctance. How such a picky, shy and conservative species, like the girl with the Alice band in the corner of the school disco, was persuaded on to the dance floor to become one of the developing world's most significant crops, is one of the vegetable kingdom's greatest success stories.

But the story of cacao and the story of chocolate are two sides of a very large and valuable coin. From an early stage in the history of each, one begins to see the preoccupations that have plagued us ever since. Was chocolate nourishing? Did it therefore 'break the fast' (a major bone of contention among seventeenth-century clerics)? Was it addictive? Did it give you acne? Was it actually a food at all? Reporters from the conquest of New Spain took note of indigenous customs regarding cacao, and were impressed and puzzled in equal measure. Even when the exotic drink became the rage in Europe, the jury was out on whether it was healthy or harmful. Various commentators noted the energetic qualities of the drink. When drunk in the morning, according to a mid-seventeenth-century Italian authority, chocolate 'comforts the stomach and aids digestion'. 'Persons who have the stomach exhausted and enfeebled by colic and diarrhea, wind, and copious evacuations, find perfectly good the usage of this drink' claimed Dufour in 1808, who warned, however, against the tendency of chocolate to produce '*des boutons sur le visage*'. Controversy raged. Chocolate was sleep-inducing. Or was it 'reviving'? It was fattening. Or did it in fact have the opposite effect? Fast forward to the year 2001, and we find Jeffrey Steingarten writing, in *American Vogue*, the following: 'Over the years we have all heard many claims about chocolate – that it gives us migraines and acne, that it contains the same chemical that circulates through our brains when we fall in love, that it is full of saturated fat to clog our arteries, that women regularly treat their PMS with chocolate, that eating chocolate kills dogs and horses, that chocolate is the Prozac of candy. More recently, the positive claims have escalated. Now chocolate is supposed to be good for our hearts; it's even said to decrease the risk of cancer.' *Plus ça change* . . .

Little by little, as I read and researched and interviewed, I came to understand the elemental binomial division between cacao and chocolate, between producing and consuming societies. In the library of the International Cocoa Organisation, hub of the chocolate trade in its widest sense, I discovered the completeness and rigour of that division, which pits north against south, First World against Third, and cold countries against hot. To all intents and purposes, cacao production is small scale and traditional, where cacao processing is large scale and industrial. In any given country there is an inverse relation, unique for an edible commodity, between the amount of cacao produced and the amount of chocolate consumed. The average Austrian eats just over 4kg a head per year, the Dane 4.436kg, and the Belgian and Luxembourgeois almost 6kg. Way down in the Ivory Coast, the world's leading cacao producer by a large margin, consumption of chocolate is just 0.488kg per head per year. In Indonesia, the second biggest producer, the figure is 0.042kg. That is less than half a gram – think of it, in British choc-gobbling terms, as the tiniest nibble of Milky Way, or a single Malteser for every 365 days.

Plainly, not all about the food of the gods is sweetness and delight. It does not take a genius to discover that the business end of the chocolate industry is beset by serious agricultural and economic problems. Tropical agriculture has traditionally respected the delicate nature of the cacao tree, which thrives in a mixed forest environment and needs for its health the shade of much taller canopy trees. 'The cacao tree is tied ecologically to the rain forest', as Allen Young puts it. When the great botanist Alexander von Humboldt visited the Venezuelan interior in 1884, he wrote of newly created cacao plantations enclosed by rainforest: 'They become there the more productive, as the lands, newly cleared and surrounded by forests, are in contact with an atmosphere more damp, more stagnant, and more loaded with mephitic exhalations.' As traditional cultivation methods inexorably give way to intensive systems, disease has become rampant. Technical manuals on the rearing of cacao make the tree sound like a delicate specimen indeed. Diseases such as pod rot, dieback, swollen shoot virus, ceratocystis wilt, and the terrible 'witches' broom', for which the only cure is to destroy the tree and burn its roots, are estimated to account for the loss of between 25 and 40 per cent of the world crop.

As the geography of chocolate took shape in my mind, I began to plan a series of journeys that would take me from the steamy cacao plantations of the equatorial zone to the workshops of Europe's chocolate artisans. I would begin at the beginning, in the cacao fields of Soconusco in tropical Mexico, hard by the Guatemalan border, whence first the Mayas, then the Mexican civilisations of the north, imported their precious cacao. From there I might move south to Venezuela, cradle of the cacao trade in the eighteenth century and still the world's greatest producer of so-called 'fine and flavour' cacao varieties. From Caracas there were fine excursions to be made, along the Caribbean coast to the villages of Choroní and Ocumare, where the descendants of Sudanese slaves still work the plantations just as their forefathers did, and to the remote hamlet of Chuao – the Montrachet of chocolate, which still attracts the great chocolatiers of France and Italy to fight over infinitesimal amounts of the finest *criollo* cacao in the world.

I might be travelling for years and still have only nibbled, so to speak, at the surface of the subject. From Venezuela the trail might go south to Brazil, for a century or more the world's major supplier of cacao and still the largest producer in the

Americas, with an area the size of the Netherlands under cultivation. It was here that the rot set in. Already in the 1930s
inferior *forastero* cacaos were being grown on a massive scale,
with a workforce so downtrodden and underpaid that it virtually amounted to slave labour. Cacao and suffering have often
gone hand in hand. Conditions on a plantation in the Ilhéus
region of Bahia were graphically described in a series of novels
by Jorge Amado (notably *Cacau*, 1934), who summed up his
themes as 'money, cacao and death'.

So much for the cacao lands, historical heartland of chocolate but no longer an important topos of its consumption. That
dubious honour passed in the sixteenth century to Europe –
initially to Spain, which for fifty years had a virtual monopoly
on the cacao trade. The Madrid of 1772 had no fewer than 150
chocolate grinders, and today a night out in Madrid still classi-
cally ends with a mug of thick dark sweet chocolate and a
length of crisp fried *churros* for dunking. When Anne of Austria,
who had grown up in Madrid and loved chocolate, married
Louis XIII, the fashion spread to France. The grand tour might,
then, take in a pilgrimage to Paris, proud possessor of the most
sophisticated chocolate culture in the world, where half a
dozen of the greatest chocolatiers of our time are to be found
poring like alchemists over their rare and fantastical and, sometimes, wildly pretentious creations.

From France to Italy, Holland, Germany, England . . . All
have retained their chocolate traditions and their fine manufacturers. Some, like Cadbury in Britain and Hershey in the
United States, have valuable historical claims to fame. But I
would need above all, for reasons of my own, to make the pilgrimage to the house of Lindt & Sprüngli in Kilchberg,
Switzerland. It was Rodolphe Lindt (1855–1909), after all, who
revolutionised the world of chocolate with his conching
machine, enabling the cacao particles to be ground into infinitesimal fineness, creating the meltingly smooth and luscious

texture that first got me hooked on chocolate as a child. Every piece of written history is also, in a sense, the history of the writer. So it went without saying that the story of humankind's relationship with chocolate, with its peculiar episodes of passion and piety laced with violence, misery and exploitation, would be nourished by my own experience.

Before I embarked on this book I worried that the scare-mongers of the past might be right, and that massive exposure to chocolate might turn me into an overweight, greasy skinned, rotten-toothed wreck of my former self. In point of fact, like the employees of certain chocolate factories who are encouraged when they join the company to eat as much of the product as they are physically able, thereby putting them off it for life, I began to find I was actually eating less chocolate, not more. Little by little I found I was no longer attracted by mass-market UK choc bars. A Mars freak in my early youth, I underwent a radical change of opinion. The Mars bar was now to me as the Big Mac: a forbidden and disgusting pleasure. As for the Creme Egg, that *monstre sacré* of the British national diet, I can't remember when I last ate one.

I suppose I have become a chocolate snob. On my desk as I write, I have a half-eaten bar of Cluizel's 85 per cent cacao-mass Grand Amer, strong and pungent, and another of Gran Samán from El Rey, a Venezuelan firm that uses only native *criollo* beans for a wild and sexy bitterness with aromatic under-tones of flowers and tropical fruit. Another current favourite is Guanaja by Valrhona with its fabulous depth and clarity of flavour. One thin square of this is enough to send my tastebuds into ecstasy, so I tend to reserve it for personal rituals of partic-ular solemnity. And there are few better examples of modern *chocolaterie* than Chantal Coady's Rococo bars, currently racked up like paperbacks along my desk, ready to bewitch me with their ethereal flavourings of cardamom, Earl Grey tea, black pepper and sea salt. Chantal's fine inventions represent a movement away from the sweet sickly fattiness of industrial chocolate, towards a very much older and wiser tradition.

In one respect at least, however, my tastes haven't changed. I would still sell my soul, if not my granny, for a Lindt Milk Chocolate Animal.

PART ONE

BEFORE THE CONQUEST

Back to the roots in Mexico,
ancient and modern

Not many tourists get to Tapachula, unless they are following the beaten Lonely Planet track from San Cristobal de las Casas to Guatemala City. And when you finally get there yourself, it's easy to understand why.

On the way down through the mountains of Chiapas, the cloudforest mists gave way little by little to a rainforest lushness. The air con was full on inside my upmarket Mexican bus, but beyond the window you could sense the steaming, stinking heat. Raging muddy rivers swept down from the peaks, past stands of dark palm trees lit up by the neon brightness of tropical birds.

The cacao tree is a modest creature and prefers to blend into the background rather than hog the rainforest limelight. Yet it sometimes gives itself away by the unusual colour of its uppermost crown of new leaves, a delicate pink fading to palest canary yellow. Scanning the roadsides, I had almost convinced myself I was seeing them flash by, when my vision was distracted by the panorama now facing me as the bus hurtled southwards; the narrow strip of vaporous tropical plain, the Pacific Ocean beyond it a mind-full of kingfisher blue.

In the outskirts of the dirty, sticky, ugly town of Huixtla I saw the first signs: the signs that said SE COMPRA CACAO: 'we buy cacao'. And there beside the big coastal highway that leads to Tapachula, in among the dense patches of luxuriant growth, cheek by jowl with banana, breadfruit, mango and palm, in a crowded orgy of fertility, I found the final giveaways: the out-of-place autumnal colours, the wide shiny leaves that could almost be chestnut but not quite – the discreet signifiers of the presence of the chocolate tree.

Tapachula was a frontier city with an edgy, down-at-heel

frontier feel. I sat in the main square and polished off three beers in quick succession, feeling the heat recede before a tropical storm that filled the air with lightning. The marimba band on their podium in the plaza weren't put off and struck up a potpourri of cheery melodies under a sky that was double black from the charcoal-black storm clouds and the deepening dusk. The square was heaving with excited people; the volume of noise was prodigious.

And then it started to rain, and it continued to rain. It rained and rained for three nights and three days, and no one in Tapachula seemed in the least bit worried, surprised or perturbed.

It would hardly occur to anyone to thank the Spanish conquistadores for their brutal subjugation of the New World. But at least we can be grateful for their letters home, without which the full extent of their bravery, their cruelty and their ingenuity would never be known.

When the Franciscan scribe Fray Antonio de Ciudad Real visited the province of Soconusco in 1586, it was a sparsely populated rural area that had fallen, from a great height, on hard times: 'It used to be very rich and prosperous, and well populated by Indians and visited by Spanish traders, due to the great quantity of cacao produced there, and the great trade in it', he wrote. 'There are resident here seven clergymen who administer the Holy Sacraments and the Christian doctrine to the Indians; they are well sustained and treated by these, because although they are few, with the cacao they make a great business.'

The arrival of the Spanish had devastated Soconusco. At the time of its conquest by Pedro Alvarado in 1524, according to the great chronicler Bernal Diaz del Castillo the region supported a population of 15,000. By 1574 there were no more than 1800 Indians left. Many had succumbed to European diseases (the common cold is believed to have been one), to which they had no resistance. Those that survived were prevented by their new masters from spending much time in the care of their cacao trees, with the result that the trade declined, effectively depriving the natives of the benefits of their land.

For the earliest colonists the cacao from this region was of such estimable quality that the word 'soconusco' was sometimes used as a generic term, synonymous with the finest chocolate. But the reputation of Soconusco went before it. For the Aztecs, cacao grown in this Pacific coastal corridor, southernmost outpost of the empire, was an item of enormous worldly and spiritual glamour. For one of the great chocophile civilisations of all time it was also a vital commodity, laboriously transported in trading canoes through the maze of coastal canals and thence overland to the markets of Tenochtitlan, six hundred miles to the north.

We are talking about a strip of land not much more than twenty miles wide at any point, sandwiched between the ocean and a mountain range whose highest peak, the volcano Mt Tajumulco, soars to 4220m. As a cacao growing region this has everything going for it: high rainfall, permanently high temperatures, a prodigiously fertile volcanic soil and good drainage provided by the area's network of canals and ditches. None of this was lost on the Aztecs. But they were merely the inheritors of a culture and agriculture that stretched back into the shadowy world of the late pre-Classic Maya civilisation which had flowered along this stretch of coast more than two thousand years earlier. Precious little is known of these almost inconceivably ancient peoples, except that they were cultural second cousins of the Olmecs of the northern Gulf Coast, that they spoke Mixe-Zoquean – from which the word *kakawa* (think cacao, cocoa) probably derives – and that they made their capital city at Izapa, in the mosquito-ridden tropical coastal zone beside the border of modern-day Guatemala.

In the context of Mexico's dazzling archaeological heritage, the grand and beautiful sites of Chichén Itzá, Palenque, Bonampak, Toniná, Tulum, Teotihuacan, Monte Albán, Cacaxtla and a hundred others, Izapa is nothing to write home about, even if you could find a postcard of the place to write on. It is merely a modest collection of low-rise remains just off the main road that leads to the border. Whether the site is not signposted because so few tourists visit, or the other way around, I am not entirely sure. If my taxi driver hadn't known where to let me out, in any case, I might have missed it altogether.

The principal interest of Izapa for archaeologists of the pre-Classic Maya period is the massive stone slabs or stelae which punctuate the site and which are carved with all manner of enigmatic designs, made more inscrutable still by three millennia of rain and natural erosion. The cacao connection is clear enough from the visual imagery of these monuments. In slab number 10, for example, a stylised tree appears to have a cacao pod attached to one of its upper left-hand branches. Numbers 5 and 25 are palpable depictions of cacao trees, with their growth of pods on the branches themselves rather than among the leaves. But the main connection is not so much archaeological as actual. Izapa stands in the midst of a great cacao plantation. Branches overhang the temple walls; their fruit practically brushes the stones. Further away from the ruins, cacao and maize grow huggermugger in neighbouring plots, a clear survival of pre-Hispanic farming practice.

Beside the stone courtyard where the sacred Mayan ball game was played, I tried to imagine myself as a spectator at this strange fusion of basketball and Buddhism, or volleyball and voodoo. I sat for a while on a flat stone structure on three squat legs with a primitive head at one end, raised and attentive as if watching the game. I had no scientific basis for my just-add-water archaeological theory, but it looked to me as if this stone table might be a symbolically oversized version of the *metate*, used in Mexico from time immemorial to grind the cacao beans into a thick brown aromatic paste.

A man slouched towards me holding an old umbrella. In theory at least it was no longer raining, but the air was still thick with humidity and droplets seemed to be forming, like condensation, within the atmosphere itself. Don Diego Tercero was the caretaker at Izapa and had his own cacao plantation just over there, beyond the last of the pyramids. He had once been the lord of more than 50 hectares, but had begun slashing and burning the trees. He had ripped up 40 hectares already and planted maize and pasture instead.

'I've been buying bullocks, fattening them up and selling them on. There's no money in cacao these days. It's the cost of herbicide, fungicide, labour ... I can take this cacao up to Tutxla and get seven pesos, eight pesos a kilo for it, but it just doesn't add up,' he told me. It was the lament of the complaining farmer: a familiar sound from Gloucestershire to Guatemala.

'Cacao is over in Soconusco. Finished. *Muerto.*' He made a cutting movement in the air with his thick dark hands, as if chopping off a plant at the stalk.

The way things were going, an agricultural tradition stretching back three thousand years would soon be drawing to a close. At least in the meantime there would always be a job here for Diego Tercero, keeping an eye on the handful of tourists who for some reason best known to themselves still felt the urge to visit these somnolent remains.

Diego was a member of the Mam tribe that still inhabits the scattered villages along the Guatemalan border. The Mam are, or were until the virtual death of their tribal culture in the early 1990s, a Maya people with a strong interest in the possibilities of cacao, both as a drink and as a spiritual talisman. The beans are dried, roasted, milled with maize and/or peanuts and sugar and made into a drink with water or milk. As Ciudad Real wrote of the Soconusco Indians, 'the cacao is eaten toasted as if it were roasted chickpeas and is thus very savoury; they also make of it many kinds of very good drinks, some of them are drunk cold and others hot, and among these there is a very common one that they call chocolate, made of ground cacao and honey and hot water, with which they mix other spicy materials: this is a very healing and healthy beverage.'

I read aloud this quotation from my notebook, and Diego nodded.

'This is correct. We call it *la bebida*. The drink. My wife makes it.'

Diego took my two pesos entrance fee and pointed me in the right direction. While he slouched back to the tin shack that served as his headquarters, I slipped into the dripping darkness of the forest.

Into the cacao zone, the crucible of chocolate's pleasure principle. The silence was total, yet contained within it an incredible volume of sound: the white noise of regeneration and decay. The forest was still, yet fizzed and buzzed with life. Insects hummed around my head; strident bird calls echoed in the distance; at the edge of the woods a chicken scratched about among the undergrowth, getting back to her genetic roots as a wild forest fowl. Hummingbirds whirred and hovered about me, playfully investigating this clumsy intruder.

Lichen, ferns, moss. A thick mulch of dead leaves crackled underfoot. I stood rooted to the spot, my heart beating faster from the airless heat and the excitement of the moment. The cacao plantation blurs the boundaries between nature and culture, being a kind of tamed or domesticated version of the jungle. No other crop that I know of, except perhaps the grape vine, gives off such a powerful charge of mystery; no fruit tree, except perhaps the fig, is more intriguing in its peculiar sensual allure. It is a noble tree, but not a proud one. Yet its fascination is progressive; it draws you in. It can often have a moth-eaten look, a tearing or crinkling of the leaves, a bluish mould bespattering the trunk. The sheer strangeness of its architecture, the size and colour and gloss and heft of the fruits as they hang there motionless in the half-light, the tiny, infinitely delicate and complex flowers – all of it forces you to look more closely at a tree than you have, possibly, ever looked before.

There have been precious few literary approximations to cacao as a crop – surprisingly, in view of its romantic and enigmatic beauty. The great exceptions are the novels of Jorge Amado, with their agonisingly realistic vision of the harshness of life on the Brazilian plantations of the 1930s. But a more subtly haunting image of the tree *in situ* is provided by V. S. Naipaul in *The Middle Passage* (1981). As a child in Trinidad, where a fine cacao is still grown, Naipaul was as familiar with the peculiar landscape of this crop as Laurie Lee was with apple orchards: 'The cocoa woods were another thing. They were like the woods of fairy-tales, dark and shadowed and cool. The cocoa-pods, hanging by thick short stems, were like wax fruit in brilliant green and yellow and red and crimson and purple. Once, on a late afternoon drive to Tamana, I found the fields flooded. Out of the flat yellow water, which gurgled in the darkness, the black trunks of the stunted trees rose.'

I drifted in and out of the woods, unsure which was the more entrancing, trees or stones. Group B, as some Mexicologist had unimaginatively christened it, was a motley collection of remains that, lying at some distance from group A, had not yet been properly excavated. Here the woods and ruins intermingled in a promiscuous embrace. In the half-darkness I stumbled – literally stumbled and stubbed my toe – on a stone stela, submerged as if by a stagnant lake in the black mulch of the forest floor. Scratching away the compost of curling cacao leaves revealed a stumpy head, perhaps meant to resemble a snake, with a gaping mouth and two huge fangs, now blunted by three thousand years of wear and tear. It was a spooky and wondrous thing to find, and a chill ran along my spine.

'It is the serpent jaguar. The guardian of this forest,' said a voice behind me, as my spine froze into an icicle.

It was Diego again. He had been thinking as he sat in his shack with the rain dripping off the tin roof, and remembered that the cacao bean played a bigger role in his life, and in the life of his tribe, than he had been able to tell me as we stood briefly by the ball court. A big man with a deeply furrowed brow and an expression that hovered between solemnity and a bad mood, the forest's low lighting gave him a fearsomely hieratic look, like the warrior priests of the pre-Classic Maya. In his right hand he carried a machete the size of a baseball bat.

'Follow me,' he grunted: it was neither an invitation nor a suggestion. He turned and plunged deep into the forest, leading me towards the minimal collection of jerry-built shacks, apparently recycled from the rubble of earlier dwellings, where the Tercero family – father, mother, granny and four little children – had their exiguous home.

The houses of the poor in tropical lands often have something of this look. The cement painted a grubby turquoise down below, a lighter shade further up the wall. Outside the front door, chickens and dogs and a pig make good use of whatever edible human by-product they can find. If the electric wires that hang around the house like garlands seem to inspire a sense of doubt, the bare lightbulb that hangs in the centre of the room is a blazing confirmation that all is well. (The lamp shade, incidentally, is surely a piece of decadent Western perversity. Once you've been blessed with the miracle of electric light, the normal thing is not to cover it up as if in shame, but to let it shine merrily into every corner of your life.)

The other important fixture of this kind of modest

equatorial residence is the TV. This one was a brand new Korean model, big enough to be visible from any point in the house and loud enough to wake the dead. But old habits die hard, and in Diego's house the top of the set had been turned into a basic sort of shrine featuring six cans of Coca-Cola (full) arranged in a pyramid, an enamel saucer heaped with dry cacao beans and a 3-D image of the Virgin Mary which smiled beatifically, repeatedly, as you moved around the room. The mild countenance of Our Lady was in dramatic contrast to the soap opera currently in progress on the TV screen below. As I watched, one teary, hysterical young woman was slapping another round the face. '*Hija de puta!*' – 'daughter of a whore!' – she screeched.

What Diego had remembered he wanted to tell me was that in his family the cacao bean had had all sorts of other uses besides its principal use in *la bebida*. For one thing, it had once had an important place in the medicine cabinet. His wife still occasionally used cacao butter as a salve for cuts, and sometimes rubbed it into her skin as a moisturiser – the ancestral origin, I suppose, of all those Body Shop cocoa butter scrubs and rubs. His mother, permanently installed in an old armchair, clung to her ancestral belief that drinking chocolate in the morning would give you a twenty-four-hour protection from snake bites. There were other families in the area, said Diego, who thought ground-up cacao a perfect cure for an upset stomach.

There was no doubt that this was a chocolate-loving household. But the Tercero family, instead of nipping down to the twenty-four-hour garage for a Wispa and a tube of Smarties, had other ways of getting their fix. Diego's young wife, a tiny woman who seemed to hop around the house on bird-like feet, had whipped up a simple hot chocolate for breakfast that morning, and, as the first foreign visitor ever to set foot in her house, I was naturally expected to partake. It was not *bebida* as such, which is usually mixed up with maize flour and spices, but a simpler everyday version. The bowlful she served me had a thick layer of oily foam quivering on its surface. The drink itself was sticky, shudderingly sweet and had a smoky or acrid aftertaste as if something had stuck to the bottom of the pan.

'*Rico*, eh?' said Maria, leading me to a chair between her mother-in-law and the TV. Clearly the closer you were to the totemic presence of the telly, the greater the honour. 'When the heat gets up in the afternoon, sometimes we drink it with ice.'

But the Mam's interest in cacao went beyond gastronomy and medicine and into the realms of ritual magic.

'We celebrate our cacao festival in the month of May. In the old days, all the cacao plantation owners used to build a cross among the trees, and decorate the cross with flowers. There would be candles and incense and prayers. Then, after the harvest, we would light the candles again and put cacao pods on the altars and say prayers to our holy Mother Earth,' Diego told me as we all sat together sipping chocolate. There was no sign around us of his four barefoot kids, who had escaped into the street and could be heard shrieking like banshees in the forest. 'What about the weddings, Diego?' his wife reminded him, turning eagerly towards me. 'When a man wants to marry, he gives cacao to the parents of the girl. We have a custom that, when the parents of the couple meet to talk about the wedding, they must give each other bread and cacao beans and flowers . . . And then after the baby is born, on the twentieth day, the parents get together with the godfather and they make a special meal with bread, cacao, rum . . .

'You see, cacao is part of our life.'

'Part of our life in the past, Maria, not in the future,' her husband told her sharply. 'If these bullocks do well, I'll soon be ripping up the last of our trees. In five years there might not be much cacao around, so we'd all better get used to it.' His wide Indian face took on a briefly grim expression, as if something had displeased him mightily.

Before I left Diego sold me a cacao pod. We went outside into the forest to choose a perfect specimen, and he hacked it off the tree with a quick neat slice of the machete. It was a curious object of a foot or so in length, as hard and heavy as an unripe melon, with a graceful tapering at one end. At ten pesos it was hardly a bargain, given the rock-bottom market price Diego had quoted earlier, but I felt I had come away with something whose value was far greater than the sum of its beans.

I clutched it to my chest, feeling like a child with a going-home present. For the rest of the journey it travelled at the side of my suitcase, in the pocket reserved for executive footwear, and now it sits on my desk as I write: a funny sort of paperweight, indeed. Originally the colour of old-fashioned mint ice cream, a bright pastel green, now spreading as it ripens with sarcoma-like splotches of dark brown. The surface of the pod is still hard and shiny, though when I pick it up now it seems lighter than ever, and as the beans begin to loose themselves a little from the sticky harness of the inner membrane, it rattles softly as I shake it.

If there were prizes to give out, one of the biggest would have to go to the pre-Classic Maya civilisation of Izapa, for its precocious appreciation of the possibilities of *Theobroma cacao* as a crop plant. But it was during the later Classic era, the sensational flowering of Maya culture, that chocolate took on its glamour, its aura of sanctity, its economic importance, and, not least, its name. The etymology of the word has elicited any number of candidates over the years. Before the science of historical linguistics arrived and blew this theory out of the water, a common explanation was that 'choco, choco' was a kind of onomatopoeia, reflecting the sound of the wooden *molinillo*, or chocolate whisk, as it whips up the foamy surface of the drink. The current orthodoxy does seem much more likely. The Maya words *chacau haa*, or *chocol haa*, mean 'hot water'. Another Maya expression, *chocola'j*, means 'to drink chocolate together'. From one of these sources, or maybe from some kind of confluence of all three, our word probably derives.

Remember the *Popul Vuh*? As well as a German progressive rock band whose memory is now almost as distant as that of the pre-Conquest Mexican peoples, it was also the sacred book of the Maya. In the *Popul Vuh* the cacao tree serves as a hanger for the severed head of the Maize God, decapitated by the lords of Xibalba, the Mayan version of Hell. Maya friezes, vases and codices depict both the cacao tree, and the taking of chocolate, in both secular palace scenes and mythical tableaux. The god Ek Chuah, patron of cacao and the merchant class – the two having a great deal in common in the context of Mayan society – is shown on a vase in the Dumbarton Oaks Collection, Washington, DC. He is elegantly attired with all manner of baubles and bangles, with a headdress resembling the waving fronds of a tree, and cacao pods apparently sprouting directly from his body. In one scene from another object, the so-called Princeton Vase, a Classic Maya production from the Petén region of northern Guatemala, a lady pours chocolate from one pot, held at chest height, to another placed on the floor. The scene has an almost Oriental quality of stylised luxury: the lady is tall, curvaceous and wears a long wraparound dress that is practically a kimono, her arms bare up to the neck and a jewelled necklace trailing down her back. The chocolate falls in a long, thin stream. Take away the bizarre distorted heads, the thick lips and nose of Classic Maya portraiture, and it could almost be a drawing by Aubrey Beardsley.

Depending on the tribe, the location and the social class of

the consumer in question, the Maya enjoyed their *chacau haa*
in various different ways: cold, hot or tepid; spiked with chilli,
sweetened with honey, flavoured with vanilla, allspice, flowers
of the itsim-te tree *Clerodendrum ligustrinum*, or 'ear flower'
Cymbopetalum penduliflorum. Tsin'te kakaw was simply a fresh
fruit juice made from the pulp; *ch'ah kakaw* was bitter, *au
naturel.* The Maya like the Aztecs sometimes added maize-flour
to make a horrid sounding, sludgy, bitter gruel. Mayan cuisine
had an Aztec-style mixture of ground cacao, maize flowers and
red annatto, and another recipe for a honey-flavoured chocolate
drink that was allowed to ferment, and acquired a few degrees
of alcohol.

The basic ingredients also varied. *Theobroma bicolor,* a related
species which produces a flatter-shaped bean with a much
coarser flavour, called in Mexico *patatxle,* was often used in
place of or in combination with *Theobroma cacao.* The white
mucilage covering the cacao beans, which I have tried more
than once – it has a tangy sweetness reminiscent of mango and
lychee – was also eaten and may have been made into a drink,
like the *pinolillo* still popular in Nicaragua. The Reverend
Thomas Gage, whose *Travels in Central America* (published
1775) is supposed to include the first English-language account
of cacao cultivation and consumption, mentions in the course
of his engaging depiction of Indian life the 'white juicy skin
which the women also love to suck off from the cacao, finding
it cool, and in the mouth dissolving into water'. In seventeenth-
century Guatemala, according to the Spanish colonist Antonio
Fuentes y Guzmán, a kind of wine was made from this pulp
by piling the beans and mucilage in a canoe and leaving them
until the pulp gave out an 'abundant liquor of the smoothest
taste, between sour and sweet, which is of the most refreshing
coolness'.

Cacao cultivation and use have been widespread across the
Maya communities of Central America in all historical periods,

from pre-Classic times until the present day. In the Yucatan peninsula only small amounts of cacao were grown – in sink-holes, or *cenotes*, where the tree had access to the abundant water it needs. Despite, or perhaps because of its difficult cul-tivation, cacao was held in the highest possible esteem. At a festival celebrated by Yucatecan plantation owners in spring-time, blue iguanas and feathers were offered to Chac and Hobnil, gods of rain and fertility, and a dog with brown mark-ings was sacrificed. A number of Maya tribes offered cacao flowers, fruit and chocolate drinks in religious rites connected with the harvest, fishing and social events such as weddings and funerals. At El Baul, once an important city in what is now Nicaragua, sacrificial victims had cacao pods attached to their legs and arms, while observers wore necklaces of cacao beans.

From sowing to harvest and from manufacture to consump-tion, the culture of cacao among the tribes of Central America was shot through with ritual, both pious and wildly sensual. In the cacao ceremonies of the Pipil in Izalco (modern El Salvador), the beans were exposed to the moon for four nights during which men and women slept in separate quarters, reuniting on the fifth day when the beans were planted. The gathering of the first cacao pods from the young trees was the excuse for a tremendous celebration. As harvest festivals go, this was as far from the typical White Anglo-Saxon Protestant arrangement of shop-bought fruit and tins of marrowfat peas as you can imagine. With an entertainment programme including sexual orgies, music, dance, transvestism and a daredevil spec-tacle somewhere between bungee jumping and the maypole, there was something for everyone.

'The effigy of the god Cacaguat was hoisted up on a pole', wrote Gonzalo Fernández de Oviedo in 1530. 'To the top was attached a revolving frame, and to this the "bird-children" were tied by ropes. At a given signal, these flung themselves into the void, spinning through the air until they touched the ground to the jubilation of the people. Around the pole danced sixty men, their heads adorned with headdresses of multi-coloured feathers, their bodies naked or painted, and some of them disguised as women. They were accompanied by musicians and a group of ten singers.'

I had hurried down to Tapachula direct from Mexico City, fired up by the idea of a journey to the place where it all began. Soconusco was not only the cradle of cacao growing, but the point of origin of chocolate's importance in the life of humanity. Having dug down to the roots, I could now spend a little time flitting among the branches. Instead of crossing into Guatemala I would make my way back northwards to San Cristobal, cultural capital of Chiapas and a major backpackers' mecca, with juice bars and funky clothes shops and groovy cafés serving banana pancakes, all in the context of a cheerfully scruffy little colonial town. High in the mountains of the Meseta Central de Chiapas, San Cristobal comes as a blessed relief to anyone arriving from the sauna-like climate of the south coast. Here, I decided, I would chill out for a while, catch up on my readings in Mexican history and carry out a little quiet investigation into Mayan chocolate rituals on the side.

I would stay at Na Bolom. Whenever I asked friends for travel tips, this was a name that came up regularly. The thing about Na Bolom, people said, was its extraordinary atmosphere. It was not a hotel as such, but a research centre for students of indigenous Maya communities, with a few rooms to rent.

In the book that has become the Bible, the Koran and the Torah of chocophiles everywhere, Michael and Sophie Coe's *The True History of Chocolate* (1996), I had just read an intriguing passage about the Lacandón Indians and their ways with cacao. The Lacandón are the last living descendants of the great

Mayan civilisations of the Classic period, now reduced to a few hundred individuals clinging to the last pathetic remnant of original rainforest in the wild lands north-east of San Cristobal. The Coes quote recipes for two Lacandón chocolate drinks, one secular and one sacred. To a non-anthropologist the differences between the two seemed minimal. Flavoured with roots and grasses and foamed up with a pulverised forest vine, neither sounds remotely appetising. The source of the recipes was an anthropological study published in 1971, before Lacandón culture was grievously harmed by the arrival of alcohol, evangelical Christianity and concerned outsiders offering money. Was it possible that such a complex piece of ritual behaviour could have survived the onslaught? I doubted it very much, though I was prepared to keep an open mind.

As a place to spend a few quiet days, Na Bolom was magical and perfect. The fabric of the house was a colonial mansion of 1891, with a series of cool courtyards full of plants and pillared walkways that gave the place the feeling of a monastery. For fifty years the house had been inseparably linked with the names of Frans Blom and Gertrudis Duby, a Danish archaeologist and a Swiss photographer respectively, who together determined that if the unique culture of the Lacandón Maya were to disappear forever, it would be over their dead bodies. It was filled with their possessions and imbued, one instinctively felt, with the spirit of their forceful, passionate double personality. An intoxicating mixture of idealism, liberalism and intellectual energy seemed to seep from the very walls of the house.

The rain pounded down. But there were fireplaces in every room, and battered old chairs to curl up in, and old books of obscure anthropology to lose yourself in. It reminded me of a professor's rooms at some old European university: Spartan but comfortable, if that isn't a contradiction in terms. There was a dark music room with a grand piano where I sat and played

Chopin nocturnes as rainy afternoons turned into rainy evenings. There were Maya bits and pieces, pots and artefacts on every available surface, and the walls were a permanent gallery of Gertrudis Duby's black and white photographs of Lacandón scenes: tribespeople hunting with bow and arrow, squatting around a fire to share a roasted whole wild pig, or messing about in boats. I had never seen an indigenous people with the minimalist chic of these tall, elegant figures with their long black hair and their astonishing long white gowns – deeply impractical for rainforest wear, one would have thought, unless the Lacandón also have access to arcane traditional wisdom in the arts of stain removal.

Na Bolom – house of Blom – was a great place in which to be studious. I spent delicious hours in the huge library, losing myself in piles of books each inscribed *Ex Libris* with a name and date: New York, 1950; Copenhagen, 1954. Alone in the museum one morning I flicked through a diary kept by Blom on one of his many journeys into the heart of the Lacandón rainforest. The little notebook bore the dates 24 September–21 October 1943. As Blom and his companions hacked their way ever deeper into the forest, they found alarming evidence that other outsiders had got there before them: rubber merchants from the north, exploiting the wild rubber trees for their valuable sap. 'In the forest both rubber and cacao grows in spots and must be hunted up by scouts', noted Blom.

Among the useful products yielded by various kinds of forest tree, Blom listed mahogany, cedar, balsa wood, rubber, *chicle* (the original chewing gum), vanilla, sarsaparilla, castor oil, wild honey, wax, and cacao. Page 419 showed Blom's rough sketch of a wild cacao pod. There were, he said, twenty-four beans in this one pod. It was elongated and pointy-ended, like the one I carried in my suitcase. On the evidence of Blom's researches, it seemed likely that chocolate, in some manifestation or other, must have formed part of Lacandón life in the mid-twentieth century, if not in the early twenty-first. A few pages later came an even clearer sign. Another rough sketch showed a length of stem with a few stubs of cut branches attached around its base. This, suggested Blom, was a 'swizzel-stick [*sic*] for beating chocolate, atole, eggs, etc. The wood is called *mahaz*.'

That night I sat at the long dining table beside a lean, dark, gently spoken gentleman who, as Director of the Centre, knew the Lacandón Maya at least as well as Blom had. What Licenciado Palma had to tell, however, did not make for happy listening. The forest was still being relentlessly destroyed for wood, he said, and the tribe was diminishing along with it. The arrival of an evangelical missionary group, openly challenging the locals to destroy their gods, had led to great swathes of its millennial culture being wiped out. Waves of change had swept over the tribe. Many of them had cut their hair and given up their long white gowns, doubtless discovering that jeans were actually far less practical than gowns in these sauna-like jungle conditions. The young had turned to drugs and alcohol. The tribe had become demanding and aggressive with those who tried to help, and some aid organisations, Palma told me *sotto voce*, were now actually unwilling to work with them.

Only in the small settlement of Nahá (pop. 180) did anything resembling the old culture still remain. Here at least the Lacandón had so far managed to resist the blandishments of the outside world. The only concession they had made to the evangelists, said my neighbour wryly, was to establish that Jesus Christ was the son of Akanthyo, the Lacandón god 'of commerce and of outsiders'. The people of Nahá still communicated with their divinities by means of the *lak il kú*, or 'god pot', a small clay vessel whose humble appearance belies its tremendous spiritual importance.

'We have one here,' said Palma, getting up from his fruit salad to bring me the object in question. It was of a roundish shape, of very rustic construction, made of white-painted clay with vertical stripes of brown and black. The front of the bowl had the form of a face, with a gaping mouth and eyes. Into this pot, when they wish to talk to their gods, the communicants put five cacao beans representing the heart, lungs, liver, stomach and diaphragm.

If the god pots are still brought out for those long-distance calls, other customs have come and gone. Those sacred and profane chocolate recipes, for example, are no more a feature of Lacandón life. They have gone out of fashion as completely as Fanny Cradock's recipe for iced doughnuts.

'Why it has happened, I cannot say,' said Licenciado Palma, turning the god pot over and over wistfully in his hands. 'Perhaps it is the bitter taste: when you connect first time with the modern world, you want sweet, you want sugar. It is a little sad. But I'm afraid it is true: the Lacandón Maya have made no chocolate drinks for ten years.'

The pre-Conquest history of Mexico is an intricate tissue of loose political coalitions based on trading patterns or ethnic ties; of military empires that spread across the map like bloodstains; of civilisations that fade into other civilisations, or are simply born and die in spectacular fashion, blazing across the sky before they burn out, vanishing inexplicably into the ether.

The Aztecs, or, as they called themselves, the Mexica, can be seen as a kind of summing-up or recapitulation of all the long string of Mesoamerican civilisations that had preceded them. The tenor and texture of their culture are hard for those not versed in them to understand. This was a militaristic state, but the Aztecs were also pleasure-lovers, hooked on luxury and exquisiteness in the fine and decorative arts and the pleasures of the table. Tenochtitlan was both Rome and Athens: imperial power and aesthetic refinement. But there was a dimension to

Mexica life that none of the dominant civilisations of the West has ever possessed in quite the same degree, with the exception of the ancient Egyptians: the all-consuming importance of the divine. This was a theocratic society, drenched with religiosity to its last fibre, in which as one historian of the Aztecs puts it, 'the sacred couldn't be separated out from the rest of life . . . it pressed in everywhere'.

I could not quite believe my luck. My hotel room overlooked the historic epicentre of the world's most populous city – the great central Zócalo, a main square on a monstrous scale and one of the most dramatic public spaces imaginable. Directly on my left as I leaned out of the window was the brooding grey bulk of the cathedral, faintly askew as the stone heart of the old city sinks little by little into the mud of the lagoon. Opposite my balcony a giant Mexican flag flapped slowly in the wind. The sky above the square was clogged with heavy summer rainclouds.

The view was heart-quickening in its grandeur. But the Zócalo is not the kind of place in which sleep comes easily. Apart from the perpetual hum of the milling crowds that seem to inhabit the square day and night, the weight of history hangs heavy on it. So much violence, so many ghosts . . . A few metres away once stood the Teocalli where thousands of human lives were sacrificed to the Aztec gods, until it and the rest of the city of Tenochtitlan was swept away by the Spanish in an unconscionable orgy of destruction. Perhaps only a culture so thoroughly imbued with fatalism could see its bad dreams come so spectacularly true. I read about rivers of human blood, coursing down the steps of the temples, congealing in the street, and the image flooded my dreams.

If it was the Maya who first took the cacao tree out of the rainforest and discovered how to make a drink from its fruits, it was the Aztecs – history's second most chocophile civilisation, the first being our own – who first developed a chocolate culture that was something akin to a way of life.

It's a mark of the importance of chocolate for the Aztecs that they even came up with a myth to explain its presence among them. In fact, as an Aztec consumer you could choose from two very different myths: a romantic tragedy of love's triumph over death, and a magical tale of gods and men. According to the latter, the cacao tree was a gift to humanity from Quetzalcoatl, warrior, high priest and god of the winds. When he was beamed down to earth on the light of the morning star, his clothes sparkling bright and his beard white as snow, Quetzalcoatl brought with him a plant of great value which he had stolen from the gods. (Shades of Wagner here, perhaps, and of Prometheus.) He planted it in the fields of Tollan, capital city of the Toltecs, and persuaded the rain god Tlaloc to water it and Xochiquetzal, the 'plumed flower', to adorn it with blossoms. He taught the Toltecs to harvest the fruit, to toast and grind it and to make a bitter drink flavoured with spices. All well and good. But the gods reacted badly when they saw mankind enjoying a delicacy hitherto reserved for them alone – especially one that had been stolen from them. They swore vengeance on Quetzalcoatl, and sent Tezcatlipoca – 'smoking mirror', god of darkness and shadows – to lead him into perdition. Disguised as a merchant, Tezcatlipoca plied him with *pulque*, the fermented juice of the maguey cactus, until he was drunk and began cavorting ridiculously in front of the disgusted populace of Tollan. When he awoke from his alcoholic slumbers, Quetzalcoatl knew he had been deliberately humiliated by his own peers. Seeing that his cacao trees had shrivelled into dry, spiny sticks, his depression was complete. Downcast, he set out on his long trek back to the stars. But on his way he stopped at the Pacific coast, on the beaches of what is today the region of Tabasco, and there he threw to the ground the last few cacao seeds he possessed, the ones that had inexplicably stuck in the corners of his jacket pockets along with the foreign coins and the empty cigarette lighter. They not only germinated, but prospered and multiplied. Which all goes to show, with the tortuous but impeccable logic of myth, why it is that cacao refuses to grow in Tollan (now Tula), or anywhere in north or central Mexico for that matter, but only along the tropical coastlines of the south.

In the Mercado de la Merced in Mexico City – plausibly described as the market with the biggest surface area anywhere in the continent of America – alongside the banks of chillies of a hundred types, the towers of cactus leaves, the pecan nuts and courgette flowers and dried grasshoppers, the flowers and fruits and roots of the Mexican table, each with its own particular use and/or medicinal value, was a sack of cacao beans.

The man brought up a handful for me to inspect. They were pale, fattish nuts, as yet untoasted and un-treated. I sniffed at them gingerly: they gave off a sour aroma, like wet wood.

'Top quality, that is. This year's crop, just in from Tabasco. Twenty pesos the kilo to you, sir.'

'What do you do with them?'

He raised his eyebrows a millimetre at my ignorance. 'You simply roast them in the oven, grind them up with sugar and cinnamon, and you've got your chocolate paste. Now if you just add milk or water to that . . . We've got the Day of the Dead coming up, and I'm expecting a big demand for this Tabasco cacao. It's the custom on the Day of the Dead to take chocolate at home with the family, or in company. We Mexicans drink a lot of chocolate, *sabes*? Eating chocolate, not so much. Drinking: *mucho*.'

If I hadn't known already about the massive predominance of drink over food, I could have guessed it from the *confiterias* of Mexico City, which specialise in brightly coloured candies to be ordered by the bagful and served up in scoops, as in old-fashioned British sweet shops and Woolworth's Pick'n'Mix counter, but offer almost no eating chocolate for sale. In the richer neighbourhoods you sometimes saw a milk chocolate

imported from Austria and boasting of its 'fine European quality'. Once or twice I found some Hershey's *chocolate con leche* –
made in Mexico, but still with the Hershey's taste of burned
leaves and toasted rubber. The only properly home-grown
brand I saw with any regularity was a small bar of milk chocolate with the brand-name Carlos V, whose wrapper depicted
the Flemish emperor in a crown and a mantle of white ermine.
The inappropriateness of the name made me smile: it was to
Charles V, king of Spain and later Holy Roman Emperor, that
Hernán Cortés wrote his famous series of letters describing the
bloody and tragic overthrow of Mexico's last great civilisation.

Around the corner from the market was the famous *chocolatería* El Moro ('the Moor') where the 'divine drink' is the
speciality of the house and its reason for being. This is one of
the most venerable chocolate houses, tile-walled and marble-
tabled, in a city that still boasts several dozen. It was founded
in 1935 but feels much older. You can have French (with
vanilla), Spanish (thick and sticky), Especial (with cinnamon),
or Mexican (with milk). All are cooked up in tin pots on the
stove at the front of the shop and, apart from the Spanish,
which has the consistency of glue, are whipped up into a froth
with the *molinillo*.

'One Mexican chocolate, *mi amor*?' said the small quick
waitress in her white clunky shoes, white cardigan and light
blue waitress skirt. She turned on her heels, leaving me to peer
about the room at my fellow partakers of the divine drink.

It was early on a Saturday morning. You might, if you were
familiar with the *chocolaterías* of Madrid, expect to see a morning-
after crowd at this hour, recharging batteries before heading
blearily for home and bed. But these customers looked rather
perky. There was a group of business people, men and women,
laughing at their big table at the back, and some silent happy couples, and a lot of nuclear families, and a few solitaries like me,
flicking through the papers. Everywhere the dark, wide, big-eyed,

solemn Mexican face crowned with the glossy black shock of
Mexican hair.

The chocolate arrives in a big white cup on a round zinc tray,
together with a plate of crisp fried *churros*. It is sweet, dark, resonant with proper chocolate flavour, and seems faintly spicy
with vanilla and cinnamon and the faint anaesthetic buzz of
cloves, though in fact the waitress assures me it has none of the
above. 'Just milk, *mi amor*, just milk.' The liquid is not much
thicker than coffee and delivers a much gentler kick to the
system than coffee's sometimes brutal upper cut. In the crisp,
oily *churros* it finds its perfect companion food, since the *churros* can be, indeed *must* be, dunked into the chocolate. This
makes for a highly soothing 'eat', in marketing parlance, and
also provides an added bonus in the flakey/chocolatey debris
that has fallen from the *churros* during dunking and collects in
a delicious layer at the bottom of the cup.

It is difficult to imagine going to work on a breakfast like
this. As I finished my chocolate and plate of *churros*, satisfied
and pleasantly mentally befuddled, what I felt most like doing
was going back to bed. Instead I dragged myself around the
cathedral, which was a hive of activity almost as buzzing as the
Zócalo outside. Five Masses were going on at the same time, filling the air with incense and chanting. In one of the chapels the
congregation was watching TV. In the chapel next door, bless-
edly free of human noise, I sat for a while to digest my *churros*.
There before me was a figure of Christ, seated, leaning pen-
sively on his wrist, behind the glass of a cabinet. This image, said
the label beside it, was made in the seventeenth century from
painted maize pulp and real human hair, and originally spent its
days out in the Zócalo, bringing in donations from passersby for
building work on the cathedral. Since there was no small
change in those days, many of the poorest made their contri-
butions in cacao beans. And this was the origin of his name: El
Señor del Cacao – Lord of Cacao.

As I began to explore the city, cacao beans and pods began to pop up all over the place, symbolic markers of a glorious past. The Diego Rivera mural in the Palacio Nacional, just across the square from my hotel, showed the hubbub of Tlatelolco market at the height of Aztec rule, with, in the foreground, a merchant tipping beans from a sack. The representation of Tlatelolco in the museum of the Templo Mayor told a similar story: cacao was part of a mixed shopping basket that included maize, beans, blue corn, tomatoes, prickly pear *nopales*, avocado, and more, all laid out on mats or displayed in square stick boxes. The *chinampa* system of agriculture, used to cultivate the waterlogged lands on the edges of the lagoon, was of a stupendous productivity, yielding two, sometimes three crops a year of maize, pumpkin, beans . . . But cacao is a tropical plant, and refuses to grow on the high, cool plains of the Mexican *altiplano*. So that for the Aztecs it remained an exotic commodity, something special and spiritually charged and expensive hailing from the distant lands of the deep south.

In a daze of awe and jetlag, I spent the best part of a day in the National Museum of Anthropology, which takes the best part of a week to see in its entirety. I spent at least half an hour examining the ninth-century wall paintings of Cacaxtla, which fuse the pictorial traditions of the Maya world with those of the holy Aztec city of Teotihuacan. Even in the context of this extraordinary museum, in which there is so much magnificence and strangeness that it exhausts the spirit, these murals have an almost hallucinatory beauty. In one image the figure of Ek Chuah is pictured with his backpack and headdress beside a cacao tree. A second panel has a sacrificial victim coloured entirely blue, symbolising his connection with the rain god Tlaloc. On either side of this figure stand a maize plant and another cacao tree – the two plants in the Aztec herbarium whose significance was such as to confer on them sacred status. The cacao tree is painted blue with pink pods sprouting on a deep red background, while an electric-blue quetzal bird – quetzal feathers were the ultimate in exotic accessories for the wealthy Aztec man about town – is to be seen swooping down on the uppermost cacao pod.

Wandering the museum's vast halls that day, I learned more than ever about the place of cacao in the Aztec economy, society, world-view and daily life. It was the merchants, or *pochteca*, a privileged class who sent their children to special schools, who imported cacao into Tenochtitlan along with other effete southern luxuries such as deer and jaguar skins, jade, turquoise, seashells and precious feathers. Their clients were the *pipiltin*, the Aztec nobility, who paid for these items in gold dust and copper tomahawks. A rigid caste system operated. Only the upper classes were allowed to wear cotton clothes or drink cacao, if among the upper classes we include the aristocracy, the priests and the warriors to whom these privileges were also granted. An edict from the emperor Moctezuma I, father of the last Aztec ruler, stipulated that the man who does not go to war 'shall not be permitted to wear cotton clothing, nor plumes, nor shall he be given roses, like other lords, nor perfume to sniff. He shall not drink cocoa, nor eat fine foods, and shall be regarded as a man of low estate . . .' According to one historian of the Mexica, the warrior class came to wield such power in Tenochtitlan society that it began to levy an unofficial tribute on the city, to be paid in the form of 'chocolate, or food'.

The question of tribute is a central theme in the study of the Mexica, for as more than one writer has remarked, by the time of the invasion there was little to suggest an empire in the classic sense of political dominion and control. The Aztec empire was essentially a gigantic machine for the gathering and processing of tribute. Partly because the rapidly expanding city of Tenochtitlan could not now feed its own people from the *chinampas*, much of this payment was made in comestibles. No less than 52,000 tons of food a year came into Tenochtitlan from its vassal states – which after 1486, when the emperor Ahuizotl conquered it for the empire, included Xoconosco (later known as Soconusco). The *Codex Mendoza*, a manuscript produced by indigenous scribes under Spanish supervision, shows in pictorial form the nature of the tribute exacted from this new province: forty jaguar skins, an unspecified quantity of pots for the preparation of *cacahuatl*, and two hundred 'loads' of cacao, a 'load' being the amount that could be carried in a trader's backpack, or around 24,000 beans. In return for their precious crop the Soconuscans gained access to *altiplano* delicacies unavailable in the deep south, such as the special cakes made from compacted red worms or the mysterious 'cheese' which the Aztecs gathered from the surface of the lagoon.

The drinking of *cacahuatl* was prohibited to commoners. Meanwhile the upper classes indulged to their hearts' content, downing jar after jar of foaming chocolate at banquets for which hundreds of turkeys and dogs had previously been slaughtered. Whenever a merchant returned from a buying trip in foreign parts, he gave a dinner at which the *cacahuatl* flowed freely and guests were given a luxurious chocolate-related present to take home: a tortoiseshell spoon for stirring *cacahuatl*, a set of calabash containers or two hundred cacao beans. Chocolate was the champagne at society weddings – the luxurious and celebratory character of both, it seems to me, having to do with the sensual frisson of hundreds of tiny bubbles bursting on the lips. 'The elaborate attire, the fine jewels and sumptuous food of the nobles were taboo for the people; the latter were unceremoniously killed if they dared to indulge in such luxuries,' writes Nigel Davies in *The Aztecs*.

When it comes to consumption of the 'divine drink', however, there were few consumers more conspicuous than the emperor and his retinue. If we are to believe the Spanish chronicler Francisco Cervantes de Salazar in his *Crónica de Nueva España*, the royal coffers of Motecuhzoma/Montezuma held a quantity of cacao – more than 40,000 'loads', or almost a thousand million beans – that would be unbelievable if we did not know about the voracious chocophilic appetites of the emperor and his court. Bernal Diaz del Castillo's description of Montezuma at table provides an unforgettable picture of imperial grandeur and sybaritism. It is frequently quoted, but I do so again partly for my own pleasure in transcribing the splendiferous scene.

'He was served on a very low table, on which they spread white cloths and large napkins. Four very beautiful women brought water for washing the hands. When he began to eat, they placed in front of him a wooden screen, richly gilded. Four leading nobles were in attendance, and as a favour he would give to each a plate of what seemed particularly good, which they ate standing up, and without looking him in the face. He ended the meal with fruit, of which he ate little. He drank cacao from cups of fine gold. Sometimes at mealtimes he was attended by hunchbacks and jesters, while others sang and danced for his amusement; to these he would give what remained of the food and the cacao.' Diaz then goes into greater detail about the number of jars of *cacahuatl* served at the meal – 'more than fifty' – and the possible aphrodisiac effects of the drink, 'which they said was for success with women'.

When the banquet was over and the emperor once more alone in his quarters, he was served up a feast of the most exquisite *cacahuatl* that money could buy or the palace kitchens prepare. One imagines him savouring the drink in solitude, much like the modern chocolate fiend who likes to unwrap a bar or two when he or she gets home from work. Fray Bernardino de Sahagún, a faithful recorder of pre-Conquest Mexican life in its most intimate detail, writes: 'Then, by himself in his house, his chocolate was served: green cacao-pods, honeyed chocolate, flowered chocolate, flavoured with green vanilla, bright red chocolate, *huitztecolli*-flower chocolate, flower-coloured chocolate, black chocolate, white chocolate.'

It is clear from this extensive menu that there was not just one type of *cacahuatl*, but a whole world of different preparations whose degree of complexity varied, as with the Mayan *chacau haa*, on the situation in hand. The basic recipe is simple. It is still followed in Mexico, with a few crucial differences. The cacao beans are toasted on the *comal*, the round, flat terracotta Mexican griddle. They are ground on a three-legged grindstone, the *metate*, with a long roller made of granite, wielded after the manner of a rolling pin. (I have seen *metates* of five hundred, one thousand years old in museums that were indistinguishable from the ones still in use by women in the house next door: the design is eternal, like the technique.) To the resulting brown, sticky mulch, water is added, and the entire concoction poured from one container into another (most likely gourd or calabash *jicaras*) until a foam appears on its surface.

The foam is crucial. The best chocolate, which the Aztecs called *tlaquetzalli* (precious thing), had a good thick head of it. In Sahagún's account of the process, the chocolate-maker 'adds water sparingly, conservatively; filters it, strains it, pours it back and forth, aerates it; she makes it form a head, makes foam; she removes the head, makes it thicken, makes it dry, pours water in, stirs water into it'. If the last step seems strange, it is because the prized foam was often skimmed off the surface to be added later after other ingredients had been incorporated.

Poor man's *cacahuatl* was really *pinolli* – the *pinole* of modern Mexico – a drink of ground toasted maize and water with only a little cacao added, and the cacao used would have been the inferior *pataxtle* – *Theobroma bicolor*, rather than true *Theobroma cacao*. Further up the social scale, the recipes take on a greater sophistication. Vanilla, allspice and ground chilli pepper were three common spicy flavourings. Sugar had not yet been invented, and anyway the Aztecs do not seem to have minded the bitterness of raw cacao, which modern palates find so problematic. Even so, they sometimes added a little honey or maguey nectar. Finally the Aztec larder contained a series of exotic flowers, harvested in the forests of the tropical south and brought back by the merchants along with the cacao and jaguar skins and quetzal feathers, which when dried, powdered and added to chocolate, sent the upper classes of Tenochtitlan into raptures. Each of these blooms brought its own distinct perfume to the 'divine drink', and, according to Francisco Hernández (1517–87), physician to King Philip II of Spain and author of a massive study of native Mexican plants, each brought its various health benefits too. The Mexican magnolia, for example, called in the Nahuatl language *yolloxochitl* ('heart flower') was supposed to be good for the heart. *Mecaxochitl* ('string flower'), in combination with cacao, says Hernández, 'gives an agreeable taste, is tonic, warms the stomach, perfumes the breath . . . combats poisons, alleviates intestinal pains and colics'.

Cacahuatl in general, without flowers or flavourings, thought Hernández, was refreshing and highly nutritional. 'This drink, adding nothing to it, is usually administered in order to temper heat and mitigate burning fevers in the seriously ill, as well as in those who suffer from irregularity of the liver and other parts.' As soon as the flowers were added, however, it took on the property of 'exciting the venereal appetite'. There is no evidence that the Aztecs themselves shared our modern belief in chocolate's aphrodisiac powers, yet the association with eroticism has been a perennial theme in its history, from the writings of the earliest Spanish commentators, for whom it was something of an obsession, to the marvellous seventeenth-century physician Doctor Stubbes, who trumpeted 'the great Use of Chocolate in Venery', right up until the Flake advertisements of the 1970s.

Which are the world's major 'chocolate towns'? One could make up a shortlist of five or six cities where, because of their size, sophistication and/or gastronomic credentials, the art of chocolate is widely practised and appreciated. This list might take in Paris, New York, San Francisco, possibly Zurich. But there are other towns (they are usually towns) where not only does chocophilia represent a popular passion, but chocolate-making somehow comes to be almost a *raison d'être* for the town's very existence. Places like Hershey, Pennsylvania, the factory town founded by Milton Snavely Hershey, he of the famous bar and Kisses. Or Brussels, home and heartbeat of the Belgian chocolate industry; or Bayonne in south-west France, with its drinking-chocolate culture and its Académie of master chocolatiers. Or Oaxaca.

Oaxaca – pronounced wa-ha-ka – has liquid chocolate running through its veins.

The Aztec *Matrícula de Tributos*, or tribute book, lists fifty-nine places obliged to provide the Aztec empire with cacao as tribute. The list includes twelve places in the Colima region, nine in Chiapas, eight in Tabasco and Veracruz and twenty-two in Oaxaca. Among the Oaxaca names is a village named Cacaotepec, now known as Cacahuatepec, frequently mentioned in early colonial chronicles as a notable centre of cultivation. In itself this is surprising, because the central valleys of Oaxaca state are much too high, and the climate too dry, for *Theobroma cacao* to grow and prosper. But two centuries later Thomas Gage wrote of the town of Nejapa: 'this is counted absolutely one of the wealthiest places of all the country of Oaxaca, for here is made much indigo, sugar, cochineal, and here grew many trees of cacao and achiote. The chocolate made of these is a commodity of much trading in those parts, though our English and Hollanders make little of it when they take a prize of it at sea, as not knowing the secret virtue and quality of it for the good of the stomach.'

Of Oaxaca itself, he commented: 'In the city there are six cloisters of nuns and friars, all of them exceedingly rich; but above all is the cloister of the Dominican friars . . . Here are also two cloisters of nuns, which are talked of far and near, not for their religious practices, but for their skill in making two drinks, which are used in these parts, the one called chocolate and the other atole, which is like unto our almond milk, but much thicker . . . This is not a commodity that can be transported from thence, but is to be drunk there where it is made. But the other, chocolate, is made up in boxes, and sent not only to Mexico and the parts thereabouts, but much of it is yearly transported into Spain.'

After a brief bout of Montezuma's revenge, I wondered as I promenaded in the Zócalo, historical hub of this handsome colonial town, what if anything I should have for dinner. The glories of the local cuisine, which combines heat and spice and sweetness in a myriad surprising ways, were off limits for the moment. Just then, however, I saw an advertisement on the back of a bus – a 1950s-style gal in a neat frilly apron holding up a packet of Guelaguetza, one of Oaxaca's four or five popular brands of drinking chocolate. I decided on a cup of chocolate, and, in a café under the arches, settled down to nursing its sweet, nutty warmth. It was a pale pinkish brown in colour, with a nice sticky foam on top. Nourishing and comforting and restorative, it was just what the doctor ordered; indeed, to judge by the number of locals around me nursing their own cups of chocolate, the doctors in this town seemed to order little else.

Chocolate here is quietly omnipresent. Or not so quietly – around the Calle 20 Noviembre, beside the market, it shouts from the rooftops. In the space of a couple of blocks are half a dozen of the chocolate mills upon which Oaxaca depends for its sustenance and livelihood, and the streets are full of the all-enveloping heady smell of freshly ground cacao – alternating with sweet-hot blasts of chilli from the heaped market baskets. The best-known chocolate house, Mayordomo, is a miniature empire with several shops in Oaxaca, a factory on the outskirts of town and 'exports' all over Mexico. Then there are the medium-sized outfits, Guelaguetza and La Soledad, right down to the hole-in-the-wall places along the Calle 20 Noviembre like Molinos La Gloria which has just three small mills rattling away in the back and the products – balls and slabs and cigar-shaped tubes of chocolate – plainly packaged in plastic bags and displayed at the front of the shop.

Chocolates La Soledad – 'Solitude Chocolates' – is a reputable old Oaxaca firm, founded sixty-nine years ago and still in the hands of the Chávez Bombo family. The shop at Calle Mina no. 212, at the epicentre of Oaxaca's chocolate culture, is old-fashioned and neon-lit. Wooden counters and wooden cabinets with the wares displayed on them, and the clatter of old machinery. Painted upon one wall is a larger version of the charming logo that adorns La Soledad's packets and boxes and leaflets and all: a standard-issue Indian gentleman complete with plumed headdress and lance, offering a bowl of something steaming – we are to assume it is hot chocolate – to a seated squaw.

Through a double door I looked into the courtyard – plant-filled, with a gentleman reading the newspaper – of the small *pensión* which forms part of the business. The Hotel Chocolate is a place it might be fun to stay in, despite being decorated almost entirely in shades of brown. The powerful aroma of freshly ground chocolate, not sweet and milky but raw, bitter, rich and sultry, drifts into the patio and up towards the rooms. What must that smell do, I wonder – lull the guests to sleep, or have them tossing and turning in gluttonous frustration?

I stood and spoke to a pretty young girl, beguiling and *bien educada*, an assistant in the shop. Did she actually still enjoy chocolate, having to be surrounded with it for so much of her life, I asked her.

Her face lit up. '*Si señor, me gusta mucho. Mucho.*' She liked chocolate so much that still, occasionally, when no one was looking, she took a fingerful of the brown sludge in a tin tray on the counter – a freshly milled and glossy chocolate paste, on its way to the moulds.

I tried it myself; it was greasy with cocoa butter, potently chocolatey, with a rough granular texture which European and American chocolate-makers expunged from their products more than a century ago. The Swiss and French visitors to the shop, Cecilia told me, are taken aback by that grainy crunch and sugariness, so different to the European hyper-smoothness, the product of hours and days in the conching machine. Yet they are always charmed into buying something – partly, I surmise, because to European eyes the price of this fine, uncomplicated, artisan product is wonderfully low.

'We do a lot of our business around the Day of the Dead,' said the girl, echoing every cacao merchant and chocolate-maker in Mexico. The idea is to place on the altar whatever your forefathers would have most appreciated. In Veracruz province, Cecilia explained, that means chocolate medallions and figures moulded from a mixture of ground cacao with maize flour, boiled egg yolks, sugar and cloves. In Oaxaca, it means cups of chocolate.

Over at the mills on the other side of the shop they were mixing up an order for a local hotel. The millers, all men, wore overalls, while the women attending to customers wore neat red aprons. Into the mill, through a hopper at the top, went the beans – skins and all – from a sack that said 'Tabasco' in big stencilled letters, together with several generous scoops of California almonds and a prodigious amount of sugar. Despite what the label may tell you, there is no such thing as a genuinely bitter chocolate in Mexico.

The old machine, Mexican-made, quivered and rumbled on the marble floor. Little by little there emerged from it a coarse-milled, damp, dark brown crumb. This was then tipped back into the hopper for a second grinding, and what came out next was a sloppy, shiny paste, so dark as to be almost black. The miracle of cacao is here in this sudden change of character, the transformation from dry and bitter to unctuous and rich as the cocoa oils, newly released from their molecular prisons, seep through the mixture.

My nose was invaded by a powerful aroma, strong and sweet and complex. As I brace myself psychologically for criticism of my flowery descriptions of chocolate flavour at various points in this book, I feel there is something I should point out. Scientists, in their wisdom, tell us that cacao as a substance may contain as many as four hundred different identified aroma chemicals, to say nothing of the unidentified ones. Is it not surely legitimate and logical, your honour, that from time to time, as in the case in question, the smell of chocolate may remind the narrator of anything from woodsmoke and hazelnuts to plums, dried apricots, orange peel, nutmeg and roses? I rest my case.

Señora Chávez, proprietress of La Soledad and leading light of the Oaxaca chocolate scene, sat in state on a high chair behind the cash desk.

'Cacao is a basic food for the country people around here,' she told me during a gap between customers. 'In the mornings people take chocolate. Not coffee. Then at midday, a nice refreshing cup of *tejate*. And in the evenings, it's back to chocolate. Cacao makes you strong. Our chocolate is all natural – no added fats or chemicals. That's the reason our country people don't get fat. You'll never see a fat person in the countryside of Oaxaca.'

I bought a thick square packet of La Soledad drinking chocolate, packaged in bright red with the Indian logo on the front.

'That'll be twelve pesos,' said Señora Chávez a little briskly. There was a long queue of customers behind me. I felt I should get out of the way, but there was something I hadn't at all understood.

What on earth was *tejate*?

'It's a drink. Nice and refreshing. The country people round here, they take it as a *refresco* around the middle of the day. Turn right out of the shop and you'll find a girl there selling it, sitting on the market steps. Take him down, would you, Cecilia.'

And the girl led me down the street through the throng of shoppers and makeshift market stalls. The temperature had been rising all morning, and the pavement now radiated heat. Sure enough, there she was: a Zapotec Indian girl who had come in from the village of San Andrés Huayapam at five o'clock that morning, bearing the raw material for her daily sale, plus a big terracotta basin to mix it all up in. The province of Oaxaca is rich in cacao-based drinks of various sorts, the best known of which, apart from chocolate itself, is a sweet lumpy mixture of maize gruel and cacao known as *champurrado*. But *tejate* represents an entirely different, and arguably much older strand of tradition. The basic element is *patatxle*, the fruit of the wild cacao, *Theobroma bicolor*. The flattish beans are submitted to a ritual the details of which are jealously guarded, but which involves burying them in the ground for six full moons, until the beans are turned chalky-white by the highly alkaline local soil. They are toasted on the *comal* along with the stones of the mamey fruit (*Pouteria sapota*) and the white flower, previously sun-dried until it turns yellow, of a tree that grows abundantly in San Andrés Huayapam. I have not been able to match this flower, Latin name *Quararibea funeraris*, with any of the flowers used as flavourings for ancient Mexican chocolate drinks. Yet it seems to me tantalisingly close. The dried flower has a sweet, sickly fragrance, like a cross between jasmine and rose, with a hint of vanilla.

Maria, in her bright striped Zapotec skirt, smiled at my interest in the product, gently stirring her strange brew in its terracotta cauldron. She had ground the toasted cacao and flowers and mamey stones on the *metate* the previous night in San Andrés Huayapam, adding to it this morning before she left a lump of fresh maize dough, and diluting the whole thing with water from a spring on the outskirts of the village. When she arrived at the market, she began frothing the whole thing up with a *molinillo*, so that the surface of the liquid was now covered with whitish grey clots of scum. Among the Mayas and Aztecs the foam, remember, was always a delicacy.

The *tejate* looks, frankly, off-putting. But, having quizzed Maria so mercilessly, I can hardly avoid trying a cupful. With a plastic cup she pushes aside the surface scum and removes a cupful, pouring it back in once or twice, finally scooping off a little of that special grey foam and sliding it into my cup, in the manner of a cappuccino. I sip at it, grimacing; the foam sticks to my upper lip. It has a mild nutty taste, not unlike the Spanish pig-nut drink *horchata*. It is indeed surprisingly refreshing, and not at all unpleasant. Though it tastes not at all of cacao, the truth is borne in on me: this is the Aztec *cacahu-atl*, or at least a blood-relation of it, still being made almost half a millennium after the Conquest. Anybody looking for the roots, the deep pre-Hispanic roots, of the history of chocolate, might have reason to think they had stumbled on some of them here.

Susana Trilling has a big house with a dome as big as a church, built on a gentle hillside in the rolling central valleys outside Oaxaca, within sight of the temple complex of Monte Albán. Her nearest village is none other than San Lorenzo Cacahuatepec, where cacao was once grown in great quantity but has now disappeared from the fields and woodlands hereabouts.

According to local lore, there was once a cacao tree where the church of San Lorenzo now stands.

Susana is American but her grandmother was Mexican. After a variegated career as a chef and caterer in the States she has gone back to her Mexican roots. Her cookery school is the only one in the world to specialise in the legacy of Oaxacan cuisine with its curious melange of sweet and spicy, rustic and urbane, ancient and modern. If the way to a nation's heart lies through its stomach, then a day or two spent at Rancho Aurora provides one of the best short cuts I know to a closer understanding of Mexican culture. Because with Susana you are not only cooking and eating, which is of course an education in itself – you are market shopping, and sightseeing, and meeting people, and talking constantly, and bombarding Susana with questions. When I heard she was running a short course in artisan Mexican chocolate-making, as practised by the Zapotec tribe from time immemorial, I leapt in a taxi and sped out of town to the big domed house on the hill.

Aurelia, a Zapotec woman from the village, had set up her *comal* on a fire outside the door. She squatted down in front of the coals, fanning them with a copy of *Bon Appétit* magazine, telling us about her son in North Carolina, until the terracotta disc was smoking hot. The beans crackled and popped as they roasted, their thin almond-like outer skins cracking and peeling to reveal the brittle, mahogany-dark flesh inside. A faintly acrid smell rose from the *comal*. Susana showed me how to shuck off the parchment-crisp skins from the hot cacao beans. Lying together in a bowl, they looked as though they had been moulded in dark chocolate. I took one and chewed on it, receiving a mouthful of tannins, as acrid as wormwood, for my reward.

Now we moved to the *metate*. Until the arrival of the Kenwood mixer and, later, the Magimix, the *metate* was as essential an element of the Mexican kitchen as the fire and the *comal.* Aurelia's *metate* was a hundred years old, its grey granite surface worn shiny smooth with constant use. She had learned to cook on this *metate*, she told us, and her mother before her. That made two generations of Mexican women and their infinite hours of milling, the daily grind of maize for the tortillas, beans, cacao, chillies, the spices and salsas . . .

Aurelia knelt on the ground with the sloping surface of the *metate* facing away from her. She began with the cinnamon sticks, pounding them lightly with the stone rolling pin, or *mano*, its originally cylindrical shape now squareish and slender towards the middle. Then she tipped the roasted cacao beans on to the *metate* and began to work them, fast and deftly, never letting a single crumb fall off the edges. I took her place for a while and she laughed at my clumsy incompetence, as her neat pile of gradually disintegrating cacao became an unruly mess and the floor around the *metate* was scattered with debris. Plainly, there are certain tricks which only a lifetime of chocolate-grinding can teach.

Back in the saddle, Aurelia ground away again, the process now back on track and the cacao beginning its miraculous transition from a dry crumbly powder to something as different as anything becomes by the application of a simple kitchen process. First the crumbs began to adhere to the pin, and had to be scraped off from time to time with a knife. Then, as the cocoa butter seeped out of the dry cacao mass, the mixture became suddenly dark and sticky. A smell came up now, recognisably chocolatey, pungent yet fresh. When a scoop of white sugar was added to the *metate* and ground up with the cacao, the mixture took on a thick, glossy, luxurious texture, and a deep burnished brown colour tinged with russet red.

Aurelia served forth her Oaxacan chocolate in a circular patty on a medlar leaf from Susana's garden, and left it on a table outside where the breeze could catch it. The contrast of those colours has scorched itself on to my visual memory: a rich red brown, glistening mahogany with cacao butter, on a background of vibrant, emerald-bright, equatorial green.

In the library of the Museo Amparo, in Puebla, I spent the morning drowning in encyclopedias, catalogues, concordances and codices. From the *Enciclopedia Mexicana* I learned that thick chocolate, in Hispanic lore, is the equivalent of rectitude and sincerity. '*Las cuentas claras y el chocolate espeso*' – 'Clear accounts and thick chocolate.' And that the phrase 'like water for chocolate', title of the novel by Laura Esquivel, is a simile applied to someone in a state of boiling indignation or fury – because good chocolate is prepared with water that is literally boiling hot.

From the *Codex Vindobonensis* I would have learned nothing were it not for the eminent scholar and librarian of the Museo Amparo, who sacrificed an hour of his time to give me a crash course in ancient Mexican hieroglyphics. The original *Codex*, a product of the Mexica culture that flourished between Puebla and Oaxaca, was sent by Hernán Cortés to Charles V on 10 July 1519 along with other documents and gifts; it arrived four months later on 5 November. Like other pre-Hispanic manuscripts the codex is made in the form of a folding screen. At first I flicked through it like a child with his first picture book, charmed by the comic-book colours of deep red, light blue and golden brown, but alarmed by the sinister, incomprehensible imagery.

What was this upside-down triangular form, repeated over and over throughout the codex? This was the *temazcal*, steambath or 'sweat lodge', still used in parts of Mexico, said Don Luis. He read from the images the poetic names for the various types of *temazcal*: of the dawn, of the cloud, of the four flowers, white, shining, of fire, of the open jewels, of turquoise and jade, and (yes!) of cacao.

Next to the steam-bath triangle is a small double form that appears to be the representation of a fruit, sometimes seen with its two halves open, sometimes closed.

'After the bath, you see, they may have taken chocolate,' suggests my teacher.

But the form is repeated again and again throughout the codex, usually coloured deep red and golden brown – the same shades, deliberately or coincidentally, as those of the ripe cacao pod in its natural habitat. Now that I understand the symbol, I race through the codex hunting it down. Here it's set in a row of six, upon a chessboard design that represents the earth. Here, placed inside a high-sided box, as if the plant is growing in a sinkhole like the ones in northern Yucatan.

What about this: the chessboard earth, a row of pods, and a group of little creatures painted red with fierce white teeth and bright blue eyes, seeming to emerge from a hole in the ground, and a florid symbol floating in the space above them, resembling a large decorative letter A?

Don Luis strokes his beard, ponders the possibilities. 'This floating symbol here represents the year. But these creatures . . . could this perhaps be some kind of rodent? Rats, or beavers? Perhaps they destroyed the crop that year?'

And what about this much more uncanny and unsettling image: a cacao pod with a shoot creeping out from between the two halves of the pod, like the shoots of those bean seeds we used to keep in a jar wedged full of tissue paper when we were kids. But – and this is the sinister thing – the shoot is coloured bright scarlet. It is a simple, powerful motif: a streak of red emerging like a tender shoot from a germinating seed. It suggests fertility, but also pain; new life, but also the vitality of death.

Thereby, says Don Luis, hangs a tale.

'Perhaps you know the myth about the origin of cacao? Not the Quetzalcoatl myth; a different one, not so well known,' he says, taking off his glasses to rub them with his handkerchief. 'It goes like this. There is a prince. He leaves the city to defend a part of his territory. Before he leaves, he tells his wife that a treasure is hiding somewhere in the palace. While he is away, robbers break in; they attack the princess. She must reveal where is the treasure. But, of course, she will not do it. Then the robbers are mad, frustrated, they are really crazy, and they kill the princess. The legend says that her blood fertilised and watered the ground. And from this spot exactly comes a tree, *un arbol maravilloso*. The story says that the fruit of this tree was bitter, like the pain the princess suffers for love. It was a strong taste, like her virtue. And it was of a colour red, like her blood. This is the myth.'

As in almost every aspect of Aztec life the cacao pod had its own powerful symbolism and the taking of *cacahuatl*, accordingly, took on an important element of ritual. The *Codex Magliabecchi* shows how the bodies of the dead were supplied with cacao for their journey into the next world. Upon the death in 1481 of Axayacatl, the emperor under whose reign the empire's frontiers expanded as never before, a splendid funeral was held at which offerings of jewels, feathers, cacao beans and gold were made to the gods. Jars of foaming chocolate and maize cakes were arranged around the emperor's shrouded body. Six hundred turkeys were slaughtered. 'Then they sounded Axayacatl's great drum, cut out the hearts of the dwarves and hunchbacks, and cast them into the eagle vessel.'

The heart and the cacao pod were united by a persuasive analogy based on their similar shape: one was a vessel for blood, the other for chocolate. Fernández de Oviedo noted that the Indians of Nicaragua seemed to have bloodied red lips, stained by the annatto in their chocolate. But the association goes even further, into the realm of the literal. The slave chosen to be sacrificed in an annual festival dedicated to Quetzalcoatl was given a drink of chocolate mixed with the blood of previous victims – the so-called 'water from the washing of the obsidian blades'. This potion was intended to keep up his spirits for the following day, when at the summit of the Great Temple his heart was to be physically extracted from his chest.

From a shelf high up near the ceiling, where the Spanish conquistador chronicles languished in acres of leather-bound, forgotten volumes, I took down the collected works of Fray Diego de Durán, looking for his commentary on the horrendous procedure in his *Historias de las Indias de Nueva España e Islas de la Tierra Firme*: '. . . and if they saw that he became melancholy, that he stopped dancing joyously, with the happiness that he had shown, and with the gaiety they desired, they prepared a heathen, a loathsome spell for him: they went immediately to procure sacrificial knives, washed off the human blood adhering to them (the result of past sacrifices), and with that filthy water prepared a gourd of chocolate, giving it to him to drink. It is said that the draught had this effect on him: he became almost unconscious and forgot what he had been told. Then he returned to his usual cheerfulness and dance . . . It is believed that he offered himself for death with great joy and gladness, bewitched by the beverage.'

I went back to the codex, flicking back and forth through the pages in silence. In another part of the manuscript four stocky Aztec gods were shown piercing their own ears with obsidian lancets, scattering showers of blood over a heap of cacao pods. The four divinities were seen in various positions – bending down, stooping as if in pain, or proudly erect as the vicious-looking blade slices through the cartilage. The gruesomeness of the Aztec obsession with violence and mutilation is striking, if no more extreme, in some ways, than our own Western fascination with gore and violent death.

And here was the seed motif again – and again and again.

'Now this image is repeated a great deal, as you see,' says Don Luis, holding a magnifying glass above the parchment. 'It might mean the necessity of making an offering of some kind: a sacrifice. You see quite often in these codices the same representation. The container is a cacao pod, or possibly a seed, and the red thing coming out of it is . . . well, I think it is clear, no?'

Indeed it is. The tender shoot is a spurt of haemoglobin, bursting from the heart of the fruit. Blood and chocolate, the two precious liquids of ancient Mexico, mingling at their symbolic source.

On the outskirts of most cities in the southern hemisphere, the farmyard fowls seen pecking by the roadsides are scrawny chickens. You know you are in Mexico when, as the bus draws into the city, what you see scratching in the roadside grime are big, black, well-nourished looking turkeys. It reminded me of a painting I had seen in the Natural History Museum in Mexico City, of a kitchen in which four young female cooks are preparing to make *mole*. One busies herself with the pots and pans; another is already kneeling on the floor, giving it some on the *metate*; while the other two are holding down a big black turkey, ready for the chop.

According to the conventional explanation, *mole* was invented in the kitchens of the convent of Santa Rosa in Puebla, where Sister Andrea was the famously gifted cook. The Viceroy of Mexico was to be received at the convent, and a fine turkey fattened on chestnuts, hazelnuts and walnuts was slaughtered in his honour. But there was no sauce to go with it until Sister Andrea, filled with divine inspiration, set about raiding practically the entire contents of the convent larder, including two tablets of drinking chocolate – a *sine qua non* of monastic catering in the Mexico of the sixteenth century. Having fried and

roasted and otherwise treated her enormous array of ingredients, she set about grinding them into a thick sauce. 'With what
saintliness, with what fervent unction she knelt before the black
metate, seeming to be about to take communion or to pray to
the Virgin for mercy!', as Mexican writer Artemio del Valle
Arizpe describes the scene. And when the other nuns saw her at
work, they exclaimed '*qué bien mole!*' – 'how well she mills!'
(Which is where this charming theory goes off the rails, since
the correct form of 'she mills' is actually '*muele*' and not '*mole*'.
Never mind.)

The convent of Santa Rosa is now a cultural centre with
craft stalls and lectures and ballroom dancing in the afternoons.
In the taxi on the way from the bus station at Puebla, the driver
told me about his mother's special *mole* – made up in a trice by
adding stock or water to a cup of instant *mole* mix.

To the caretaker of the convent this sounded like a sacrilege.
He tut-tutted under his breath as he led me across a central
patio and through a maze of nondescript rooms towards the
back of the building, finally unlocking a door that led suddenly
into a dazzling interior: the original convent kitchen, tiled from
floor to vaulted ceiling with antique Talavera tiles, jewel-like in
their colours of yellow and blue, their floral and geometric
motifs. Outside in the Huerta Vieja a ten-piece band with a
wobbly Herb Alpert trumpet was playing the *danzón*, while a
group of elderly couples went through its slow, wobbly
motions.

Mole-making for Sunday lunch began on Friday, my guide
told me, with the visit to the market. On Saturday morning the
housewife started frying, and the grinding went on all afternoon. On Sunday morning the sauce bubbled away in a thick
glazed cauldron with two handles, allowing the diverse flavours
to orchestrate themselves into one harmonious whole. The
chocolate used was always La Abuelita ('Granny') brand – long
since absorbed, sad to say, into the mighty Nestlé empire.

To one side of the kitchen was a tiny alcove, lined with coloured tiles now higgledy-piggledy with age, with a gap just big enough to hold a cooking pot, and a space underneath where the fire would have been.

'This was where *mole* was born,' said the caretaker in a reverent near-whisper.

Mole has become a symbol of Mexican-ness. When Mexicans live abroad, it becomes a dish that they cook up with enormous ceremony, taking hours over the preparation and agonising over the difficulty of obtaining the right ingredients so far from home. There is a nice example of Expatriate *Mole* Syndrome in an essay by Laura Esquivel in which she describes trying to make *mole* in a New York apartment with a roommate who complains about the smell. At the heart of the piece is a strong association between food and family, food and fatherland.

'In the middle of winter, so dark and cold, how nice it would be to feel a little warmth: the heat of my mother's kitchen, the heat from the plants in our house at midday, the heat that stays in my throat and stomach after eating *mole*,' sighs the homesick narrator.

Mole is essentially a sauce for turkey or chicken – albeit an extremely complex sauce, made by reducing to a purée a huge number of ingredients most of which have previously been fried or roasted. The two great rival centres of *mole* are Puebla and Oaxaca, the difference being that a) *poblanos* claim Puebla as the birthplace of the dish, whereas *oaxaqueños* do not seem to mind either way, and that b) Puebla has just the one *mole poblano*, essentially a black *mole*, whereas Oaxaca has no fewer than seven types of various different colours. *Mole negro* is certainly a highly inclusive anthology of the Mexican larder, requiring fruits and vegetables, nuts and leaves, herbs and spices, garlic and chillies, and various baked goods both sweet and salty. Notorious, and essential to both cities' conception of black *mole*, however, is the presence of chocolate. It is the final addition of black chocolate that crowns the dish, sanctifying its shotgun marriage of piquant bitterness and fruity sweetness.

Esquivel's ingredient list for *mole negro* is not definitive, but then almost nothing about *mole* is truly definitive. I reproduce it below in all its comprehensive, preposterous glory.

a whole turkey
2 tablespoons of peanuts
1 cup of black chilhuacle chillies
2 tablespoons of walnuts
1 cup of red chilhuacle chillies
1 tablespoon of anise
1 cup of ancho chillies
2 onions
5 pasilla chillies
1 head of garlic
5 chipotle chillies
1 strip of cinnamon
4 cups of tomatoes
5 cloves
1 cup of lard
5 black peppercorns
2 dry tortillas
5 large green peppers
1 piece of *pan dulce*, sweet Mexican bread
3 bay leaves
3 bars of chocolate
3 branches of sweet marjoram
15 tomatillos
3 branches of thyme
2 tablespoons of almonds
1 tablespoon of oregano
2 tablespoons of sesame seeds
1 tablespoon of cumin

2 tablespoons of pumpkin seeds
10 avocado leaves
salt

Well before I tried my first *mole negro*, I had a feeling it would not be – how shall I put it? – quite to my taste. The culinary credo of British chef Alastair Little, 'keep it simple', is also mine, and this dish is about as far from simplicity as cookery ever gets.

Staring at my plate that night in the Fonda Santa Clara in Puebla, I saw only a lump of white meat enrobed in chocolate-coloured gunk and incomprehensibly, though traditionally, sprinkled with sesame seeds. The sauce is thick and cloying in texture; it is like eating mud. And the taste, sweet and salty and spicy and smoky and fruity and chocolatey all at the same time, is an experience of baroque excess to make even the strongest stomach quail. I found myself craving the freshness and crunch and herbaceous zest and dazzling colours of Mexican street food, as opposed to this murky prehistoric monster of *haute cuisine*. I drank up my bottle of Mexican wine, ate as much as I could of my haunch of brown-slathered turkey and limped into the night.

PART TWO

THE COLONIAL HERITAGE

Travels in Venezuela,
heartland of fine cacao

There are so many things to catch the eye and engage the mind about Venezuela – to name but three, the wildly varied landscapes, the unique and impressive racial mix, and the eternal mystery of how it is that a nation with such a fabulous wealth of natural resources should be permanently poised on the brink of bankruptcy – that it is a while before one is invited to consider its relationship to the 'food of the gods'.

Neither cacao nor chocolate seem to count for much these days in the Venezuelan national value system. This is a cruel historical irony, because for at least two hundred years, roughly during the period of Spanish colonial influence, cacao was a crop and culture of the greatest possible importance. When Columbus first set foot on the continental American mainland at the tip of the Paria peninsula in eastern Venezuela in 1498, cacao was already growing in a wild state in the tropical forests south of Lake Maracaibo and in the jungles of the upper Orinoco River, where it was known as 'mountain cacao', or *bacao*. We know very much less about the pre-Hispanic tribes of the Caribbean than we do about their Mexican contemporaries. But it's thought that, much like the Maya or Aztecs, the indigenous people of New Granada used cacao beans as a form of currency, burned cacao butter in their votive lamps and even made a kind of medicinal drink from the raw beans.

On 5 August 1612 the colonist Juan Benjumea Escalante wrote in a letter to the governor of Venezuela that he had discovered 'a mountain of more than one hundred thousand very large cacao trees' near Lake Maracaibo. The problem was that the trees gave forth a bean that was 'very slight, being wild and not cultivated'. The Spanish had begun to cultivate their own cacao in the fertile valleys of the Caribbean coast, chiefly as a means of supplying the market of New Spain (Mexico) where local production could not keep up with insatiable demand. Cacao beans were loaded at the colonial ports of La Guaira, Puerto Cabello and Coro on ships plying the so-called Veracruz Route to New Spain.

In the mid-seventeenth century Venezuela overtook Mexico to become the world's major cacao producer, a position it would maintain for more than a hundred years. At the end of the century cacao accounted for 78 per cent of all Venezuela's exports, making this once forlorn backwater one of the most profitable Spanish colonies after the wealthy *virreinatos* of Mexico and Peru. The cacao barons lived like kings, and their wives sipped fine chocolate in the salons of Caracas. Before the discovery of oil in 1920 and the rise of Venezuela as the number one supplier of petrol to the United States, currently producing more than three million barrels a day, cacao was the great wealth creator, the single most dynamic factor in Venezuela's economic development and a symbol of civilisation that has lost ground forever to something somehow uglier and much more single-mindedly mercantile.

Cacao cultivation took hold wherever the tree would grow. The first plantations in Barlovento, the coastal region east of Caracas, were founded by Aragonese Capuchin monks in Curiepe and Panaguire. Orituco, on the shores of the River Tuy, became famous for an especially fine and aromatic bean. In the eastern part of Venezuela, where the Paria peninsula juts out into the Caribbean towards Trinidad and Tobago, huge haciendas were founded; their owners grew rich and lived like princes.

The haciendas were microcosms of the colonial society, with the slaves at the bottom and their white or Creole masters, the so-called *grandes cacaos*, at the top. Some of the haciendas were Church-owned, and their profits went to fund hospitals, schools and prisons. The most important *hacendados* listed in the Spanish consulate in 1786 included the Bolivar family –

forebears of the great liberator Simon Bolivar, who relinquished a cacao estate of 200,000 trees in addition to a substantial fortune in order to follow his revolutionary path.

From the earliest days of the industry the excellence of Venezuelan cacao was well known. The nineteenth-century gastronome Jean Anthelme Brillat-Savarin wrote in his masterpiece *The Physiology of Taste* (1826): 'The cocoa tree is indigenous to South America. It is found equally in the islands and on the continent; but one agrees that the trees giving the best fruit are those which grow on the shores of Maracaibo lake, in the valleys of Caracas and in the rich Province of Soconusco.' Its superiority over the products of other newly established growing areas, however, was a matter of debate. Under the name Caracas, used to define the whole central part of the Caribbean coast, a French map of 1731 appends the words '*d'où vient le bon cacao*'. The Spaniard Antonio Lavedán understood the cacao grown on the coast of Caracas to be 'juicier and less bitter than that of the French Islands; and so in Spain and France that of Caracas is preferred to all others, but in Germany and the North, their taste is completely the reverse'. Père Labat (Jean-Baptiste Labat) was reluctant to accept the hegemony of the Spanish in the matter of quality. 'Many people claim that Caracas cacao is better than that of the islands . . . It is not surprising that the Spaniards should think the same; everyone knows that their natural vanity will not allow them to appreciate anything that is not Spanish . . .' Another major competitor was the Guayaquil region of southern Ecuador, then as now an important source of so-called 'fine flavour' cacaos.

From the window of the plane as we came into land, through the tropical heat haze I could see the little harbour town of La Guaira, where most of the dwindling production of Venezuelan cacao is still loaded into boats for London, Rotterdam and Hamburg. Above the coastline began the immense sprawl of shanty housing, lawless and comfortless, in which several million of the people of Caracas are apparently condemned to live.

After customs and immigration I took a taxi in the stifling heat a mile or so from the airport back along the coast. La Guaira, like the rest of Venezuela, is a wrack and ruin of its former self. In December 1999, torrential rains caused the slopes of the El Avila mountain range to disintegrate, creating a tide of mud and rocks that swept down towards the sea, destroying everything in its path. The disaster spared La Guaira's cathedral and its few streets of colonial houses, but the place still looked a mess – grand colonial mansions, their roofs a tangle of broken beams, up to the eaves in dried mud mixed with old mattresses and broken furniture. Many of the bodies are still in there, said my driver quietly as we cruised along filthy and near-deserted streets.

Almost the only building still in a reasonable state, either because it escaped the mudslides or as a result of a dutiful restoration, was a grandiose white palazzo on what would have been the old seafront, with balconies and a sloping beamed roof and a covered walkway out in front. This was the headquarters of the famous Real Compañía Guipuzcoana, a company created by the Spanish in 1728 to protect their cacao monopoly from smuggling operations based on the Caribbean islands of Curaçao, Aruba and Bonaire. The Compañía was founded by Basque merchants following a Royal Decree signed by Philip V on 25 September 1728. It was charged with ensuring that the colony's entire production of fine cacao reached Spain without let or hindrance. In this, however, it was a notable failure. The huge profitability of cacao contraband made it an irresistible temptation for Dutch, French and English pirates, despite the death sentence imposed by the Spanish for convicted smugglers, and one estimate suggests that an average of 30 per cent of total cacao production was sold on the black market.

For a fortnight I made my base in a big house in the Altamira district of Caracas, just below the great green wall of the Avila mountains where, from the city, waterfalls looked like shreds of whiteness and, so it was said, jaguars and bears still lived cheek by jowl with one of the most vibrant, violent and over-populated cities in the world. Altamira, like the other rich neighbourhoods of northern Caracas, strung out along the south-facing slopes of the Avilas, sheltered from gales and the heat of La Guaira, was once the name of a great cacao planta-tion. (In his 1621 description of the town of Santiago de León de Caracas, at the time no more than a collection of adobe huts, the Carmelite friar Antonio Vázquez de Espinosa wrote: 'It has in its district by the sea coast which is of a warm climate, fertile valleys and plains of more than forty leagues width where since 1615 have been sown great orchards and cacao fields which give forth cacao in great abundance. They brought the cacao from the mountain ranges of the interior where there were great hillsides and stands of wild cacao . . .') There was now no trace of *Theobroma*, but plenty of evidence of other noble fruits: above my bedroom terrace a huge mango tree was in full ripeness, dropping its orange fruit all about with heavy thuds, sending me out with plastic bags to gather them greed-ily, remembering the price fruit shops in European cities charge for a single mango hard and green inside and impregnated with preservatives. I ate my mangoes in the classical style: naked in the shower, or leaning over a sink as the juice ran down my arms. More than once I asked myself whether the luscious flesh and acid sweetness of fridge-cooled tropical fruit, in the sticky heat of a tropical afternoon, wasn't an even greater luxury, for a northern European, than chocolate itself.

The cacao growing regions of Venezuela traditionally fell into three groups: western, central and eastern. Nowhere is cacao a major crop any more, and in the western region it has almost disappeared. The eastern region has fallen on difficult times, with only a few haciendas still flying the flag of *criollo* excellence and technical know-how. Only the centre has held on to something of its reputation. Barlovento, an hour or so east of Caracas, accounts for half of all the Venezuelan crop and almost three quarters of its exports, and still manages to produce a high quality cacao that finds its way to the best European chocolatiers. Hacienda La Concepción, where I spent a day in the company of manager Silvino Reyes, provides the fermented and sun dried *criollo* and *trinitario* beans that go towards a single-estate, high-cacao, black-as-the-devil, absolutely super-duper chocolate bar made by Parisian wizard Michel Cluizel.

But the legendary names of Venezuelan cacao are the string of villages along the Caribbean coast, about a hundred miles west of the capital. Cuyagua, Cumboto, Cata, Ocumare, Cepe, Choroní and Chuao . . . to the serious chocolate-worshipper, these names are sacrosanct.

When I grew tired of the whisky and paella parties of the Spanish expatriate set in Caracas, I took a long-distance bus to Maracay and a taxi to the coast via a long-unrepaired switch-back road that wound breathtakingly upward and gaspingly downward through the jungles of the Parque Nacional Henri Pittier, depositing me eventually in the Venezuelan equivalent of a country house hotel.

The Hacienda La Aljorra had looked nice on the Internet, but there is something about being the only guest in a rambling, ramshackle hotel in the low season, especially when one happens to be a writer, that always brings to mind that scariest of scary movies, *The Shining*. La Aljorra had its fair share of ghosts. The house was a former cacao plantation and depot, built in the eighteenth century, and still had its handsome covered walk-ways and the classicizing columns of colonial Hispanic architecture. But the old place was soulless, silent and sad. At the front of the house was the drying floor, now cracked and weed-infested after years of disuse. The great plantation was long since overgrown, and a last handful of cacao trees left out in the garden were slowly dying, their leaves littering the ground as in an English autumn. Cacao likes to hide in the shade of the forest and responds to all attempts at cultivation in direct sunlight with a two-fingered gesture of contempt, in the shape of falling yields and debilitating illnesses.

The Aljorra was miles from anywhere and a long way from Choroní, beside the switchback road that brought me down the mountainside. All morning I waited for a bus. When none came, I started walking. The air was full of a suffocating grey mist of heat, but I found a path along a forest stream that played foot-sie with the road, crisscrossing it under bridges and then losing itself for a while amid clumps of giant bamboo that creaked and groaned like seagoing galleons.

Choroní itself was a pretty little town of low colonial houses, some painted garish tropical shades of blue and orange, others slapdash with whitewash. One house had a stucco ornament above the door: three plump cacao pods, hanging there like a talisman. Several hand-scrawled signs advertised *pasta de cacao*, a hard ball of chocolate paste to be ground into milk or water. This was clearly a chocolate town of sorts, though the business end had shrunk into a cottage industry.

In the low whitewashed house with the tiled roof opposite the church in Choroní, Pedro Ramón Sosa offered me a drink of fresh lemonade in a dirty porcelain cup. He was a wiry, very white-skinned, elderly man in a grubby shirt and trousers and a grey-brown beard of a month or so. His father had been a *gran cacao* of the old school, owner of several big haciendas in the Choroní area who passed them on to his son, who sold them off one by one.

Señor Sosa's own house was a fine colonial house in a town consisting largely of them, with a tiled roof sloping inwards towards a central patio overgrown with dazzling scarlet flowers the size of flamethrowers. There was junk everywhere; old radios, pages ripped from magazines, unmade beds with torn and yellowed sheets. I had an impression of decay and tedium.

'The girl comes once a week,' he said apologetically, surveying the squalor.

His family had made its fortune with a trinity of luxury crops: coconut, coffee and cacao. Coconut down on the beach. For as far as an hour's walk would take you inland, cacao. And on the higher slopes, coffee. That was what his father used to say.

'We once had five haciendas. San Miguel, La Sabaneta, Santa Apolonia, Santa Clara and La Aljorra. Our cacao was *criollo*, the very best. You could tell by the size of the bean, and it was white, white, white inside. We had five or six workers on each farm. They used to make their fiestas down at the port. We never had any trouble with labour relations, as far as I can remember – not like the problems you get these days. The workers all lived nearby, on the estates.'

He waved his hand in the air dismissively, as if to say 'good riddance'.

Of the Sosa family's five haciendas, two were now hotels. Two more had fallen into abandonment and disrepair. But the fifth had taken on a surprising new lease of life. Word was that the only flourishing plantation in the area was owned by a wealthy foreigner who had already restored the house and was now busy sorting out the land. Clearly things were going well for the man, because rumour also had it that the Choroní house with the cacao pods above the door had recently come into his possession – a town house to go with his hacienda up there in the forest.

There would be buses today, I was told in the main square. When did they leave?

'Soon. Don't worry, mister. Bus come, no problem.'

The rhythm of life in Choroní was adagio. It was pointless to try and accomplish very much in this climate, with this Caribbean soon-come mentality. After another morning's wait I began to doubt the existence of a bus, and set off once more on foot, following the same river path that led past La Aljorra and up through the forest to La Sabaneta.

The big house was some way back from the road, invisible behind a thick swathe of cacao groves. I turned off the path and plunged into the forest's almost frighteningly exuberant vegetative profusion, feeling dwarfed and enclosed, both protected and vaguely intimidated by this overarching shade and humid stillness. When I looked up, I could see the canopy of treetops interspersed with jungle vines and pendulous parasitical plants and bukaré trees that flower in a surreal explosion of flaming red-orange; ficus and Swiss cheese plant grown to monstrous size in this tropical sauna; and the skeletal strands of the Lady of the Night which blooms once a year in the early hours of the morning and dies at dawn. Looking down, I saw the ferns, the creepers, the clouds of minuscule flies that pollinate *Theobroma*'s tiny flowers, and the thick mulch or crust of dead leaves in which they breed.

As a plantation, you could see this one meant business. Under their great marquee the cacao trees themselves were laid out in a grid formation, although, perverse creatures that they are, they had since grown into chaotically irregular shapes and sizes. In a slow period for fruit, workers were giving them some TLC. While one man delicately pruned them with a huge machete, another cleared away the dead leaves and tendrils from around the roots of each tree, while a third dug in some kind of animal manure.

The forest hummed with echoing sound. If I stopped and listened hard, I could hear the thud of falling fruit and the quiet dry sounds of leaves tumbling to the forest floor. I felt myself falling into a mildly hypnotic state; for a moment I wondered whether I might be about to faint.

Kids in school uniform skipped along the forest path to their homes, a group of tied cottages on the estate. Their voices echoed under the canopy, mingling with the liquid notes of tropical birds. They caught up with me and interrogated me mercilessly. Afterwards one of them, a sweet little black girl with braided hair, took me by the hand and led me up to the big house. As we passed a ramshackle shrine hung with torn coloured garlands and peopled with plastic virgins and rustic wooden saints, she said gaily: *'Nosotros hicimos eso.'* 'We made that.'

The focal point of all Venezuelan cacao haciendas is the drying floor, and this one was no exception. The house was a collection of pitched roofs whose old brown tiles sloped gently down over a wide columned corridor running around the side of the wide square patio. The living quarters were decorated in eclectic style, with bright coloured abstract paintings on cool white walls, terracotta floors and a minimum of clutter. It was the kind of house you wouldn't be surprised to find in one of those books of architectural pornography called things like *Caribbean Style, Venezuelan Interiors, Fabulous Dwellings You'll Never Be Able to Afford* . . .

When I arrived, the cook and the major-domo were in the kitchen making breakfast. Though it was halfway through the morning, the master of the house, who had arrived from Germany the night before, was still snoring in his bed.

I sat in the shade with a cup of coffee as the tropical morning worked up through the gears and drank in the sense of order and continuity and fruitfulness that emanated from this forest setting, this river gurgling and gushing in the valley floor below me, and this marvellous house, a colonial *casa grande* functioning more or less as it would have done in the eighteenth century – minus the electricity and the abstract paintings. At the edge of the drying floor stood a whitewashed shrine decorated with a naif design of cacao pods, leaves and bunches of flowers; within the niche a cross wrapped in multi-coloured paper garlands – the Cruz de Mayo (May Cross) that has been a tradition among cacao estate workers ever since the arrival of the Spanish.

There were sounds of stirring from the bedroom, and in due course the Master emerged, wearing Bermuda shorts and a T-shirt and nothing on his feet. He was a pale-skinned figure with a generous belly and skinny limbs, yet clearly a person of tremendous physical vitality with a business brain to match. Señor Rosenberg was a German who had Hispanicised himself so efficiently that there was almost no German-ness visible any more, apart from the pale northern European skin. His Spanish was an impeccable counterfeit of the local variant, practically accent-free. When he answered his mobile phone he said, as only genuine Venezuelans do: '*Alo?*'

He sat down at the table under the eaves, called for coffee, and told me about himself and his hacienda.

'I first bought the place as a holiday home. It hadn't been touched for fifty, sixty, seventy years. And the plantation was worse – totally overgrown. But I soon realised that there was some very fine *criollo* cacao here. Very fine indeed. It took three or four years to get started, and now I'm pleased to say we have twenty hectares in full production.'

The telephone rang.

'*Alo? Alo?*'

Pause. '*Ah, bonjour. Ça va?* Yes, it's all organised, the flights are booked. Yes, for next Friday. We'll be flying straight down to see the new plantations, as agreed. Yes, *merveilleux*, I'm sure you'll enjoy the trip. We'll be flying direct to El Vigía.' Pause. '*Mais oui, bien sûr.* I'll get an itinerary over to you in the next few days. *Voilà. Merci. A bientôt.*' And he hung up and hurried to explain.

The call was from Valrhona, the famous French company who have led the way in making chocolate from special cacao sourced in particular places. By analogy with fine wine, they use the term *grand cru*. The company is always on the lookout for new sources of fine cacao and have found from experience that Venezuela, with its heritage of rare *criollo* varieties, represents the happiest of hunting grounds. Kai Rosenberg's job is to act as a kind of talent scout.

'I am managing a plantation for them in the south of Lake Maracaibo, and they're coming over to see it. It's a very exciting thing – we've got a lot of real old *criollos* down there. Some real old famous types, Porcelana, Guasare, Novillero, all absolutely 100 per cent pure . . .' He swigged his coffee to the dregs and waved it above his head, whereupon the cook bustled out of the kitchen with a fresh pot.

Until after 1825, when the so-called *forastero trinitario* was introduced from Trinidad, the Venezuelan haciendas planted only *criollo* varieties. Swiss naturalist Henri Pittier, writing in 1935, traced the arrival of *criollo* cacao to a group of Spanish Capuchin missionaries who brought seeds from Costa Rica, or possibly Cuba, during the early seventeenth century. It seems more probable, however, that *criollo* had its origin in the forests around Lake Maracaibo – not far from the site of Valrhona's new plantation – from which it was taken north to Mexico by indigenous traders and brought south again by Spanish missionaries.

What Kai Rosenberg doesn't know about *criollo* cacao probably isn't worth knowing. He is Mister Criollo. So I felt justified in asking him the crucial and urgent, though dumbly obvious question:

'What is the difference, then, between *criollo* and *forastero*?'

'I won't tell you that,' he said loudly, springing from his chair. 'I'll show you instead.' He disappeared into the bedroom again and reappeared in a pair of leather sandals, brandishing a stick. 'Come.'

He disappeared down a path that led to a small gate, beyond

which was the bottle-green curtain of the forest. When I caught up with him he was standing beside one of the young trees in the newest part of the plantation, examining a slender pod that had barely reached half-size. It was a deep and luscious russet red.

'Of course, all this goes to Valrhona. All *criollo*. All top quality. Look. See the long shaped pod, the furrows along it, the point at the end? The *forastero* is wider, rounder. And there's one other big difference. This one isn't yet ripe. But when you open up a ripe *criollo* pod, you'll see the beans are white inside. *Forastero* has more purple. A good *criollo* bean is white. White like a pearl, and not at all bitter.'

We made a brief tour of the hacienda, a brisk morning walk that brought me out in a sticky sweat. Kai took great deep breaths of humid forest air, beaming with satisfaction. He was happy to be home. In Europe he was just a businessman. At La Sabaneta he seemed to grow in stature. As he strode around his domain, whacking the weeds with his stick, it was tempting to see him as a neo-colonial gentleman farmer, a contemporary version of the *grandes cacaos* of the eighteenth century.

At another tree he knelt down to show me the flowers in their delicate clusters up the trunk. Pigs were forbidden on plantations in the old days, because their rubbing on the tree trunks took its toll on the crop.

'See how pale the flowers are? That's another sign of *criollo*,' he told me in a whisper, brushing the tiny petals with his forefinger. 'But you want to know the clearest sign of all? It's the taste.' He was on his feet again, marching back to the house. 'Come. Breakfast time.'

While we were out a big dining table had been laid out on the terrace, with fine china and silver forks and a linen tablecloth. More than a mere breakfast, this was a tropical mid-morning feast of sweet maize pancakes, spiced shredded meat and black bean chilli, fresh goat's cheese and avocado, and a big bowl of pineapple and mango and breadfruit – all from the hacienda – and bunches of miniature bananas called *titiaro*, tastier and finer textured than any banana in the world ever.

It was all washed down with a thick sweet foaming hot chocolate, aromatic with allspice, served in terracotta cups. It was sensational. But then it would be. The chocolate had been made that morning, with beans from the trees whose shapes I could see, just beyond the terrace. And it was all *criollo*, all *grand cru*. What I was drinking was liquid Valrhona.

'Yes, of course you should go to Chuao. Nice place. OK cacao,' said Kai as I left.

In the little harbour at Choroní, where the jungle river meets the sea and the fishermen swig their Polar beers in the bar with the blaring salsa music, I stood on the sand and waited for a lift along the coast. The population around here was 90 per cent black, with a lustrous sub-Saharan blue-blackness that spoke volumes of history. These are the descendants of the Sudanese slaves that worked the vast coastal cacao plantations in colonial times. In the pockets of cacao production that remain, their descendants continue to do so. At the fiestas of Saint John the roots come right to the surface in the drumming parties held every night on the harbourside, when local guys beat away on enormous drums laid on their sides, and couples shake the night away to a wild jittery African dance.

It is no secret that the economic importance of cacao to the province of New Granada was largely underpinned by slavery. In 1788 there were no fewer than 60,000 African slaves among a total population of 300,000, mostly employed on the cacao haciendas. An eighteenth-century handbook of cacao production, *Modo de fundar hacienda de cacao y sus comodidades*, recommends that, 'to care for every thousand trees . . . one only needs one useful slave'. So central was slave labour to the industry that when the Venezuelan President José Gregorio Monagas decreed its abolition in 1854, there was a dramatic fall in productivity.

I drank a cup of passion fruit juice and sat on the harbour wall, watching the fishing boats come and go and the sun slowly bleach away the colours of the morning. A white girl called Rosa Elena, owner of a flat-based fishing boat, needed to pop over to Chuao to pick up a bunch of bananas. Here was my lift! We sped out of the harbour into a sea that pitched the boat into the air before pulling it back down with frightening force. We passed beaches of wild and unvisited beauty and distant mountains. Rosa Elena left me at Chuao beach and went to look for her bananas, pointing the way inland to the village along a valley floor dense with greenery.

The sandy path wound among the forest. I walked alone in the shade and silence, flip-flops clacking. Villagers carrying machetes muttered '*a la orden*' – 'at your service' – as they passed, or creaked by on ancient bicycles. People on this Caribbean coast moved slowly through the damp heat, languidly, as if swimming in warm soup.

The midday heat buzzed and whirred. Clouds of tiny flies attacked my eyes and nose; mosquitoes assailed my shins and forearms. Among the forest trees threaded with vines and parasitic succulents and the giant banana fronds swaying gently, I began to make out the modest and unassuming trees that have brought worldwide fame to Chuao, their few fruits dangling from the slender trunks, coloured deep purple or pale apple green. The trees looked cared for and healthy, comfortable perhaps in the knowledge that their precious beans were destined not just for any old industrial chocolate-making process, but only for the finest chocolatiers of old Europe.

An hour's walk brought me to the diminutive and scraggy

village, a few streets of low houses, a little white church splashily whitewashed, its façade picked out in cheap electric blue. At the end of the square beyond the church was the original dwelling house of the hacienda, a white balconied building on two floors, the ground floor of which was now a small and exceedingly scruffy and sadly padlocked museum. Through the keyhole I saw skulls, coloured tribal masks from the rituals of Corpus Christi, an immense wooden mortar apparently made from the trunk of a tree, all unkempt and gathering dust.

Black barefoot kids played marbles in the street. The heat was scorching, African. I took refuge under the pitched roofs around the square, where there was a village bar selling ice cold beers and shots of rum, and a shop that sold two very different kinds of chocolate: handmade tablets of ground local cacao spiced with cinnamon and nutmeg, meant as the basis for a drink, and cheap bars of industrial chocolate of infinitely inferior quality, pale, dry and crumbly and tasting of practically nothing. It was like finding Blue Nun in a village shop in Burgundy – an absurdity.

Chuao is often described as a *ne plus ultra* of excellence where cacao is concerned. The mere mention of the name sends a certain kind of ultra-sophisticated chocolate fiend into a poetic frenzy. The French, with their propensity for drawing outrageous gastronomic analogies, have compared the village both to Château d'Yquem, the home of the famously exquisite and expensive wine of Sauternes, and to the Burgundy domaine of Romanée-Conti. I have compared it, earlier in this book, to the village of Montrachet, which, I dare say, seems a better comparison than either.

The Japanese magazine *Eat*, that madly fashionable cult publication for ice-cool foodies, once carried an article on Pierre Hermé, an avant-garde patissier whose work has more in common with contemporary sculpture than cooking. A full-page close-up of one of his oeuvres showed a sinuous slender wall of dark chocolate, reminiscent of Richard Serra's vast iron forms at the Guggenheim in Bilbao. The caption read: 'Fresh chocolate ganache filled with cassis and crème de cassis, coated with Chuao chocolate and gold leaf.'

Chuao has been told so many times that it grows the Best Cacao in the World that it has started to believe its own publicity. 'Chuao: home of the Best Cacao in the World' announced a welcoming sign beside the village square. This may not be true; but then again it may be.

Around the edges of the patio was a series of spaces dedicated to the processing and storage of Chuao's precious crop. On the wall beside the factory door was a twice-lifesize portrait of Simon Bolivar, saviour and idol of the Venezuelan people, and a handwritten notice that spoke volumes about the importance of cacao in the village, given the general poverty of its inhabitants and the enormity of the mentioned sum: 'Any *macho* found burning, cutting or uprooting cacao trees on the estate will be fined $80 per tree.'

Good cacao, and therefore good chocolate, depends largely on what happens to the product directly after its removal from the tree. Nothing decent can be done, for example, with any cacao that hasn't been properly fermented and properly dried. The post-harvest process in Chuao is highly rustic and basic and traditional, and can't have changed substantially for hundreds of years. Here was the fermenting room, lit with a single hanging bulb, where the beans still drenched in their sticky white pulp lay in wood-lined boxes, covered with banana leaves, for nearly a week, while the chocolate-flavoured alkaloids surged and grew within their pale flesh. And in front of the church was the great *patio secadero*, the drying floor doubling as a churchyard where the cacao is laid out in circles in the blistering sun for five whole days to toast and dry and darken to the colour of mahogany.

Through the heat haze on the patio moved three women in

brightly coloured African dresses, pushing the beans around the patio with long wooden paddles.

'By San Juan Bautista!' one of them swore at me, wiping her brow with the back of her hand. She was a big black mama with a bad temper. 'I said no photographs when I'm bending down!'

In the darkened warehouse beside the square lay a pile of finished beans, jute sacks thrown over them to keep the flies off. The room was dark, the floor and half the walls lined with planks, a symphony in ancient dark brown, pungent with ancient and dark brown aromas. I picked up a handful of beans and breathed in the surprising smells of wine and bread and vinegar, then peeled off the rust brown skin and crunched one in my mouth. It was edible though not very tasty: faintly bitter, toasty and astringent. There was almost nothing, except for the bitterness and the deep brown blackness, to tell my tastebuds that this had anything at all to do with the sweet, smooth and voluptuous substance they were used to wrapping themselves around so often.

The women had moved into the shade to sort and grade an earlier batch of sun-dried beans. They sang quietly as they worked, fanning their faces with their hands. Beside them stood the sorting machine, a cast-iron contraption of unknown vintage, by which the beans rattled around in a central drum and emerged at the bottom through a series of tubes. A label on the side of the machine read J LABASSON, CONSTRUCTEUR, MECANICIEN, 108 RUE ST MAUR, PARIS.

'It is two hundred years old,' said Angel Herrera, reading my thoughts. Señor Herrera was the elected President of the Empresa Campesina de Chuao, the cooperative that now runs the village hacienda after a string of private owners stretching all the way back to 1560. He invited me into his office for an ice-cold beer and a chat, telling me how the entire production of Chuao was once bought by Valrhona, but had now been snapped up by the Italian chocolatier Amedei, based in Pisa, who were prepared to pay almost twice as much. Angel grinned from ear to ear, entertained by the fact that prestigious European companies were fighting over the produce of his snoozy scruffy Venezuelan village.

'Until a few years ago, production was falling. The trees were never cared for. Then we decided to give the trees a good prune, and the yield started to increase. From 90kg a hectare, we some-times get up to 160kg.' The harvest is tiny. So tiny, in fact, that one wonders how all the prestigious European chocolate bars described as being made from Chuao cacao can possibly be kosher.

'We make 17 tons a year. Next year we are aiming for 20 tons,' said Angel. The Empresa Campesina was on the move. They had just signed a deal with the Ministry of Agriculture by which Chuao would soon have its own Denominación de Origen, like the fine foodstuffs of Europe. Children at the vil-lage school were already busy with their pencils, designing logos and labels which would one day accompany the local cacao in its journey across the Atlantic.

When I left the office the big bad-tempered mama was snoozing on a chair in the darkened warehouse, guarding the pile of precious Chuao beans. I grabbed a handful from under her nose and tiptoed out into the sun.

Back at the beach, Rosa Elena sat in a beach bar where the big-bellied owner, known as Velocidad (Speedy), lay snoring in a hammock. Salsa blared from the radio. Rosa had picked up her bananas, eaten half of them and given away the rest, swum a little and drunk a number of ice-cold beers. It had been a busy day.

Five hundred years to the year after cacao's first brush with Western consciousness, a world without chocolate is one that

few Westerners would care to imagine. Chocolate has become
central to our psychic geography, taking its place among the
'base flavours', the primary colours of our sense of taste.
Though the professional chocolate-taster (that lucky breed)
may find echoes of flowers and fruits, suggestions of smoke and
honey and leather, there are no words to describe the basic
taste of chocolate. Like oranges, coffee, bread, and olive oil, it
tastes only of itself – 'chocolatey'. But how strange this substance must have seemed to eyes and palates that had never
encountered it before: a murky, foaming liquid whose bitterness
was undisguised by sugar, and often accentuated by the pun-
gency of spices and the heat of chillies.

Early travellers in the New World were overwhelmingly
struck by one thing about this 'almond' and the peculiar drink
made from it: the high esteem in which both were held by the
barbaric peoples who had so recently submitted to European
domination. When tribute collectors arrived at a provincial
village from Montezuma's court, Bernal Diaz del Castillo
describes how the locals, quaking with fear, received them with
much ceremony and a banquet including '*mucho* cacao, which
is the best thing that they drink'. Chocolate as the Spanish saw
it formed part of the luxurious and exotic lifestyle of the Aztec
upper classes, who consumed it in prodigious quantities.
Chroniclers like Fray Bernardino de Sahagún were fascinated by
the imperial wealth and prestige it seemed to epitomise.
Sahagún gleefully records that, for example, two thousand pots
of foaming *xocolatl* were once drunk at a single banquet in
Tenochtitlan – though as one modern historian usefully points
out, these pots would have been less than half full of liquid,
since it was the foam above all that was the object of the
exercise.

But it was the value of chocolate in monetary terms that initially drew the attention of the foreigners. On the island of
Guanaja in 1502, at the historic moment of its first sighting by

Europeans, Christopher Columbus' younger brother Ferdinand astutely observed that the natives 'seemed to hold these almonds at great price; for when they were brought on board ship together with all their goods, I observed that when any of these almonds fell, they all stooped to pick it up, as if an eye had fallen'. Eighteen years later, in his first letter to the Emperor Charles V, Hernán Cortés told how Moctezuma had created for the emperor an *estancia* (plantation) including two thousand cacao trees, explaining that cacao gave a 'fruit like almonds, which they sell milled, and set so much store by it, that it is used as money across the land, and with it are bought all things necessary in the markets and in other places'. For centuries after the Spanish conquest cacao continued to be used as money; it is said that well into the twentieth century the beans were still common currency in the markets of rural Mexico. There was even a suggestion by Pedro Flores de León, a seventeenth-century professor at Salamanca University, that the cacao bean should be made valid as a form of currency back home in Castile. The phrase *'no vale un cacao'* – literally 'not worth a bean' – originated in colonial Mexico but passed into the language of the mother country and is still occasionally heard on the streets of Madrid even today.

Few of the writers of post-Conquest chronicles bothered to say much about the appearance and taste of the chocolate drink – partly because they simply had nothing to compare it with, and partly because very few of them had actually tasted it at first hand. Even the so-called Anonymous Conquistador, who wrote at some length about the monetary use of cacao and its correct method of cultivation, concluding that chocolate was 'the healthiest and of most substance of so many foods and drinks that are known in the world', declined to say a single word about its taste. Bartolomé de las Casas, who almost certainly had tried the drink, calls it 'very substantial, very cooling, tasty and agreeable', and remarked that it 'does not intoxicate'.

Not least among the oddities of this new drink must have been
that it did not contain alcohol – for there were as yet in Europe,
before the arrival of tea and coffee, no non-alcoholic drinks
besides milk and water.

Early European attitudes to chocolate ran the gamut of
reactions, from curiosity and scepticism to outright hostility.
What some visitors were made to feel was sheer physical
revulsion. Since the drink was often laced with *achiote*
(annatto) it tended to stain the lips and teeth bright red, giving
the impression that the natives had been drinking blood.
Perhaps the most authentic description of sixteenth-century
chocolate tasted *sur place* comes from the Italian soldier
Girolamo Benzoni, who famously compared it to pig food.
What is interesting about Benzoni's subsequent remarks, however, is just how quickly his initial disgust turns to grudging
tolerance, and thence almost to respect – a volte-face which
seems to enact in microcosm the process of cacao's assim-
ilation by the Western palate: '. . . this [drink] seems more like
the swill of pigs than a drink for men. I was in this country for
more than a year, and came to loathe it for a season, but given
that I did not have a store of wine and could not always drink
water, I decided to do as the others. This [drink] is hot, in
flavour somewhat bitter, it satisfies and refreshes the body,
inebriates a little, it is the most expensive and important merchandise of that country and there is nothing that costs more
for the Indians, among whom, however, it is of common use.'

As the level of contact increased, so did the degree of curiosity. Theories regarding cacao and its virtues and defects from
points of view medical, ethical and gastronomic, began to come
forth and multiply. One of the most fascinating early descriptions of chocolate as a drink and as a medicine comes to us
from Francisco Hernández who visited Mexico in 1572 and
published the results of his findings in an encyclopedic work on
the plants of New Spain, including their names in the nahuatl

language of the Aztecs. 'Some abominate chocolate, making it the cause of all the illnesses that are. Others say that there is nothing better in the world, and that with it they fatten and restore the appetite and a good colour to the face', he wrote. One man's meat . . .

The ambivalent, even ambiguous nature of chocolate has always allowed for widely diverging opinions. The nature of this controversial substance was a subject dealt with at great length by one of the earliest English travellers in post-Conquest Mesoamerica, Thomas Gage. Gage was an apostate, a Catholic who converted to Protestantism and cheerfully betrayed a number of his former confessors in the process. Following Gage's testimony a certain Father Thomas Holland was hung, drawn and quartered in 1642 for the crime of being a Roman Catholic who had said Mass in England. Revolted by his behaviour, Gage's brother offered him £1000 to leave the country – an offer which the errant Gage found impossible to refuse.

He was plainly in some ways an unpleasant character, yet his writings reveal a fine degree of sensitivity to the world around him, not to mention a wicked sense of humour. Apart from providing perhaps the first description of transatlantic 'culture shock' in literature – 'thus as we were truly transported from Europe to America, so the world seemed truly to be altered, our senses changed from what they were the night and day before . . .' – Gage was as finely responsive as all travellers ought to be to the new foods and flavours of his journey, be they tortoise meat ('sea-veal'), shark, banana or *chicosapote*, a rubbery sap extracted from the sapodilla tree which provided a kind of chewing gum.

Gage was what would be called nowadays a chocoholic. For the twelve years he spent abroad he drank five cups of chocolate every day, 'without any obstructions or oppilations, not knowing what either ague or fever was'. He had heard rumours that the use of chocolate makes you 'fat and corpulent', and had seen evidence of this in other people, but never in himself. As made by the nuns and gentlewomen of the colony, with cinnamon, amber or musk, and sugar, it was a 'strong and nourishing drink, which the physicians do prescribe unto a weak body as we do here our almond milk'. Nowhere in his narrative does Gage describe the taste of chocolate; as a health drink, on the other hand, it was efficacious in every way.

One of the urgent questions first asked in the century after chocolate's 'discovery' was whether it caused blockages, or 'stoppages', in the digestive system. According to Gage, if cacao were eaten in raw form, without grinding or otherwise treating the beans, the result might be grievous: 'if it be not stirred, grinded, and compounded to make the chocolate, but be eaten as it is in the fruit (as many Creole and Indian women eat it), it doth notably obstruct and cause stoppings, and make them look of a broken, pale and earthy colour'. During the process of chocolate-making, however, by which 'the divers parts which nature hath given it do artificially and intimately mix themselves one with another', the 'cold and dry' character of cacao would be partly transmuted into 'warm and moist'. Result: no more stoppings or obstructions.

The image is unsettling in its false, kitschy jollity. A monk wearing a voluminous hooded cape – its dark brown woollen weave perhaps suggesting the Franciscan order – is enjoying a cup of chocolate. A thick-set, portly man, his ruddy face framed by squarish folds and jowls that remind the viewer of the deep folds of his cape, he seems to loom out of the shadows, lit brightly from the front in an echo of baroque chiaroscuro. His hands look preternaturally large as they grip the small cup (right hand, tip of forefinger barely fitting into the handle) and tin plate (held underneath in the left hand). The predominant colours are white and brown. White cup and plate, whites of eyes half-closed in bliss, and an array of white, pointed teeth as the monk smiles a beatific yet oddly sinister smile. Two dark drips can be seen running down the side of the cup, perhaps suggesting a less than lilywhite reputation.

Long before the laity caught on to it, the monks and nuns of New Spain were already avid consumers of the chocolate drink. The hundreds of monasteries and convents in New Spain were hotbeds of chocophilia. The evening before the feast days of Saint Francis and Saint Dominic, patrons of the Franciscans and Dominicans respectively, saw a traditional meeting between the two orders after which a 'simple *merienda*' was served – *merienda* translating roughly into modern English as 'afternoon snack', and into the customs of New Spain as a chocolate feast including at least a dozen different varieties of sweetmeats. 'With such exquisite things to dip, there was no friar who took a single sip of chocolate; all the reverend *señores* raised it genteelly by hand to their mouths, cup after cup', wrote Artemio del Valle Arizpe, adding in their defence: 'That was an everlasting delight, but an innocent one. Saint Francis of Sales has said that what enters the mouth, does not harm the soul.'

The presence of chocolate in monastic life continued at least until the early nineteenth century, when Brillat-Savarin was given a hot tip by the Mother Superior of the Convent of the Visitation in his home town of Belley: '. . . it is sufficient to prepare it the evening before in a ceramic coffee pot and to leave it. The night's rest concentrates it and gives it a velvety smoothness which makes it much better.'

Yet the Church, historically responsible at least in part for chocolate's triumph in Europe, could not quite make up its mind whether it was a good thing. In 1616 a committee of Doctors of the Church condemned it as the 'damnable agent of necromancers and sorcerers'; the cacao bean, it was said, 'carried within it malignity and the ferment of revolt'. In 1650 the

Jesuits of New Spain attempted to ban the drink among the Society of Jesus: the prohibition was a disaster, since members preferred to leave the order rather than be deprived of their favourite indulgence. The Jesuits had also made a successful business out of cacao trading.

The great debate about whether or not chocolate 'broke the fast' was to rage for two centuries or more after Pope Pius V pronounced in 1569 that, if made with water, the new drink might be consumed in the course of a ritual fast, since although it was restorative it was not actually a food. This decision appeared to make it safe for monastic consumption. After Pius' death, however, the controversy reignited. Doctor Juan de Cardenas argued in 1591 that any kind of solid food could be liquefied and thereby get around the rules, but Fray Agustín Dávila Padilla, consulted by the viceroy of Mexico, once again came down on the side of the pro-chocolate lobby – as did a succession of prelates from the sixteenth century to the eighteenth. It is hard to see how they could do otherwise, when so many of their members depended on chocolate for their physical wellbeing, not to mention their livelihood.

There were always dissenting voices. Some authorities espoused the liberal view of Tomás Hurtado, theology professor at Seville University, that if anything solid was added to the drink, such as eggs or milk (maize flour, oddly, was allowed, thus saving atole from the prohibition), it logically became a food, and thus 'broke the fast'. Others saw this as mere casuistry. 'For all the subtleties of Father Hurtado, I see that all the ingredients of which [chocolate] is composed are edible and very substantial, and that this drink gives great strength, heat and sustenance and relieves hunger for considerable time, and thus contains all the requisites of those drinks that for such reasons break the fast', wrote Juan de Solorzano y Pereyra.

Nevertheless, the more ascetic orders came down harshly on the consumption of chocolate. The Barefoot Carmelites, for example, decided that whatever the nature of the substance, it was so closely allied to the sinful pleasures of the flesh that its use by any Carmelite should be punished by a three-day penance of bread and water. This harsh sentence was eventually overturned by Pope Pius VI (1717–99) who allowed the monks to take chocolate, but only outside the walls of the monastery or, as a special exception, in case of sickness – bearing in mind the high nutritious value of chocolate, which of course was never in doubt.

By the eighteenth century, in any case, the battle had been largely won, and cacao had been thoroughly rehabilitated in the eyes of the Church. In 1743 Pope Benedict XIV presented chocolate pastilles as gifts to each of his Vatican guardsmen, and in 1799 the Chapter of Escuelas Pias of Catalonia approved a proposal for all priests more than sixty years old to receive a daily ration of chocolate. The powerful commercial association of chocolate with the Christian festivals of Christmas and Easter dates essentially from around 1830, when the new technique of 'tempering' made it possible to mould chocolate on an industrial scale into the delicate shapes of eggs, rabbits, and so on. At the start of the third millennium, more than eighty million chocolate eggs are sold every year in the United Kingdom. Either this means that Easter as a festival of rebirth and renewal is more popular than ever, or that the confectionery industry has found a way of satisfying our deepest spiritual yearnings with the shallowest of physical gratifications. Either way, the 'food of the gods' is still a consummation devoutly to be wished.

After an initial period of uncertainty, the Spanish colonies quickly became stalwart consumers of chocolate. Before the sixteenth century was over they had almost certainly surpassed their Aztec predecessors in the passion and quantity of their consumption. Chocolate was drunk at all hours, from morning until night, and accompanied all meals. The phrase *a la chocolatada* came to mean 'at eight in the morning' – the time of the day's first chocolate. *Chocolaterías* sprang up in most of the colonial cities and at strategic points along major roads, so that travellers and those away from home would not have to break their accustomed chocolate regime. Chocolate was manufactured in the form of round, square or cylindrical pastilles to be crumbled or grated into boiling water. It could be bought either from small *obrajes* (workshops) or from the convents of Mexico City; the best producers, it was generally agreed, being the nuns of Saint Jerome, the Capuchins and the Poor Clares.

As the chocolate-drinking fashion took hold, New Spanish society was gripped by a benign madness. The ladies of the colony in particular took to the drink with a vengeance, demanding to have their chocolate served to them even in the Cathedral of Chiapas (contemporary San Cristobal). The women of the city, said Gage, 'pretend much weakness and squeamishness of stomach, which they say is so great that they are not able to continue in the church while a Mass is briefly huddled over, much less while a solemn high Mass (as they call it) is sung and a sermon preached, unless they drink a cup of hot chocolate, and eat a bit of sweetmeats to strengthen their stomachs'. Gage's story of the goings-on in the cathedral has been much repeated, but neatly serves to illustrate the extremes to which the true chocolate-lover will go in pursuit of her quarry. Don Bernardino de Salazar, bishop of Chiapas, became tired of the constant interruptions of maidservants bringing their mistresses cups of steaming chocolate as they sat in their pews in the chilly cathedral. It was not only a distraction from the holy sacrament, reasoned Salazar, but consumed in such gluttonous quantities came dangerously close to vice. When gentle persuasion had no effect, he threatened to excommunicate anyone eating or drinking in church. The response from the ladies was furious: if the bishop would not allow them to take their chocolate in his church, they would take it, and their custom, elsewhere. There were uproarious scenes as the priests tried to confiscate the ladies' chocolate cups as they arrived from the kitchens of the city's grand houses. Before long the cathedral was empty and the ladies comfortably ensconced in one or other of the convents around the city, where the chocolate tradition was deeply rooted and perfectly acceptable.

But the saga was not quite over. The bishop fell ill and not only his symptoms, but the rapid decomposition of his body after death, seemed to suggest that he had been poisoned. Furthermore, the finger of guilt seemed to point to a particular lady who, according to Chiapas gossips, had persuaded the bishop's page to administer the poison to his master in – irony of ironies – a cup of chocolate. The bishop, says Gage, 'lay not above a week in the cloister, and as soon as he was dead, all his body, his head and face, did so swell that the least touch upon any part of him caused the skin to break and cast out white matter, which had corrupted and overflown all his body'. This unsavoury episode gave rise to the expression '*le dieron su chocolate*' – 'he got his chocolate', or 'he got what was coming to him' – which, according to the Mexican writer Ana Maria de Benitez, is still a common expression in San Cristobal de las Casas. For his part, from that day forth, Thomas Gage refused to take chocolate in any household where he couldn't be 100 per cent sure of coming out alive. He was particularly cautious of the notorious Ladies of Chiapas. 'The women of this city are somewhat light in their carriage, and have learned from the Devil many enticing lessons and baits to draw poor souls to sin and damnation', he sentenced; 'and if they cannot have their wills, they will surely work revenge either by chocolate or conserves, or some fair present, which shall surely carry death along with it.'

For some time after the Conquest the basic colonial recipe for the chocolate drink continued to be the same as that of the indigenous peoples – indeed, it was they who mostly continued to prepare it, in their new roles as cooks and servants. Little by little however, European tastes began to prevail. Doctor Juan de Cardeñas, who in 1591 published a work appetisingly entitled *The Problems and Marvellous Secrets of the Indies*, writes as follows: 'Though it is true that each lady enjoys making her own invention and mode of chocolate, even so, the most generally used in the Indies, is in the form of tablets, the which had its origin with the Guatemalan ladies; and this type is that which is dissolved in hot water and a touch of sweetness, which favours it greatly.' There was also another type, served cold with powdered toasted maize or atole, which was popular among the common people, and sold in all the streets and squares of Mexico. The atole drink was 'the coolest chocolate of all, that which best quenches the thirst and gives most sustenance'.

It was common practice, as in the Aztec court, to whip up the drink into a foam. But no longer was this achieved by pouring the chocolate from one container into another from a great height. For reasons which are not at all clear, the pre-Conquest custom was suddenly replaced by a quite different technique. The *molinillo* was the first great Spanish contribution to chocolate culture. The word is supposed to be a diminutive of the Spanish *molino*, meaning mill, although one eminent scholar traces its etymology back to the nahuatl verb *molinia*, 'to shake, waggle or move'. The object is made of wood, with a long handle and a kind of bulb with deep cuts and loose wooden rings and other complications with which to form air bubbles when the *molinillo* is whisked in the liquid, the handle rubbed to and fro between the palms of both hands. It is, I suppose, the ancestor of the hand-held mixer.

Along with the *molinillo* came a series of other innovations.

The Aztecs had drunk their *xocolatl* from the same dried pumpkin shells in which they prepared the drink – the *xicalli*, later Hispanicised to *jicara* – though for ceremonial and palace use the vessels were often exquisitely painted. Under Spanish colonial rule preparation and consumption became distinct activities, perhaps owing to the newly imposed class system by which servants prepared, and masters consumed, and two new objects duly appeared. The *chocolatera* was a stout pot-bellied jug with feet, originally made of terracotta or copper, then of tin, pewter, porcelain, enamel and precious metals, incorporating the *molinillo* whose handle emerged through a hole in the lid. The earliest known example in silver was presented to Louis XIV by the ambassador of Siam in 1686; the first in porcelain was made at Sèvres in 1784. Madame de Sévigné, the celebrated lady of letters, declared it an essential element of stylish living, writing to her daughter in the provinces on 11 February 1671: '*Mais vous n'avez point de chocolatière, j'y ai pensé mille fois: comment ferez-vous?*' The *chocolatière* was to reach the heights of decorative sophistication in the eighteenth and nineteenth centuries, before disappearing with the invention of soluble cocoa powder.

As in so many other ways, the arrival of the Spanish brought about a series of irremediable changes within the agriculture of cacao in Mesoamerica. At the time of the Conquest most cacao was grown in the coastal lands of tropical Central America, major areas of cultivation being Xoconochco (Soconusco) and Tabasco in modern Mexico, Izalco in El Salvador, Nito in Belize, and other pockets in Nicaragua, Guatemala and Costa Rica. Most cacao was still grown on small family-owned plantations as part of a mixed regime of cacao, maize, cotton, tobacco and kitchen-garden crops such as beans, tomatoes, avocados, chillies, squash, yucca and peanuts, known in the Pipil-Nicarao region as *cacao de la tierra*. We know from the testimony of Fernández de Oviedo y Valdés, chronicler for the Spanish crown between

1532 and 1557, that indigenous farmers' cultivation methods took account of the importance of shade trees, the so-called 'mothers of cacao'. '. . . Some years the sun scalds [the trees] in such a way that it fruits in vain and doesn't form correctly and is lost. To remedy this they put other trees in between, the Indians call these other trees Yaquaquyt and the Christians call them blackwood. They grow almost twice the size of cacao and they protect them from the sun, and make shade with their branches and leaves.' Some tribal peoples understood the value of maintaining soil moisture through irrigation and even planted leguminous species among the cacao groves – a technique now known to 'fix' nitrogen in the soil.

At least at first the cacao plantations of New Spain gave a very good yield, possibly as much as a hundred pods per tree per year. It was a stroke of luck for the colony to stumble on an industry that was not only up and running, but, as the chocolate fashion began to spread, promised to be highly profitable. The *encomienda* system by which colonists were rewarded by the Spanish crown with lands and the workers who happened to live on them – in effect, providing a free source of labour – was another important incentive towards wealth creation among the governing class of New Spain.

But there were bad times just around the corner. In the mid- to late sixteenth century cacao production underwent a sharp decline – for reasons unknown, but possibly because Spanish pressure for greater productivity soon led to its opposite: the exhaustion of the land. Concurrently, the Indians began to succumb in huge numbers to 'imported' diseases to which they had no immunity, leading to a dramatic fall in the local workforce. (Let us not forget that the Spanish conquest wiped out, by one means or another, no less than 90 per cent of the original population of the Americas.) The growing demand for cacao in the markets of New Spain, with 'Old' Spain on the point of taking up the chocolate habit too, only added to the urgent need for new plantation sites in hitherto unexploited areas.

And so cacao set forth into its great diaspora. How it travelled is something of an enigma, since cacao beans lose their ability to germinate after a couple of weeks and the portable Wardian greenhouse, much used in the nineteenth century for transporting young plant specimens, had not yet been invented. The broad brushstrokes of its progress are at least clear enough. First it travelled to Venezuela, Trinidad and Ecuador, then the Philippines, before passing out of the Spanish colonial orbit and swimming into the ken of other empires – Portuguese, French and British. Under Portuguese rule Brazil became an important producer in the late eighteenth century, and remains so today. The Dutch took it to Indonesia, the British to Jamaica and Ceylon, the French to Martinique and Guadeloupe. From Brazil it crossed the Atlantic in 1822 to São Tomé, Fernando Po, Ghana (then the Gold Coast), Nigeria, and finally to the Ivory Coast in 1905 – the latter now by far the world's greatest producer. In four hundred years *Theobroma cacao* had circled the globe – paving the way for the coffee plant *Coffea arabica*, which tended to pitch up in the same place at a slightly later date.

A watershed in chocolate's history was the appearance in South America of another crop with which it was to be intimately associated. The Aztecs had added honey to their cacao on occasion, but it was left to the Spanish colonists – which of them exactly we will never know, though the convents seem a likely point of origin – to discover that ground cacao was made more pleasant to the European palate by the addition of sugar. At first sugar cane was brought from southern Spain, where it had been cultivated since the time of the Arabs on the south coast near Malaga (where, incidentally, it is still grown to produce the Spanish rum which is the historical progenitor of all other rums). Sugar cane was produced in great quantities on

Hernán Cortés' enormous private estate near Oaxaca. But a
cheaper source of sugar would soon become imperative if, as
seemed likely, chocolate were to find a larger market.

With the establishment of sugar cane plantations in Brazil
and the Caribbean from 1640 to 1680, the price of sugar plum-
meted. A papal bull from Paul III had forbidden the enslavement
of native Indians, but no one said anything about slaves from
outside the colonies. With the local population decimated, a new
source of cheap labour was required. Black slaves were shipped
from the ports of West Africa by Spanish, English, Portuguese,
French and Dutch companies to work the cacao and sugar
plantations of the New World. The growing Western lust for
sweetness was therefore underpinned by human suffering on a
massive scale. Historically, chocolate had been a drink consumed
by the elite, whose exclusivity only confirmed its aura of
spiritual glamour. Thanks to the influx of unpaid labour, it now
worked out at a price that everyone could afford. The stage was
set for chocolate's conquest of the Old World.

I had seen cacao pods before. But the very first time I really
looked at one, up close and personal, opening it up to see the
surprising contents, was a moment that has snagged on a corner
of my mind. It took place at the remote Hacienda Bukaré in the
paradisical Paria peninsula, in the far east of Venezuela, a few
miles from the point at which Columbus first set foot on the
continental mainland of America on 1 August 1498. Paria was
colonised first by the Spanish in the sixteenth century, then
again by Corsican landowners fleeing from the slave revolt in
Haiti and the Dominican Republic in the early nineteenth century. Even today the names that dominate the rural economy
are of Corsican origin – Pietri, Benedetti, Franceschi at the 300
hectare Hacienda San José near Carúpano. Bukaré, which dates

from 1908, belonged to the Luciani family until it was bought by the German/Venezuelan Essers, whose plan for the hacienda included restoring the abandoned cacao plantings and converting part of the buildings into a small, unpretentious hotel.

Apart from being a delectably restful place to stay, the Bukaré provides its guests with a useful basic education in cacao and chocolate culture. Billy Esser, the gentleman *hacendado*, is grey-haired and sinewy, mild-mannered and kind. He takes me on a private tour of the plantations, explaining every step of the production process. Just now we have entered a period of little fruit but much flowering. The trunks of the trees are sprinkled with legions of the tiny cacao flower, an exquisite construction of five whitish outer sepals, five star-shaped curling pink petals above them, from each petal a yellowish prolongation or lip which leans back out of the flower and an elegant crown of long purple stamens protecting the greenish-yellow ovary at their centre – all contained within a space of between one and three millimetres. These flowers grow all the way up and down the trunk, almost to the ground. A few have already been fertilised, and baby cacao pods the size of my little finger are emerging from warty excrescences on the wood. Even fewer have reached maturity, and hang heavily from the trunk, a tropical equivalent of ripe autumnal pears and apples in our temperate zone.

Billy Esser takes his machete and deftly whacks a cacao cob from the tree. The golden yellow pod is elongated, the tip thinning to a point, with a longitude of ten furrows running from base to tip – telltale signs, says Billy, that the cacao in question belongs to a pedigree *criollo* variety. I cradle it in my hand; the skin is hard and ridged, shiny and cool to the touch. Billy then takes the pod back and slashes it open. There inside is a loose worm-like blob, the cacao beans clinging in circles to a central membrane and enveloped in white mucilage. Deploying the machete blade with surgical precision, he slices delicately into one of the beans, revealing the pale flesh within: another sign of *criollo* class.

'Ah, this lady has white blood,' says Billy.

The aroma of tropical fruit emanates from the open pod, sweet and a little sickly. What propagates the species in its wild state is not the bean itself, which holds no attraction for the squirrels, monkeys and parrots which are its main consumers, but the sticky white pulp around it. At my host's suggestion I suck on a bean in its gooey casing – it is acid and refreshing, with the richness of mango and the piquancy of lychee.

Three black workers are pruning a tree nearby. '*A la orden*,' they say automatically when they catch sight of us. The care of a traditional cacao plantation is exclusively and exhaustively manual. The machete, used for clearing and pruning and chopping and the execution of dangerous snakes, becomes almost an extension of the hand. After harvest the pods are split open, the outer husks discarded or composted, the beans piled into baskets and removed to the hacienda, where they are covered in banana leaves and fermented.

Back at the ranch, Billy pulls away the cover from a basket that has been fermenting for three days, testing the sticky mass for temperature and consistency. The process of fermentation brings about chemical changes in the bean, releasing enzymes which react with the polyphenols and proteins and setting off hydrolytic reactions which give rise to the precursors of chocolate flavour. All this happens at a temperature of around 45 degrees centigrade. To my hands the mass of beans seems even hotter than that, the stickiness now more concentrated and darkening with the heat. But there is still no hint of a real chocolate aroma, only a dizzying gaseous mix of carbon dioxide, vinegar and rotting fruit.

Now I am to make my own chocolate. Not modern hi-tech eating chocolate, but the hardened cacao paste sold in Chuao as *panela*, and in the villages of Barlovento and the Paria peninsula as *bola de cacao* (so called because it is rolled into balls). This was a chocolate used for drinking, in the days when hot chocolate formed an elegant alternative to coffee and no society gathering was complete without it. Billy Esser remembers that a cup of chocolate was always offered at funeral wakes. Ladies took the drink with great enthusiasm at the fashionable Caracas establishments known as *salones de familias*. Special cups called *bigoteros* were designed in such a way as to prevent the chocolate messing up the gentlemen's moustaches.

First we coarsely mill the toasted winnowed cacao beans in a huge old-fashioned kitchen grinder. During their restoration of the hacienda the Essers found a giant wooden mortar, just like the one in the village museum at Chuao, that would have been used for this purpose in pre-electricity days. Then we mill them again. By the third milling what emerges from the machine is a thick, sticky, brown mass, grainy to the touch and increasingly oily as the cocoa butter seeps out of what seemed a dry substance that would simply reduce to a powder. At this stage the Venezuelan village chocolate-maker often adds cloves, cinnamon, nutmeg, following the pre-Columbian tradition of spiced drinking *cacahuatl*. We add vanilla and sugar, and the bitter brown paste undergoes the now-familiar transformation. Though the chocolate is still greasy and a little granular, I am suddenly licking my fingers obsessively; my white T-shirt is stained an oily brown. With its acids and sugars, its occasional overtones of peach and orange, its richness cut by a clean and tangy freshness, this wholesome homemade plain chocolate reminds me that cacao is genuinely a fruit.

Billy Andrés Esser, son of Billy senior and presiding genius of the hacienda kitchen, is a notable and adventurous user of the family's own produce. On other occasions during my stay at the farm, I am served roast meat with a gravy thickened with grated chocolate, and bananas from the estate with chocolate sauce –

thick, pungent, fruity, the world's best chocolate sauce. The hacienda makes a sweet liqueur with roasted cacao beans macerated in rum. On a boat trip to the mangrove swamps of Turuepano, northernmost corner of Venezuela's vast coastal deltas, this Licor de Cacao came in handy for one of the strangest culinary experiments I have ever witnessed. We were on our way to the remote swamp village of Querepe, where the tribespeople grow their own rustic cacao, when Billy Andrés stopped the motor and we glided alongside the forest where the water lapped among a mass of slender roots. He pulled up a mangrove root from the depths; it was encrusted with oysters. With a machete he delicately removed and opened them. Being freshwater oysters, they were very sweet and subtly flavoured, and a squeeze of lime would almost overwhelm them entirely. But Billy Andrés had another idea.

'You must try it. Please try it; for my sake,' he pleaded. 'It's like nothing you've ever tried in your life before, I promise.'

As food and drink combinations go, oysters and chocolate sounds like one of the worst ever. If the oysters had been salty, the sticky richness of the alcohol would have made it purely and simply emetic. As it was, the mixture was certainly disconcerting to the palate. But the palate also requires a gentle stimulus from time to time if it's not to become complacent. And there were reasons for thinking a dash of cacao liqueur in each small oyster might not be such a bad idea. Two sublime and elemental foods; two famous aphrodisiacs; two products that could hardly be more local if they tried . . . In the event, it was just too surreal a concept, too offensive to common sense, for the resulting cocktail to be genuinely pleasurable. I remain grateful for the experience, but politely unconvinced. I shall consider it part of my aesthetic education.

Venezuelan cacao, Venezuelan chocolate, have fallen from grace. If you could plot their economic progress over the last fifty years on a graph, the trend would be firmly downwards, as a once great industry tumbled headlong from the peaks of an economic boom into the low plains of dereliction. Of the 2.5 million tons of cacao produced per year worldwide, Venezuela now accounts for just 14,000 tons, or a mere 0.5 per cent of the world total. Alongside the massive plantations of West Africa and Brazil where *forastero* trees are grown intensively, Venezuela cannot compete. A glorious past counts for nothing in the face of political insecurity, economic instability and the world's changing needs. But the plain fact is that cacao has been killed off by oil. Brown gold has finally been swamped, drowned, enveloped and contaminated by black gold.

Jorge Redmond of Chocolates El Rey, one of the few signs of vibrant life amid the prevailing decline, reclines in his leather boardroom chair and speaks frankly to me.

'It is sad. We are reducing production slowly, mainly because of lack of interest. The government has abandoned agriculture altogether. Politicians are much more enthusiastic about petroleum – after all, there's a whole lot more money involved.'

El Rey was founded in 1929 by José Rafael Zozaya and his Italian father-in-law Carmelo Tuozzo, taking its place among a number of thriving *chocolaterías* in Caracas – the most famous of which, La India, also ran its own elegant 'Dancing Salon for the aristocracy and foreign colonies' (as a contemporary advertisement describes it). The basis of El Rey's enterprise, then as now, was the excellence of local cacao, which was brought in by mule and, where possible, on the rickety coastal railway line.

But El Rey was both more ambitious and shrewder than its rivals. While they continued to concentrate on the local market, El Rey soon realised there was better business to be done overseas, in the US, Europe and Japan. As the Venezuelan economy falters and earnings plummet in real terms, local demand for gourmet eating chocolate – never substantial, one imagines, outside aristocratic and foreign colonial circles – is lower than ever. Exports now account for half of the company's business, a figure that will rise to three quarters by 2005.

Señor Redmond has the kind of shape and character – very large and extremely amiable – one would expect and hope to find in a dealer in the finest chocolate. There is a mixture of pride and exasperation in his voice as he describes how El Rey has overcome the international stigma attached to anything made in the Third World to win the hearts and minds of connoisseurs the world over. 'People think the Third World is inconsistent, knows nothing about quality. Chefs in Paris used to tell us: "Why should we buy chocolate from Venezuela, when we can pick up the phone and order the best French *couverture*?" But when people put our product to the test, they find that the reality is different.'

All his company's proper chocolate is made with Venezuelan *criollo* or *trinitario* beans, fermented and sun-dried. Their milk chocolate has a higher proportion of cacao (41 per cent) than most milk chocolates on the market. But the real achievement of El Rey is its range of dark chocolates, all made with the Carenero Superior bean, and its single-estate San Joaquín bar, all of which goes to the Japanese market and which I have never managed to get my greedy hands on. But the Apamate, Bucare and Gran Samán, each named after a tree used for shade in the cacao plantations, are all splendid black bitter chocolates with a high proportion of cacao solids and plenty of wild, aromatic and spicy aromas.

In Caracas airport, stuck with a sheaf of useless local Monopoly money, I bought a block of Gran Samán, stuck it in my hand-luggage, and sneaked it out when the in-flight movie was over, the lights were down and the rest of the passengers were snoring under their polyester blankets. It was a half-kilo bar with chunks so thick they were quite impossible to break off, but had to be nibbled at instead, leaving mouse-like tooth marks down the side.

I bit off a small brittle chunk and waited. The taste made a smooth landing on my palate, my tongue relishing the feel of the chocolate as it melted. I see, said my tastebuds – this will be another dark chocolate experience – very pleasant, certainly, but not so much as to interrupt the conversation or private train of thought. But then the curtain opened, and the aria of flavours began. Once again I apologise to readers sensitive to the inappropriate use of flowery adjectives, but in this case there is no alternative. The taste of this chocolate was a billowing crescendo of smoky, earthy, fruity and spicy notes that grew in intensity with every moment. It was full of tropical memories, like the *macedoine* that morning at La Sabaneta, and the allspice in that breakfast chocolate. The flavours lingered on in the mouth and in the mind, reaching a nice sort of closure with a brilliant final twist of espresso coffee.

Infused with a sensation of physical contentment, together with a feeling that I would not be requiring for some time another bite, another nibble, another whiff of this twenty-four-carat black gold, I pushed the recline button and lay back in my seat, still chewing and savouring and swallowing mentally. I slept like a baby all the way to Spain.

PART THREE

CHOCOLATE IN THE OLD WORLD

Spain – Decline and fall of a chocolate culture

Italy – Beyond Nutella

France – The return of the high priests

The first cacao beans to arrive in Europe may have been brought back in the pockets of some minor conquistador, for all anyone knows. The beans were probably familiar on this side of the Atlantic as a botanical curiosity, a kind of New World souvenir, before anything chocolate-related was actually made from them. As for the historical facts, the only practical certainties are that Spain was *Theobroma*'s first European port of call, and that the religious orders, closely involved from an early stage in the enterprise of New Spain, must have had a hand in its acceptance by colonial, and thereafter by European, society.

Many of the existing theories as to how chocolate crossed the Atlantic have taken on the character of legends. Even the most colourful of them probably has at least a grain of truth. Some of the most oft-recounted of these hypotheses are: 1) Hernán Cortés, having praised the energy-giving virtues of cacao in his letters to Charles V, included among his first gifts to the emperor in 1528 (along with a box of enormous emeralds) a sack of beans with a list of instructions on how to prepare the 'Indian Nectar'; 2) Padre Olmedo, a Franciscan monk travelling in Cortés' entourage, brought the sacks back with him; and 3) a Cistercian monk called Fray Aguilar, who had travelled to Mexico in the first wave of conquistadores, sent back the first cacao beans, together with a recipe for the drink, to Don Antonio de Alvaro, abbot of the monastery of Piedra in Aragon. If this last is correct, it would explain the strong chocolate tradition of the Cistercian order and its reformed wing, the Trappists. The monastery of Poblet, near Barcelona, where I once stayed for a five-day bout of self-denial, has a vaulted hall with a great chimney known as the *chocolatería* – the only place within monastery walls where monks were permitted to indulge in the heavenly beverage.

Certainly by the mid-sixteenth century it was already being consumed by a small number of Spanish monks and nuns. The earliest European consumers must have relied on occasional 'drops' of cacao, perhaps from missionaries returning from New Spain, because it wasn't until 1585 that imports began to arrive in Seville from Mexico on a regular basis.

Seville was the entry point, but it was Madrid that saw the first flowering of a European chocolate culture. In 1600 Madrid was still a small provincial town that had been the nation's capital for only forty years, yet in the century that followed its growth was prodigious, both in population and material splendour. By the second half of the seventeenth century it had become a city of renown to which other Europeans came to observe and absorb the latest fashions. Courtly life was at its apogee, a whirl of receptions and salons at which the refreshment of choice was a foaming beverage recently brought from the Indies. According to the testimony of one English traveller of the time who appreciated this novelty, the Spaniards were 'the only People in Europe, that have the Reputation of making Chocolate to perfection'. The drink was commonly spiced with vanilla, cinnamon, annatto and musk. Sweetened in a proportion of roughly four parts of cacao to one of sugar, it would still have had a bitter, tangy taste, comparable in modern terms to that of an 80 per cent cacao chocolate bar. A French lady of quality, the Countess of Aulnoy, Marie-Cathérine Jumel de Barneville, visited the Spanish court during the years 1672–9 and relates in great detail the afternoon she spent in an aristocratic household in Madrid, noting with disapproval the state of the ladies' teeth, and their skinny bodies – physical failings which she was quick to attribute to their extraordinary liking for chocolate. 'After the sweets they gave us a good chocolate, served in elegant porcelain *jicaras*. There was cold chocolate, hot chocolate, and chocolate made with milk and egg yolks. We took it with sponge cakes; there was one *señora* who sipped six cupfuls, one after another, and some of them do this two or three times a day.'

Fads tend to be downwardly mobile. They start at the upper levels of society and filter down through its ranks. Madrid was a small town in which the goings-on at court one day would have been the talk of the Plaza Mayor the next. Even so, chocolate-drinking took a while to catch on among the lower orders. High taxes on cacao, the small amount of material available in the market and the relatively high price of sugar may all have had something to do with it. The municipal authorities, worried that unbridled chocolate consumption, associated as it was with decadence and libertinage, might present the wrong image of the city to the world, did their best to kill off the nascent chocolate trade. In 1644 the mayor of Madrid issued a decree to the effect that 'no one, either in a shop or from home or in any place whatever may sell chocolate as a drink'. This however was not the same thing as prohibiting its sale in solid form, as *pastillas* for dissolving in water; nor was it forbidden to take chocolate at home. And this was the loophole in which the fashion grew and prospered. In 1772 there were no fewer than 150 chocolate-grinders in a city of some 150,000 inhabitants. 'Chocolate, and the taste for chocolate, has been introduced in such a manner, that scarcely a street can be found where there is not one, two, and three stalls where it is made and sold; moreover there is no confectionery, nor shop in the calle de Postas, in the calle Mayor and others, where it is not sold, and it only remains for it to be available in oil and vinegar shops . . . Apart from those who busy themselves with milling and treating it, are many other men and women who sell it door to door . . . So that there is a large number of people occupied in this, in particular those robust young men who might otherwise serve in the war and in other mechanical trades of greater use to the state', explains a handwritten document dating from the late eighteenth century.

Since then Madrid has had a number of stimulating fashions to contend with, from coffee to Coca-Cola to cocaine, but the taking of chocolate is one Spanish tradition that will never be superseded. Or so I believed, until I set foot on the streets of Madrid and found that the former world capital of chocoholism is currently immersed in the painful process of kicking the habit.

As I stepped out of the Metro at Plaza de España, I asked myself what I knew about chocolate in Spain. I knew that it was still popular among the generation that was young during the Civil War; elderly folk who saw the steaming cups of thick dark chocolate as a symbol of the good life against the post-war backdrop of creeping impoverishment and cultural stagnation. *Chocolate con churros* was classic fiesta fare, a double hit of sugar and grease that, taken as a palliative after a long night's carousing, settled the stomach and prepared the body for sleep.

Spanish chocolate is unlike any other drinking chocolate. Having the consistency of custard makes it hard to get down, unless you chase it with a big glass of water. In a sense the real point of *chocolate* is *churros*, and vice versa; the one exists as a vehicle for the other. After the death of Franco, as Madrid transformed itself into Europe's wildest party town, the custom lived on, only now it was young people tipping out of discotheques at six in the morning who patronised the city's *chocolaterías*.

In the glory days of the *movida* – the 'movement' – there was no after-hours venue more famous than the Chocolatería San Ginés. The San Ginés (est. 1894) is to be found in an alleyway off the Calle Arenal, between the Puerta del Sol and the opera house. It also happens to be right next door to a nightclub called Joy Eslava, which in the early 1980s served as the unofficial headquarters of Madrid's movers and shakers, including Pedro Almodóvar, Carmen Maura, Rossy de Palma and the rest of the city's alternative crowd. When the disco shut its doors at dawn they would all roll out and over the road into the San Ginés. In the Madrid of the 1980s chocolate was just one (the mildest) of a range of available stimulants. Cups of chocolate shared a table at the San Ginés, often literally, with lines of cocaine and joints of marijuana.

I set the alarm for 6.30 and walked to the Puerta del Sol, through streets still dark and damp from the autumn rainstorm that had nearly turned Saturday night fever into a bad case of the flu. It was a miserable morning to have woken up in, but the tiled interior of the *chocolatería* was warm and comforting. You could see your face in the polished brass fittings of the bar. As I stood at the counter a gang of rich Spanish kids in their twenties stumbled through the door laughing and shouting and installed themselves at two marble tables beside the wall. Their equivalents in the Madrid of an earlier time would have positively lusted after a nourishing cup of chocolate and a plate of piping hot *churros* sprinkled with plenty of sugar. But these young people hummed and hahed and cackled and fooled about and lit cigarettes, and then ordered five beers, a rum and coke, a freshly squeezed orange juice and a mint tea.

'We don't get too many people wanting *chocolate con churros* any more. *Cada vez menos*. Less and less,' said the waitress tiredly, running her hands through her hair. She had been up all night and was nearing the end of her shift.

'It's not the fashion any more. People think it's fattening; of course, they're right. All that oil and sugar . . . heavy on the stomach. Times have changed. But it tastes good, no?'

There is no doubt that the *chocolaterías* of Madrid are not what they were. The Casa de Vacas, up towards the fancy Salamanca district, used to be famous, and the name above the doorway still proclaims its vocation loud and clear. But the place is now a high-class restaurant, and limits itself to announcing via a photocopied sheet stuck into the corner of the window, '*Hay Chocolate Con Churros*', as if this were an irrelevance, a mere sideline, which of course it now is. At another well-known chocolate house, the Brillante, in the Iglesia neighbourhood, there is so little interest nowadays in the house speciality that the owners have taken diversification to an extreme. They have branched out into cheap lunches of paella and lentil stews at midday and display shriekingly garish photographs of chicken and chips and the like around the neon-lit interior. A prominent sign reads, bizarrely: 'The best squid sandwich in Madrid'. Yet the all-in breakfast of *churros* or *porras*, a thicker type of *churro*, plus a cup of chocolate, is still on the menu, costing just one and a half Euros, or a few pence more than a pound. Despite having eaten one such breakfast already that day, I ordered it and sat at the zinc bar trying to relax while the TV blared incomprehensibly, cups clattered madly and a piledriver roared in the street outside.

Choc 'n' churros, a bit like fish 'n' chips, is a dish that exists on a permanent knife edge. Fresh and properly made, the crisp fried golden dough and the thick rich chocolate go together like a dream. Cold, greasy *churros* and weakly flavoured, half-congealed chocolate upon which a skin has already formed are not nearly such an enticing proposition. As is often the case with this kind of traditional food, waning interest leads to waning quality. The Brillante's offering, at any rate – old, chewy *churros*, and a chocolate whose acquaintance with the cacao bean seemed sketchy at best – was far from brilliant.

Strange, the reversal of fortune that has taken place since the chocolate-crazy seventeenth century, when chocolate was served at all the great public events, including bullfights, official receptions of various sorts and the trials and executions of the Inquisition. One foreign resident, the wife of the French ambassador, complained that her 'chocolate diet, to which I owe my health' was practically the only satisfactory thing about her life in Spain.

The Fábrica de Chocolates El Indio stood on the corner of the Calle Luna and the Calle San Roque, in the working-class *barrio* that lies behind the roaring metal river of the Gran Via.

Inhabitants of the neighbourhood still remember it well. It was the kind of establishment you wouldn't easily forget, with its imposing dark façade with the legend: 'Superior Chocolates, We Undertake Orders in the Presence and to the Taste of the Client, Established 1847'. Children in particular were enchanted by the interior of the shop, a smart and shiny old-fashioned place full of quaint contraptions like the splendid brass scales topped with an eagle's head, and the ancient telephone which continued to bear the original Madrid number (five figures, rather than the eventual seven). From the counter, through a glass screen, customers could watch the operation of a cacao mill fashioned in the shape of a generic 'Indian' in a grass skirt, his arms strangely akimbo and a large inverted cone on top of his head into which the cacao beans were poured. The ground cacao then emerged from his outstretched hands.

For the Fábrica was not just a retail establishment, but a maker of chocolate on the premises. It had been passed down from father to son within the Ruiz family for nearly 150 years, during which time its recipe for chocolate *a la taza* ('in the cup') had remained completely unchanged. In its heyday during the 1950s El Indio supplied the Chocolatería San Ginés and Lhardy, Madrid's grandest restaurant. Its clientele included the Generalísimo himself, Don Francisco Franco y Bahamonde. But in the early 1990s, when the Ruiz family ran out of direct heirs, it began to seem that the business was finally running out of steam. The last owners, Josefa and Maria Ruiz, two sisters in their eighties, had become tired of the daily struggle. When finally, reluctantly, in the spring of 1993, they decided to put their beloved *chocolatería* up for sale, the sisters had no very clear idea of the historical value of the jewel they held in their tremulous hands.

The Chocolatería El Indio had fallen so far behind in the rat race that it was practically a museum piece already. All that was needed was a museum to put it in. When the National Museum of Anthropology got wind of the sale, a group of curators was dispatched to the Calle Luna. A deal was struck, and in 1994 the work of dismantling began. The chocolate shop and mill were to be preserved for posterity. There was satisfaction all round. What no one can have known, however, was that posterity would have little chance to enjoy the old place. Thanks to a wholesale reorganisation of Spanish state museums and the endless politicking involved, it would be scuttled away in the vaults of a museum which is currently closed to the public and shows no signs of opening 'any time soon', as they say in America.

In order to see the little Indian, a certain amount of bureaucracy is therefore necessary. Applications must be made, forms filled in, faxes sent stating your reasons, area of research, qualifications . . . I duly filled in my form and sent my fax, and I had entirely forgotten about the whole thing when a few months later my appointment finally came up.

The director, a busy man, led me briskly down the echoing corridors of his moribund museum into a great storeroom with Dexion shelves stacked with pottery, baskets, farm implements and other items of significance in the anthropology of Spain, each tagged with its identifying label.

'It should be down here somewhere. We've done what we can to restore the thing, but of course there's only so much you can do. I think it's all here. I've brought some documentation, photos and so on, which might interest you. It should be fairly self-explanatory. And now, if you'll excuse me, I must be on my way, already late for a meeting; you were lucky to find me in the office at all.'

He disappeared in a flap of his curator's white coat.

It certainly did seem to be 'all here'. There were slabs of chocolate still in their original packets, and chocolate moulds that, alarmingly, appeared to be made of lead, and archaic appliances like the massive wooden fridge, surely one of the first to be seen in Madrid, and the 1950s fire-extinguisher. Piles of cardboard boxes contained the office equipment of a bygone age – stamps and sealing wax and leather-bound ledgers filled out in triplicate, and sheafs of invoices dating back before the Civil War. The dust had settled over everything like a layer of snow.

Stacked back to back against the wall were the doors of the cabinets that lined the interior of the shop, each with its painted scene of maritime themes. I cleaned one off with a finger. It showed galleons arriving at a harbour, and bundles of merchandise being unloaded on the dockside. Until the last day of business at El Indio, the merchandise was weighed out in a massive brass balance crowned with the head of an eagle. I had seen it in photographs, but here it was before me, lying on its side on a shelf, the shine of the brass dulled by long neglect and verdigris.

And here in the corner of the room, incongruous in his palm-leaf skirt and his quiver full of arrows, was the little Indian himself. His arms, held at an angle from his body, would once have deposited the ground cacao in the bins at either side. But now they gave him a melancholy look. There could hardly have been a better symbol of the decline of chocolate-drinking in Spanish society than this sad little blackamoor, once admired by poets and politicians, now dumped in the corner of a cold warehouse. From the look of him, he knew it too.

'Can you believe I've been reduced to this?' he seemed to be saying as he raised his jet-black hands in exasperation.

The Spanish monopoly on cacao put the brakes on its expansion through Europe, and for a century or more the custom of chocolate-drinking remained an exotic Spanish speciality. When Dutch pirates ambushed a Spanish galleon headed for Europe in 1585, they tipped overboard its valuable cargo of cacao beans, believing them to be sheep droppings.

But foreign ignorance did not last for long. By the end of the seventeenth century the Dutch East India Company was growing cacao in their new colony of Surinam, which had passed from British to Dutch domination in 1667, and shipping it to the port of Amsterdam. The volume of shipments had reached such a pitch that by the late eighteenth century there were some thirty chocolate factories in Amsterdam, forcing many of the old mustard mills on the banks of the River Zaam to reinvent themselves as cacao mills. According to industry figures, a fifth of the world's trade in raw cacao still passes through Amsterdam, and Holland is the largest exporter of cacao powder, cacao butter and chocolate. (If this sounds like an anomaly, consider that Holland effectively acts as a cacao entrepôt, receiving the beans and bringing them to a certain stage of the manufacturing process, before re-exporting the cacao products to their final destination.)

Chocophilia took off in Italy partly owing to existing connections between the various religious orders, and partly thanks to export of Spanish customs to their possessions in Naples and Sicily. News had already reached Italy via Girolamo Benzoni and his description of chocolate as 'a food for pigs', and via Pietro Martir and his 'happie money'. Cacao had been known to Italian commentators, botanists and pharmacists at least since 1686, the year in which Giuseppe Donzelli published his *Teatro Farmaceutico*. But it was chiefly as a medicine rather than as a pleasant drink that it was recommended, and Donzelli gives his recipe for the chocolate '*medicamento*' – generously spiced with cinnamon, aniseed, vanilla, nutmeg and annatto, plus ground almonds, maize flour and sugar – mainly to 'satisfy the delicate taste of the curious'. As for the medicinal value of this preparation, 'They say it comforts the stomach, aids digestion and is very nourishing', writes Donzelli, his reference to hearsay implying that he has never tried it himself.

As Europe began to echo with rumours of a wondrous new drink, the Italian upper classes quickly saw the possibilities of *cioccolato* as a delightful adjunct to a sybaritic lifestyle, and lost no time in creating a refined chocolate culture of their own. On the occasion of his visit to Madrid in 1668 Cosimo de' Medici was served chocolate in 'huge cups' along with sweetmeats and glasses of cold water.

By the mid-eighteenth century the taking of *cioccolato* was so deeply embedded in Italian social mores that a book of etiquette entitled *Precetti necessari alla nobile e pulita gioventú* (1751) advised the young gentleman always to carry two white handkerchiefs with him, 'one for peeling fruit and the other for the lady when she takes sorbets, coffee and chocolate'. The first merchant to put the product on sale was Antonio Ari of Turin, a city which was to become the undisputed chocolate capital of Italy. Eighteenth-century Turin was the birthplace of such sophistications as *bavareisa*, chocolate mousse and *bicerin*, a rich mixture of coffee, chocolate and cream which can still be enjoyed in the city's elegant cafés. At the end of the century chocolate production in Turin had reached 350kg per day, some of which undoubtedly filtered north into Austria, Switzerland

and Germany, extending the chocolate habit deep into central Europe.

It is a sad fact, but a true one nonetheless, that most people's idea of contemporary Italian chocolate culture is summed up by two words: Ferrero Rocher.

Actually, there is a piggish kind of pleasure to be had from a box of 'rocks'. A large part of the appeal lies in their sexy packaging: first you have the transparent plastic box, displaying its wares unashamedly, as if they were tarts in an Amsterdam window; then come the chocolates themselves, a much more complicated proposition, wrapped up in Victorian ruffles of foil and chastely buttoned up with a paper seal. As a brand it is an anomaly. It has tried its level best to come over as a luxury item, spending millions of euros on advertising that shows the 'rocks' being consumed by the denizens of a pan-European high society. Yet the market has a mind of its own and persists in seeing Ferrero Rocher as a regular bit of trashy late-night-garage choc, with no more class than a tube of Pringles. As for those ads, with their fatuous and much-quoted tag-lines – 'The ambassador's receptions were noted for their elegance . . .' – and their deeply unconvincing evocation of the high life, they have become camp classics. We saw through them instantly, yet our affection for the brand was, if anything, increased. When Ferrero finally realised that their products were having the mickey taken out of them and killed off the ads in the UK (they are still to be seen in Spain, where irony is not quite such a way of life), British lovers of kitsch felt a terrible sense of loss. During the 1997 siege of the Japanese embassy in Lima, I at least felt that no one would die of starvation, since there was bound to be plenty of Ferrero Rocher in the pantry.

The irony is that Ferrero is actually a fine old Italian chocolate firm (originally from the town of Alba in Piemonte) and the Rocher, though spoiled by overexposure, certainly has something to say about the Italian chocolate tradition with its fondness for elaborate confections based around sweet hazelnut, walnut or almond pastes. Close to the heart of this same tradition lies the *gianduja* – a name that has come to apply equally to the brand of ingot-shaped gold-wrapped chocolates made by several Italian manufacturers, and to the hazelnut–milk chocolate paste they contain. *Gianduja* was invented by Isidore Caffarel (1817–67), son of the founder of Italian industrial chocolate Paolo Caffarelli, who opened his first steam-driven factory in Turin as early as 1826.

Italians' love of chocolate is only equalled by their fetish for nuts. Indoctrinated from an early age by Nutella (also a Ferrero product, first marketed in 1964), the hazelnut and chocolate spread which Italian children consume by the gallon, they spend the rest of their lives trying to duplicate that primordial childhood pleasure. With the result that two out of every three chocolate products currently on the market contain nuts in some form or another, from La Perugina's hazelnut Baci, sold by the million, to Majani's Cremino, created in 1911 to mark the launch of the Fiat Tipo 4. But the choc–nut association goes back a great deal further: in the course of their meticulous historical research, Michael and Sophie Coe found a 1786 recipe for lasagne with a sauce made of almonds, walnuts, anchovies and chocolate, and another for 'black polenta' with chocolate, almonds, breadcrumbs, butter and cinnamon.

Almost all the great Western cuisines have a savoury chocolate dish, or, to be more precise, a dish in which small amounts of bitter chocolate are used as a flavouring and thickening agent. Even British cuisine has one, though I have never tasted it and do not wish to. A work entitled *Chocolate and Confectionery Manufacture*, published in London in 1913, contains a recipe for Beef Chocolate (ingredients 5lb 'chocolate dough', 1lb 'dried beef in powder'). The Spanish add chocolate to braised partridge and stuffed squid, and a friend's mother in Extremadura makes a strange-sounding gratin of hake fillets baked in the oven with white wine and a sprinkling of grated black chocolate, producing a sauce which is not so much sweet as aromatic and creamy. Dark meat, particularly game, has a long relationship with chocolate. British chef and writer Rowley Leigh, apropos of his fine dish of venison, baby onions, chestnuts and chocolate, judiciously remarks that too much chocolate can make a sauce sickly and sticky, whereas in the right proportion it adds a wonderful smokiness to the dish. I was recently making a rabbit ragú for tagliatelle when I remembered Rowley's advice and sneaked a square of Michel Cluizel's 85 per cent-cacao Grand Amer into the already rich and gamy sauce. My guests were puzzled by the mild smoky peppery sweetness of that sauce, and the guessing-game that followed was a lot of fun.

No one is more interested in exploiting the possibilities of chocolate in cooking than the Italians. Some of their recipes do indeed stretch the imagination. Sicily, whose rich chocolate tradition is in part a legacy of Spanish domination during the fifteenth century, has two outstanding dishes. One is the chocolate granita from Catania which Jeffrey Steingarten samples in *The Man Who Ate Everything* (1998), a mild milky sorbet made with cocoa powder. (If you add to your granita a little vanilla, orange zest and jasmine essence, says Steingarten, it becomes something called *cioccolato in garapegra*, a 'holy and noble elixir of fresh life' which sounds reminiscent of Cosimo de' Medici's jasmine-scented drinking chocolate.) The other is *'mpanatigghi*, a speciality of the pastry shops of Modica. The name had me puzzled for a while until I remembered the Spanish *empanadilla*, a kind of turnover usually stuffed with red peppers and tuna, or with spinach and pine nuts and raisins, or simply with ground meat and onions – but never, as far as I know, with the *'mpanatigghi*'s distinctive combination of spices, sugar, minced meat and chocolate . . .

If this is not exotic enough for you, there is a traditional

Italian dish which is so outlandish that some people might be repelled by the whole idea of it. Readers of a delicate constitution may like to turn over a few pages at this point, if they do not wish to have their tender stomachs turned instead.

When I arrive, on the Ryan Air express from Stansted to Pescara, the Mediterranean is not so much wine-dark as gun-metal grey. Luigina comes to meet me from the village, and the motorway takes us inland and upward towards a range of forbidding mountains. We are heading for Prezza, a village of a few hundred people, 150km in distance, but thirty years in time, from Rome.

Luigina diMeo and her husband Antonio run a restaurant in the Spanish village where I live, in which the menu is a confluence of robust Spanish rural food and the refined simplicity of Italian *alta cocina*. For a long time I had been hunting down a rare Italian dish that used chocolate in a unique and extraordinary manner. I was becoming tired of the search when I met Luigina and the wheels of synchronicity began to turn. The dish I referred to was a speciality of her home village in the Abruzzi mountains, she told me brightly, while the hairs on the back of my neck stood to attention. Few people now made it any more, for reasons the reader will shortly understand, but her sister-in-law and elderly mother were acknowledged in the village as experts.

Happy to be back home for a few days, Luigina takes me out on to the balcony to show me the view. A wide plateau ringed by serious mountains, their lower slopes dotted with villages. Pratola Perigna, Roccacasale, Bugnara, and, just over the hilltop, Pacentro. The latter is best known, or indeed only known, as the village from which the singer Madonna's grandparents emigrated to Detroit and where apparently she still has distant cousins. (Trivia junkies may be interested to know that Ciccone is a common surname in Pacentro and Rocco, the name of Madonna's son, a common Christian name.) Emigration has

been a constant factor in Luigina's village throughout the twentieth century, gradually leaching the life out of it. Now there are
more *prezzani* in Boston than in Prezza itself, and its medieval
streets are ivy-choked, slowly collapsing, silent but for the flut-
ter of pigeons.

I am installed in a chair beside the cast-iron stove in the
kitchen and the first waves of Italian hospitality begin to wash
over me. Luigina's mother is a tiny lady wearing little black
lace-up shoes and long stockings with the occasional hole, and
a blue and white check apron accessorised with an olive-green
woolly hat. She offers me a basket of *pizzelle*, a local sweetmeat
resembling waffles.

And with the *pizzelle*, a surprise. With some reverence, a tin
container of the sort used for Chinese takeaways is brought to
the table. Within is a dark-brown substance, almost black, but
with a sinister gleam of green. I am invited to taste it with a tea-
spoon, while the entire extended diMeo family watches me in
hushed anticipation. The texture is thick and sticky yet faintly
granular; the taste, an intensely sweet, aromatic concoction of
caramel, nuts and citrus fruit.

This is the gastronomic spectacle I have come to witness, and
the truth is I am privileged to witness it. In the days of Old
Europe, when every rural family kept a pig, the turning of the
year saw an event of unparalleled importance in the life of the
household: the killing and transformation of the pig into hams
and other joints of meat, sausages, lard and soap. One of the
most highly valued products of the pig-killing was the blood
which gushed from the animal's jugular when its throat was
cut. In most of Europe the blood was used in a range of sausages,
from black pudding to *morcilla*. But in certain regions of eastern
and southern Italy, notably in Molise, Basilicata, Calabria and
Apulia, there was another traditional recipe: the *sanguinaccio*, in
which the blood was stewed with concentrated grape juice and
other sweet things, thereby effectively preserving it for later

consumption. And in a few villages of the Abruzzo, the sweet things added to the blood included chocolate.

Agata and Antonio diMeo have kept a pig all their lives, until last year, when they felt they could no longer physically cope with the work involved. It is the familiar southern European story of millennial customs abandoned after centuries of continuous life. Agata takes me out to see the pigsty in its field of closely planted almond trees, just now on the point of bursting into pink blossom. The door of the sty hangs open, its dark interior cavernously empty.

The pig's blood for this year's *sanguinaccio* will not, therefore, be of the freshly home-produced variety, but has been bought from a butcher's shop. It stands in a preserving jar on the dining-room table, having separated out like vinaigrette into thick dark scarlet and translucent watery layers. Around it are bowls containing the other ingredients: crushed toasted almonds, pork fat, breadcrumbs, finely chopped orange and lemon rind, concentrated grape juice, or *mosto cotto*, and a big bowl of grated black chocolate. This is the classic *prezzano* recipe. Other villages and households have their slightly different versions – one adds chopped dried figs, another adds milk, yet another substitutes powdered sweet biscuits for breadcrumbs.

Early next morning the kitchen is a fug of warmth and feminine presence. Teresa, sister-in-law of Luigina and a glorious cook in the maternal Italian manner whose polenta with fresh tomato sugo and whose ravioli stuffed with goat's cheese and artichokes will be two of the lasting memories of my visit, takes charge of the *sanguinaccio*. Another girl arrives from Pratola with her baby daughter in tow. She is a modern girl for whom this blood and chocolate jam is as much of an anomaly as it would be for anyone from Paris, Potsdam or Peterborough.

The lard is heated in a big brown enamel pot, the strained

blood added along with the *mosto cotto* and the other ingredients, one by one. When Teresa tips in the chocolate the mixture becomes a glossy black liquid which must be simmered on a very low heat, stirring constantly with a wooden spoon. I peer into the depths of the cauldron at the dark spluttering mess within: it looks like some Dantesque nether region of hell. Half an hour later it starts to boil, leaving spattering stains around the white enamel oven top.

Now it can be poured into a saucer for testing. A deep brown liquid on a white plate. It has a tangy bitterness of plain chocolate combined with the caramelised tang of citrus fruits and *mosto cotto*, which reminds me suddenly of a childhood taste which has latterly fallen out of favour: the Terry's Chocolate Orange. Rather to my relief, you cannot taste the blood.

Whatever you think of the dish, you have to admit it is fantastically nutritious, packing as much protein, fat and sugar as possible into a single spoonful. Agata remembers that in the bad times when there was not much food – 'we ate polenta for lunch and dinner' – eating *sanguinaccio* was like ascending into heaven. It was often poured into a pig's colon and hung up with the sausages, where it dried and could be cut off in slices. With a loaf of bread and some wine, this made an excellent portable food at harvest time, or whenever meals were taken *in campo*.

The history of this weird culinary phenomenon is beyond any of the *prezzani* here present. Clearly it cannot be older than chocolate's widespread acceptance in Italy, which is to say the late eighteenth century. Yet it cannot help reminding us of a very much older set of customs, far distant in time and space, with which it doubtless has no historical connection whatsoever. In the symbolic universe of ancient Mexican religion, blood and *cacahuatl* were the two great life-forces, intimately combined in grisly rituals of death and rebirth.

While it cools in its jars, the ladies sing strange Abruzzese songs in a dialect as impenetrable as Portuguese. Agata gets up and dances a few faltering steps around the kitchen, holding her skirts in front of her with finger and thumb.

The girl from Pratola tries to persuade her daughter to try a little *sanguinaccio*. '*E cioccolato, ma non é Kinder*,' she tells her. The little girl is not convinced, and squirms with reluctance.

It is not the Kinder Egg, however, that I would suggest as the obvious point of comparison here, but another mega-brand loved to distraction by Italian children. Smear a thick layer of *sanguinaccio* on a piece of bread and what have you got? Answer: the mother and father of all chocolate spreads.

Nutella, eat your heart out.

Though Italy runs it close, no nation in the world has a more obsessively refined approach to the domestic arts of cooking, clothing and the home than France. The French believe that chocolate, along with the various branches of gastronomy, wine, fashion and interior decoration is an element of the quasi-philosophical entity known as '*l'art de vivre*'. The nearest English equivalent of this concept might be something along the lines of 'lifestyle', which may sound cheap and nasty alongside it, but faithfully reflects a basic cultural difference.

I think I always knew about this basic difference. My generation was perhaps the last to have it drilled into us that France was the epitome of style, and that the French were incontrovertibly the world's best manufacturers of cheese, wine, philosophy, arty cinema and women's dresses. In our own lifetime their superiority in nearly all these fields has been gradually chiselled away. Though in other fields it's true that they have come along in leaps and bounds – football, for instance, and pop music, which they now make quite a decent stab at – it is also true that, in general, the world no longer sings to a French melody. French is no longer the language of diplomacy. Classic French food and wine have lost ground to the daring novelties of 'fusion food' and New World wines. But in the world of fine chocolate, there can be no doubt who still rules the roost.

The French have their own Université du Chocolat. It forms a part of the Institut d'Etudes Supérieures des Arts, recognised by the Ministry of Culture and Communication. They have their own professional Académie. Chocolate clubs, so exclusive as to resemble secret societies. Chocolatiers have their own trade union. An entire bureaucracy in chocolate. The only things missing are chocolate soldiers and chocolate money.

And now they have the Salon du Chocolat, a five-day orgy disguised as a trade fair at which more than 150 of the world's great chocolatiers are present – almost all of them French, it goes without saying, although a few Belgians are generously admitted. There are tastings, workshops, demonstrations and lectures of all sorts, and an event that has predictably captured the attention of the world's media: the famous catwalk fashion show, with models clad in chocolate gowns, sporting chocolate hats and clutching chocolate handbags, all of which they are mysteriously able to do without any of the items melting away into dark brown oil slicks on their immaculate bodies.

The central geographical location of the Salon only seemed to reinforce its cultural centrality. Underneath the Louvre is a vast shiny shopping centre, but a high-class version of the shopping centre as is usually understood, with branches of museum gift shops and fashion boutiques and a fancy French interpretation of that horrid and unavoidable fact of modern life, the 'food court'. In among all this are the subterranean halls of the Carrousel du Louvre, into which I strolled on my first morning at the Salon, losing myself like one bewitched among the countless stalls and exhibits and the heady, intoxicating aroma that hung in the air like some exotic perfume. The crowds that thronged the place seemed caught up in the same mild ecstasy of sensual excitement; we were all acolytes in a great basilica of pleasure. There were children leading their grandparents by the hand; there were Day-Glo ravers with dreadlocks and fashion queens in high-heeled shoes; there were chocolate-coloured people both black and white; there was a troop of mentally retarded folk having the time of their lives. It was a democracy of the most excellent sort. The true grandeur of Western civilisation, I decided at the Salon, lies in its generous and scientific attitude to pleasure. We are all entitled to have as much of it as our lives will take, as long as we take on board the essential fact that greatest pleasure comes with greatest understanding.

The size of the show was bewildering in itself, a labyrinth in which new and rare sensations presented themselves at every turn. Wherever I went in the maze, it seemed that smiling people were holding out plates of sweet stuff for the tasting – truffles, pralines, patisserie, chocolate filled and flavoured with nuts and fruit and spices and aromas of a hundred different sorts, and dark chocolate tablettes broken into shards – thrusting out the plates as you went by, cajoling, friendly, like drug dealers in a playground. Most of the great names in contemporary French *chocolaterie* were here: the famous-name companies – Weiss, Poulain, Hédiard, Valrhona – and the Parisian wizards with their chic boutiques, artist–artisans like Michel Cluizel, Pierre Hermé, Christian Constant, and perhaps the true genius among them, Jean-Paul Hévin. Conspicuous by his absence was one of the pioneers of chocolate modernism, Michel Chaudun, a modest man whose low public profile belies his enormous influence. Chaudun's inspired combination of bitter chocolate with nibs of toasted cacao bean, and the legion of inferior imitations it has spawned, has become an oft-recounted legend in the business.

There was creativity here in enormous melting mouthfuls and novelties aplenty. Chocolate and fashion have always been comfortable bedfellows, and at this year's Salon a number of fads were peering out from under the duvet. Chocolate caviar, tiny black balls that popped on your tongue, was all the rage. *Pâte à tartiner*, those little pots of chocolate cream for spreading on bread or toast, seemed to be everywhere, suggesting that a traditional French children's treat had come back for the adults. Had I not seen and tasted it myself as prepared by one of France's greatest young masters of chocolate patisserie, Jean-Luc Pélé, I would never have believed in the triumphant return of the chocolate éclair – an item which I thought had died a death in the late 1970s, drowned forever in vats of oversweetened fake cream.

The vogue for so-called *grands crus* – chocolate of exceptional purity whose origins can be traced not only to particular countries but to particular plantations and particular years – was now a general frenzy. The presence of my old Venezuelan friends El Rey was a reminder that what upmarket chocolate-lovers want nowadays is to return to the source. The anonymities of the industrial era have brought about a backlash, and now to be geographically identifiable is *à la mode*. Yet, with every chocolatier from Lille to Lyon apparently boasting a range of *grand cru* chocolate bars bearing the names of Chuao, Choroní, Trinidad, Ecuador and so on, you wondered how there could possibly be enough of this rare and precious cacao to go around.

At the Valrhona stand, I spent a happy half-hour reacquainting myself with the work of the Rhône Valley company that virtually invented the concept of *grand cru* chocolate back in the 1980s. My palate was sent into orbit by a glorious 70 per cent cacao-mass 'Guanaja' (named, of course, after the site of the first European encounter with the cacao bean), one of the first and most successful of Valrhona's forceful lessons in the way chocolate ought to taste. It came, as do all the classic plain chocs produced by the people from Tain l'Hermitage, in a neat, austerely packaged square, thin enough to dissolve on the tongue like a communion wafer. It smelt fruity, rich and fresh; it tasted of Ovaltine, wood smoke, molasses and tropical fruit. I wondered what proportion of its contents, if any, had its origins in the cacao woods of La Sabaneta.

Valrhona is a name more usually associated with magisterial minimalism than wild feats of experiment. Here at the Salon, however, even the high priests of chocolate purity seemed caught up in the new mood of adventure. I joined a group of fascinated gourmands at a cookery workshop where the dish being prepared was one of the oddest applications of chocolate I had ever seen – odder even than hake with chocolate, *sanguinaccio* and Mexican black *mole*.

'*Ça, c'est bizarre,*' whispered an impeccable Parisian grandmother at my side.

'*C'est la folie,*' murmured a younger lady solemnly, scandalised by this outbreak of culinary impropriety.

In truth, there was something outrageous about the combination of bacon, onions, cream and Guanaja chocolate, however bravely the young chef explained to us the *raison d'être* of his experiment, which was not to create a sweet and savoury interface as such, but to see if the chocolate's dark hint of smoke might result in some fruitful liaison with the smokiness of the bacon. The resulting creamy soup, light beige in colour, was served in miniature plastic beakers and garnished with crisped onions and bacon – '*pour suivre le goût*', 'to follow the taste'. Unfortunately the taste, we decided as we sipped the soup, grimacing in disgust, was not really worth following. It wasn't so much the bacon that was the problem. It was the onion. If there is one plant family that is not at all friendly towards *Theobroma cacao*, it is *Allium* – though *garlic* and chocolate would be even worse.

Such is the nature of human creativity, however, that for every experiment that fails, there is another that works. Pierre

Marcolini, the young revolutionary of Belgian chocolate, is the man doing most to save Belgian chocolate from the curse of excessive sweetness and creamy, sickly centres. As a lover of bitterness in chocolate and a great respecter of *terroir*, Marcolini is one of the few Brussels chocolatiers the French take seriously. His collection of *pralinés*, tiny bombshells of intense flavour rather than the usual unwieldy Belgian blobs, amazed me with its silky fresh-cream ganache fillings flavoured with cardamom, with ginger, with liquorice, with jasmine tea, and, best of all, with a celestial mixture of orange and thyme, the herbal aroma coming through crystal clear and pungent, like a memory of Mediterranean hillsides in the heat of the afternoon.

Chocolate in myriad forms, mixed and matched with everything under the sun. I ate *pralinés* filled with ganaches made with goat's cheese, with three different honeys, with basil, lime, chicory, aniseed, lavender, fennel and curry. Truffles flavoured with pumpkin, from Godiva in Brussels. Tablettes whose percentage of cacao mass was dizzyingly high: 85 per cent and rising, 90 per cent – even 100 per cent, for a bitterness that was too extreme to be pleasurable. Dark chocolate bars made of fine cacao not only from the great centres of *criollo* excellence, but from bastions of *forastero* and *trinitario* production like the Ivory Coast, Ghana, Madagascar and São Tomé, a tiny island off the coast of West Africa which was the first place in Africa to cultivate the *forastero* brought over from Brazil in 1824 and became for a few years in the early twentieth century the world's leading producer.

Several Parisian galleries had taken stands at the fair in order to show paintings and sculptures made in chocolate. These varied in seriousness of intent and degree of success, from the appallingly kitsch models of Santa Claus and Godzilla in chocolate artificially coloured red, green and blue, to the skilful floral still lifes in black and white chocolate, and the solemnly abstract daubs in which melted chocolate was used as paint and built up in layers on the canvas. The message seemed to be that *la choco-laterie* was not just a particularly lucrative branch of the confectionery industry, not just a sophisticated artisan calling, nor even just another aspect of the *art de vivre*, but actually an art form in itself; a minor one perhaps, but allied to the greats.

You have to admire the French for the hard-headed dedication with which they follow through their most outrageous whims. That night at seven o'clock I took my seat in the front row of the notorious catwalk fashion show at which each of the garments, designed by a famous chocolatier with help from a famous couturier, was a confection of moulded, sculpted and otherwise manipulated chocolate. The models looked more than usually cool as they stalked the stage, doubtless aware that the merest rise in body temperature might have devastating results.

And next morning I embarked on my first session at the Université. Later in the day, I saw from my printed sheet as I took my place in the lecture hall, feeling as nervous as a student on his first day at the faculty, that there would be talks on the relationship between beer and chocolate (*'un mariage délicat'*), on the cosmetic uses of cacao butter, and on the hard-headed commercial transactions of the cacao industry in the Ivory Coast and Ghana. But the first lecture of the day was one that thoroughly interested me. A noted expert on toxicology from the prestigious Fernand-Widal hospital in Paris had been engaged to talk on the subject of 'Chocolate Addiction: Pathology or Pleasure?', of which she had made a rigorous statistical study.

Doctor Chantal Favre-Bismuth was an elegant lady of a certain age, her grey hair severely coiffed, who stood ramrod-straight on the dais and delivered her speech with the impeccable, porcelain diction which is the pride of all good *intellectuels*. I scribbled away in my student's notepad.

First of all, we need to define our criteria.

'The term chocoholism is misleading. I therefore propose

two new terms: chocophilia, for those whose love is essentially hedonistic, and chocomania, for those who feel their consumption has taken on the character of a necessity.'

Her subjects were not ill or mad, said the doctor, but otherwise perfectly healthy and sane. She had ruthlessly excluded from her survey all fans of milk chocolate, since what those unfortunate folk were addicted to was sugar, and the psychological effects of sugar were '*très, très différents*'.

And what had she found about the others, the ones who like it black and bitter? That they had certain fascinating things in common. As personalities, she claimed, they were often intensely energetic, competitive types. They enjoyed both physical sports and the less sedate intellectual games, particularly card games like poker, which require a high degree of mental agility and cunning. Chess, it seemed, was a particular favourite. Madame did not speculate on the wherefores of her findings, but I wondered about the connection between the endorphins produced by the body in states of physical excitement and the similarly pleasure-inducing chemicals which scientific research has lately been finding in chocolate.

They were compulsive people, many of them, who got their kicks from large doses of reading, housework or sex. (*Naturellement*.) They tended to be 'great consumers of cinema and entertainment'. Their physical needs extended to other types of drug, from cigarettes and, particularly, cigars, to caffeine, alcohol, cannabis, cocaine and Ecstasy. Most of them were on a regular fix of 100g per day – the equivalent of a standard bar of black chocolate. Their dependence required them to hoard the stuff at home, so as never to be without it when the need arose. Whenever chocolate was offered to them, they found it impossible to refuse: a widespread phenomenon among the French, said Doctor Favre-Bismuth sagely.

It was important not to demonise excessive consumption of chocolate, she insisted, since it could hardly be said to constitute a social problem. The only fatality she could think of was an extreme case: a woman sunk in the depths of depression whose massive ingestion of chocolate was really a form of suicide. Chocolate is extremely rich in potassium, and the woman simply overdosed. She poisoned herself, dying a lingering and painful death as her stomach wall dissolved.

Questions from the floor; confessions, testimonies. One of the questioners was a nervous young man who confessed to eating almost half a kilo of chocolate every day. There were gasps from the audience, titters of amazement.

'*Mais oui, je suis complètement dépendant du chocolat au lait*,' he murmured with a faint, dazed smile.

'Ah, milk chocolate. You are not at all interested in black chocolate?' said the doctor, worried by this turn of events.

'Only when I cannot get my usual milk. I keep some in the cupboard, just in case.'

'Well, *monsieur*, I am afraid you are a genuine *chocomane*,' she said gravely.

A young girl stood up to tell us she ate two or three bars every day. 'When I arrive in a provincial town, the first thing I do is to look for a chocolatier. Somewhere I know I can find my peace of mind. Last summer I was travelling in Sikkim and Burma. There was no chocolate to be found. I was becoming desperate. Finally after fifteen days without a single bite of chocolate, I came to a town where there were a few European-style shops. In one of these I discovered a Mars bar. To my great shame, I could not resist it. I wolfed it down in a minute.'

More gasps from the audience. '*Quelle horreur, un Mars!*' muttered the woman behind me.

The lecture came to an end. There was a brief pause before business at the Université resumed with an art historical disquisition on the subject of '*Chocolat et "l'art de vivre"* in the paintings of the eighteenth century'. It was given by a professor at the Sorbonne, a flamboyant and witty man who spoke without notes, strolling among us like a Parisian *flâneur* as he searched each painting for its secret meaning.

Art works flashed up on the screen. A Tiepolo mural from the Palacio Real in Madrid showing a triumphantly big-breasted Indian figure in a feathered headdress, symbolising America, alongside an overspilling cornucopia, sounded the keynote from the start. The New World in these pictorial terms, said Professor Belhaouari, was all about *'l'import de richesse'*. Homing in on a 1776 still life by Luis Meléndez, picking up on the textural richness of the painting, the deep red gleam of the copper *chocolatera*, the delicacy of the porcelain cup and its intricate floral decoration, the long thin pastry that seems to be drooping suggestively off the edge of the table, he adduced from the painting *'une condition sociale extrêmement aisée'*. Chocolate was in fact 'a commodity indicating your position in society'. A status symbol, in so many words.

We move on to another eighteenth-century still life, equally pregnant with symbolism. Around a marble balustrade is arranged a series of objects, each with its metaphorical meaning. Upon the balustrade itself stands a Roman vase, a parrot (symbolising paradise) and a set of musical instruments: harmony, the orderly functioning of family and society. A basket of oranges. The orange was, well into the twentieth century, a rare and precious fruit which could only be obtained from glasshouse 'orangeries' like the fabulous example at Versailles. Chocolate was a similarly exotic and elegant item, but in this painting the chocolate service is depicted in the lower left-hand corner – a position which, in the traditional hierarchy of Western painting, often served to point up a suggestion of moral inferiority.

The slides clicked back and forth in the projector – a comforting sound, remembered from slideshows at home and a university I once attended which had nothing whatever to do with the Université du Chocolat.

Further into the eighteenth century, and a painting by

François Boucher, *Le Déjeuner*, which hangs in the Louvre, a few hundred metres from the sweet delirium of the Salon du Chocolat. I imagined it somewhere far above me, among the miles of corridors stuffed with priceless art. This time there is no sense of rarefied or sinister decadence, even though the sense of luxury and elegance lingers on. The scene is that of a bourgeois family at breakfast – the chocolate pot, held by a young male member of the household, occupying the centre of the picture.

'*On descend un peu, socialement*,' said M. Belhaouari. Indeed, this is a relaxed kind of middle-class family scene. One child is being fed with a spoon, while another is called to the breakfast table but seems to be otherwise occupied with her dolls.

What is intriguing is the persistence in Boucher's picture, and in the society it reflects, of associations with wealth, with the exotic and with the kind of sumptuous, relaxed intimacy that the French call *feutré* ('felted'). The large mirror that dominates the top right-hand corner of the painting would have been an enormously expensive object for the time, and would have therefore suggested to contemporary viewers a leisured, prosperous class. Equally, the objects in the shelves beside the mirror – a teapot, a smiling Buddha – might seem to indicate sophistication, exoticism and refinement. Oddly enough, these are the qualities with which chocolate is still often associated, especially by marketeers and advertisers, two and a half centuries later. But the professor's point still stands. The painting prefigures a minor social revolution. It comes from an era when chocolate is still a handmade product destined for the religious and social elite, but is just on the point of being transformed into an industrial commodity for the mass market. The way things are looking, it won't be long before the arrival of the Mars bar – and there is nothing the French can do about it.

Chocolate arrived in France by a two-pronged, or perhaps a three-pronged route. But not all these prongs penetrated the culture with equal force. As in Spain and Italy, chocolate first caught on among French monks and nuns as an antidote to the rigours of fasting. Among the first wave of French chocophiles – France having produced more of that noble breed than any other country in the world – was the cardinal archbishop of Lyon, Alphonse Louis du Plessis (1634–80), brother of the more famous Cardinal Richelieu, who confessed to using this drug to 'moderate the vapours of his spleen, and had the secret from certain Spanish monks who brought it to France'.

The citizens of Bayonne, at the very south of the French Basque country next to the border with Spain, can plausibly claim that theirs was the first town in France in which the chocolate habit took root. According to the theory, when the Jews were hounded out of Portugal in 1609 (having already been hounded out of Spain in 1492), the first place they settled was Bayonne – one of the few Atlantic ports open to Jewish refugees. Chocolate manufacture in Portugal had been dominated by the Jews and Bayonne duly became a chocolate town *par excellence*. The tradition continues today, courtesy of firms like Daranatz, Andrieu, Mauriac and, above all, Cazenave, whose gloriously rich hot chocolate, whipped into a froth with a *molinillo* and served with cream, has been swooned over by *bayonnais* children of all ages since 1854. The Corporation of Chocolatiers of Bayonne was founded in 1661; the town also boasts an Académie du Chocolat which runs the annual 'Chocolate Days' festival in springtime, when the artisan chocolatiers of Bayonne open their kitchen doors and thousands of chocophiles from all over France converge like bees to a honeypot. Something like a provincial version of the Salon du Chocolat, in fact.

While the Jews were setting up shop in the Basque country, the Spanish were arriving in Paris. In 1615 Anne of Austria, eldest daughter of Philip II, was married to Louis XIII of France. In a portrait of the time she looks like the teenage girl she must have been, her rosy cheeks standing out against a white ruff collar. Chocolate was already the *dernier cri* in Spanish court circles, and it is thought that Anne's dowry included a large amount of cacao in the form of tablets, to be crumbled into boiling water. After the death of the king in 1643, the most coveted invitation in Paris became 'to the chocolate of her Royal Highness'.

The fashion was slow to catch on, however, until it received the additional boost of another royal wedding, that of Louis XIV to another Spanish *infanta*, Maria Teresa of Austria, in 1660. The Sun King's mother, Anne, had passed on the habit not only to him, but to the other great power in the land, Cardinal Mazarin. In 1657 Mazarin and the Maréchal de Gramont sent to Italy for two 'skilful cooks', Salvatore and More, whose presence was required in Paris in order to 'distil all sorts of flowers, and to prepare chocolate, tea and coffee, which few people still know in France'. The new queen was herself notably fond of the chocolate drink: 'I have two loves: the king, and chocolate', she famously remarked. Among the retinue she brought from Madrid was a servant whose sole duty it was to prepare her multiple cups of *chocolat*.

The year before the wedding, an apothecary from Toulouse named David Chaillou was given the royal warrant to sell chocolate on an exclusive basis. In 1671 he opened the first chocolate shop in Paris, in the rue de l'Arbre-Sec. For twenty-nine years Chaillou was the only authorised manufacturer in France. A letter signed by the king suggests that the apothecary had travelled widely 'in Spain, in Poland and other places of Europe, during which he has applied himself to the search for secrets which might be useful to the human body; he had among other things become acquainted with a certain composition which is called chocolate, the use of which is very healthful'. It's interesting to note that the use of cacao as a medicine continued well into the nineteenth century in France, long after it had lost such associations elsewhere.

When Chaillou's monopoly ended in 1688 the new choco-latiers who sprang up in Paris were more likely to be medical men than practitioners of the culinary arts. The druggist Delandre invented a 'homogeneous, stomachic and pectoral' chocolate, while Lefebvre, a doctor, concocted two new recipes, one aphrodisiac, the other 'anti-venereal'. Even Marie-Antoinette had her *'chocolats hygiéniques'* with orange flower water (to calm the nerves), with ground orchid root (to fortify) and with sweet almond milk (to aid digestion), made specially by Debauve, apothecary to the royal family. I believe that some-thing of this sense of chocolate's intimate connection with health must linger on in the French popular imagination even today. Perhaps this is why Christiane Teixier, scientific director of the Université du Chocolat and, like Chaillou, a chemist by trade in her home town of Toulouse, defines chocolate-makers as 'pharmacists of pleasure'.

But it was a series of bewigged and bejewelled young ladies, the 'favourites' of Louis XV, who finally set the social seal on chocolate. Each of them made her contribution to its conquest of the French court, the upper classes and the intelligentsia: Madame de Maintenon convinced the king to serve the drink at Versailles on special occasions; Ninon de Lenclos introduced it to Voltaire, who is known to have become a major chocoholic, drinking twelve cups between five in the morning and three in the afternoon; Madame du Barry is seen in an engraving by Jacques-Fabien Gautier-Dagoty (1710–81) stirring her chocolate in a minuscule cup served to her by a little black boy in a red turban, while she stares at the painter with big, beguiling blue eyes. Rumour had it that Madame du Barry, perhaps thinking of Montezuma in his harem, had chocolate served to all her lovers before taking them to her bed. Madame de Pompadour also used the newfangled drink to stimulate her flagging sexual powers. According to Stanley Loomis in his biography of Madame du Barry (1959), Pompadour represents the 'paradox of some great concert pianist born with insufficient fingers, for this woman who is one of history's most celebrated courtesans was, in fact, frigid. To warm a temperament that was by nature cool, to stir a sensuality that was at best sluggish, she had recourse to curious aphrodisiacs and diets. At breakfast she drank truffle and celery soup washed down by hot chocolate . . .'

Chocolate was so much the rage that, increasingly, it might be taken at all times of the day and in all places. If the craving for chocolate caught the user far from home or from public *chocolateries*, there was now an ingenious solution. In 1690 the Parisian newspaper *Le Libre Conmode* advertised a portable *chocolatière* which, it was said, would fit into any pocket. Seventeenth-century pockets must have been more commodious than ours, since the device in question came with a cooker, a set of cups and saucers, spoons, alcohol for burning and enough chocolate and sugar for three servings.

Gradually the taste and texture of the drink began to set European chocolate apart from its New World origins. Manufacturing techniques which had not changed at all since the Aztecs were beginning to give way to a series of tentative innovations. In 1732 the engineer Du Buisson designed a grinder which was heated from below by a wood fire, thus combining two of the chocolate-making processes in one. One imagines this, or something very like it, must have been the device illustrated in Denis Diderot's multi-volume *Encyclopedia or the classified dictionary of the sciences, arts and trades* (1751–72). We also know that at Chaillou's shop in the rue de l'Arbre-Sec the cacao had been ground twice on a heated *metate*. This double grinding and heating was an attempt to improve the texture of the finished product by rendering the cacao particles as small as possible.

The traditional 'American' flavourings of the chocolate drink, such as ginger, chilli, annatto and vanilla, were no longer added as a matter of course, indeed some influential commentators actively disapproved of them. Diderot himself had this to say of vanilla: 'The pleasant scent and heightened taste it gives to chocolate has made it very popular, but long experience having taught us that it is extremely heating, its use has become less frequent, and people who prefer to care for their health rather than please their senses abstain completely.' (Vanilla is now the only spice admitted by the master chocolatiers of our time, so Diderot was wrong about something.) And Dufour, in his *Traitez Nouveaux*, admits that chocolate made according to European tastes would be thought dull by the 'Americans', who 'demand that the pimento [hot pepper] should dominate, and that which those Peoples compose would be unbearable for our taste, because it would be too piquant on our palate'. It was a case of *chacun à son goût*: 'It is the same with chocolate as with other drinks: one could scarcely find one which pleases everybody.'

Since its arrival in Europe, chocolate had begun to acquire an aura of indolent sensuality, tinged with a suggestion of decadence and vice. In his *Tastes of Paradise* (1993), Wolfgang Schivelbusch describes how, as it shook off its clerical and monastic associations, chocolate-drinking became part of a very different social milieu. Unlike coffee, which was essentially a Protestant drink, providing a jolt of sobering energy to fuel the working day, chocolate had to do with the baroque Catholic universe of eroticism and languid pleasure. 'Whereas the middle-class family sat erect at the breakfast table, with a sense of disciplined propriety, the essence of the chocolate ritual was fluid, lazy, languid motion. If coffee virtually shook drinkers awake for the workday that lay ahead, chocolate was meant to create an intermediary state between lying down and sitting up.'

Coffee was the bourgeois stimulant *par excellence*; chocolate belonged to the aristocratic and conservative *ancien régime* and the *demi-monde*. The two most famous 'chocolate moments' in opera neatly emphasise the class identity of the drink: in Mozart's *Così fan tutte* the maid Despina complains that she has spent half an hour preparing the chocolate for her mistresses and yet is forbidden to taste it herself. And in the opening scene of Richard Strauss's opera *Der Rosenkavalier*, set in an idealised, high-camp version of eighteenth-century Vienna, the Marschallin is still lying in bed after her night of passion with Octavian – von Hofmannsthal's stage direction reads 'raising herself on the cushion' – when the little black boy brings in her chocolate. When the baron arrives later in the morning the chocolate is still there, and he shouts for it not to be removed: this is the most leisurely sort of breakfast imaginable. For the Marschallin and her romantic reveries, coffee would have been a terribly rude awakening.

<hr />

THREE GREAT FRENCH CHOCOPHILES

1. Madame de Sévigné

Marie de Rabutin-Chantal (1626–96), otherwise and better known as Madame de Sévigné, could not quite make up her mind about the virtues, or indeed the failings, of chocolate. In this as in other respects she shows the modern cast of her sensibility – for a love-hate relationship with chocolate is now thought of as the most natural thing in the world. She was capable of praising it to the skies, such as in the letter to her daughter in 1671, in which she enthuses: 'The day before yesterday I took chocolate in order to digest my lunch and be able to dine well, and today I have taken it to nourish me so that I can do without food until nightfall. What I find most wonderful about chocolate is that it is efficacious – for whatever reason you take it.' She worries that her daughter, who lived in Provence, far from the fashionable whirligig of Paris, does not possess a chocolate pot, and she cannot understand how a person can live without one. Yet in another letter a few months later she inveighs against the drink and her own capacity to be swayed by the dictates of Parisian mores.

'Chocolate, for me, is not what it was', she complains. 'Fashion has taken me with it, as it always does. All those who spoke well of it now tell me bad things about it, cursing it, and accusing it of all the ills that exist. It is the cause of vapours and palpitations. It is pleasant for a while, but then suddenly lights up a continuous fever which leads to death.' Even if the chocolate-drinker were lucky enough to be spared such grievous effects on her health, she might still be stricken with other misfortunes of a different sort. As Madame de Sévigné writes to her daughter, in one of history's most scandalous pieces of gossip, 'The Marquise of Coetlogon took so much chocolate during her pregnancy that she gave birth to a little boy as black as the devil, who immediately died.'

As a mark of respect for her early, if somewhat capricious passion, a fine brand of French chocolates now bears her name.

━━━◦◦◦◦━━━

2. The Marquis de Sade

In the life of Donatien Alphonse François, Marquis de Sade (1740–1814), as in his writings, pleasure and suffering were always intimately related. Chocolate would never be a simple matter of sweetness and delight, therefore, but a complex interplay between voluptuous sensuality and cruelty and death. 'As a substance both invigorating and deadly, chocolate functions in his novels as the sign of a double alimentary economy', suggested Roland Barthes in *Sade, Fourier, Loyola* (1970). In Sade's practically unreadable novel *Juliette, ou les prospérités du vice*, companion piece to *Justine, ou les malheurs de la vertu*, chocolate duly appears in a wholly unexpected guise. Both Rose and Madame Brissac fall victim to cups of the drink laced with poison, and Menski takes a draught of chocolate which has been spiced without his knowledge with *datura* (*estramonio*), 'one of the most powerful narcotics known, and one of the most dangerous, taken internally'.

Sade's inflammatory fictions and his heterodox political beliefs (he was a convinced monarchist) made him many enemies, and he spent most of his adult life either in jail or, later, in the lunatic asylum of Charenton where he died in 1814. He was an enthusiastic lover of chocolate, and sent frequent letters from prison begging his wife to send chocolate biscuits, bars, pastilles, *crème au chocolat*, and on one occasion, 'a cake with icing . . . but I want it to be chocolate and black inside from chocolate as the devil's arse is black from smoke. And the icing is to be the same.' He also asked for cacao butter suppositories – which, according to one source, were once popular in Martinique as a remedy for piles.

His last book, the notorious *120 Days of Sodom*, was written in the madhouse shortly before his death, and has become a popular choice for browsing among students in the Rare Books rooms of university libraries ever since. 'At eleven o'clock they passed through to the ladies' quarters, where the eight young sultanas presented themselves naked, and in that state served chocolate, aided and directed by Marie and Lovison, who presided over this seraglio . . .'

With infinite delicacy, Barthes draws a comparison which is so horribly, disgustingly obvious that no other writer has dared consider it – though Michael and Sophie Coe do make the point that the first Spanish colonists of the New World must have been put off by a brown substance the natives called *caca*, or something very like it. 'Sadean chocolate ends up by functioning as the pure sign of this dual alimentary economy . . . The victim's food is always copious for two libertine reasons: First these victims too must be refreshed . . . and fattened up to furnish vice with fat dimpled "altars"; second, coprophagic passion demands an "abundant, delicate soft food" . . .

Thus the function of food in the Sadean city: to restore, to poison, to fatten, to evacuate; everything planned in relation to vice.'

———•◦•———

3. Brillat-Savarin

Jean-Anthelme Brillat-Savarin (1755–1826) knew what was good for him. And for his readers. His essential meditation on food, life, the universe and everything, *The Physiology of Taste*, has a whole chapter on chocolate giving the history, the method of preparation and the difficulty of making it properly – for, as he pronounces, an enormous amount of 'care, skill and experience are needed to pro-duce chocolate which is sweet but not insipid, strong but not bitter, aromatic but not sickly, and thick but free from sediment'.

Brillat-Savarin was a magistrate in the town of Belley, and subse-quently mayor of the town. Though the Revolution forced him into exile abroad, he returned to Paris and was made a judge at the Supreme Courts of Appeal. As a cousin by marriage of the hostess Madame Recamier he must surely have attended her famous Parisian salon and was most likely served chocolate on these occasions. To judge by his comments on flavourings, it seems the more piquant 'American' spices were now reserved for particular medicinal appli-cations of the drink; the basic chocolate recipe as prepared in Paris at the start of the nineteenth century would have been a relatively simple affair.

'When the delicious flavour of vanilla is added to the sugar, cinnamon and cacao, the *nec plus ultra* is attained of the perfection to which this preparation can be brought. It is to this small number of substances that taste and experience have reduced the numerous ingredients which had been successively tried as adjuncts to cocoa, such as pepper, pimento, aniseed, ginger, annatto and others.'

But there was one very exotic and expensive flavouring of which he certainly approved: ambergris, a waxy excretion of whales sometimes found washed up on tropical beaches. A pint of 'ambered chocolate', he pronounced, could work wonders in the man who 'has drunk too deeply of the cup of pleasure, or given to work a notable portion of the time which should belong to sleep; who finds his wit temporarily losing its edge, the atmosphere humid, time dragging, and the air hard to breathe, or who is tortured by a fixed idea which robs him of all freedom of thought . . .'

The question as to whether chocolate was a 'heating' substance or a 'cooling' one had bedevilled scientific debate on the subject for years. Brillat-Savarin, refreshingly commonsensical to the last, dismisses the dilemma out of hand. The days of the Galenic, or 'humoural', system of medicine were evidently numbered. For 'time and experience, those two great teachers, have conclusively proved that chocolate, when carefully prepared, is a wholesome and agreeable form of food; that it is nourishing and easily digestible; that, unlike coffee, of which indeed it is the antidote, it holds no terrors for the fair sex; that it is very suitable for persons faced with great mental exertion, preachers, lawyers, and above all travellers; and finally that it agrees with the feeblest stomachs, has proved beneficial in cases of chronic illness, and remains the last resource in diseases of the pylorus'. He agrees with Madame de Sévigné that, far from being indigestible, chocolate actually aids digestion. 'Happy chocolate, which having circled the globe through women's smiles, finds its death at their lips in a delectable, melting kiss.'

As for the best suppliers of chocolate, he is in no doubt. 'Being ourselves very fond of chocolate, we have run the gamut of nearly all the dealers, and we have now settled upon Monsieur Debauve, of no.26 rue des Saints-Pères; he is a purveyor of chocolate to the King, and we rejoice to see that the sun's rays have lighted on the worthiest of all.' In 1825, when Brillat-Savarin published his *The Physiology of Taste*, Debauve's range featured a 'body-building' chocolate flavoured with lotus root, and 'anti-spasmodic' chocolate with orange-flower water, as enjoyed by Marie-Antoinette forty years earlier. But it is his 'everyday chocolate', equally suitable for breakfast, dinner and drawing-room entertainments, that the great gastronome singles out for special praise.

'Our only acquaintance with Monsieur Debauve is through his wares; we have never set eyes on him; but we know that he is helping considerably to free France from the tribute she used to pay to Spain, by providing Paris and the provinces with a chocolate whose reputation is constantly increasing.'

<hr>

. . . AND AN AMERICAN CHOCOPHILE IN FRANCE

M. F. K. Fisher's mother recommended chocolate to her daughter as a remedy for lovesickness. As a child in the country she remembered eating 'chocolate puddings with chopped nuts and heavy cream. The thought of them makes me dizzy now, but we loved them.' But Fisher's formative chocolate experience seems to have been in France, during her time as an au pair in the 1930s.

She was out walking in the countryside on a winter's day when she was offered her first revelatory taste of *pain au chocolat*.

'"Here! Try some of this, young lady!" And he held out a piece of chocolate, pale brown with cold. I smiled and took it . . . In my mouth the chocolate broke at first like gravel into many separate, disagreeable bits. I began to wonder if I could swallow them. Then they grew soft, and melted voluptuously into a warm stream down my throat.

'The little doctor came bustling up . . . "Here! Wait, wait!" he cried. "Never eat chocolate without bread, young lady! Very bad for the interior, very bad . . ." And in two minutes my mouth was full of fresh bread, and melting chocolate, and as we sat gingerly, the three of us, on the frozen hill . . . we peered shyly and silently at each other and smiled and chewed at one of the most satisfying things I have ever eaten' (*Serve It Forth*, 1937).

———◇◇◇◇———

There are a few cities in the world, very few, which not only live up to their self-publicity but go way beyond it, conferring on the visitor a magical frisson of wellbeing which makes him feel that he has been singled out for special treatment.

Central Paris – the Paris within the *périphérique*, for life beyond the ring road is a very different matter – is a theme park of urban romanticism. There are synchronicities, bewitching coincidences, conjunctions of the seasons and the fall of the light on the city's already luminous physical topography . . . Let's just say that Things happen. Like the night I was walking home after dinner, my mind still reverberating with the pleasure of a rich and velvety *petit pot au chocolat*. A giant full moon sparkled on the waters of the Seine, polishing up the great silver spider of Notre Dame. I crossed the river by the Pont du Carrousel, feeling that I was floating in the crisp autumn air, and turned south along the rue des Saints-Pères. And it was still there at no. 26, unperturbed by more than two centuries of revolution and restoration, change and decay: Debauve et Gallais, founded in 1800 and probably the world's oldest continuously functioning *chocolaterie*.

The façade, blue and gold, gives off an unmistakable air of monarchistic pride. '*Fournisseurs des anciens rois de France*' says the legend – which is about as close as you can get in French to a 'By Royal Appointment'. I peered at the window display, the boxes all tied with blue and gold ribbon and stamped with the royal coat of arms: three fleurs-de-lys and a crown. Beyond the window the darkened interior of the shop was wonderfully grand, the high-ceilinged room defined by a semicircle of slender Grecian columns. A temple, indeed, to the mysterious and sacred arts of chocolate.

But Paris is full of such temples – not all of such historical pedigree, maybe, but equally hushed and reverent. No other city treats chocolate with the same quasi-religious seriousness. Its chocolatiers are the new high priests, and the legion of chocophiles are their congregation. For those who do not know their *criollo* from their *forastero*, their ganache from their *gianduja*, shopping in one of the grand Paris chocolate boutiques can be as intimidating as *haute couture*. The same values apply: design, chic, luxury, aesthetic beauty, and, above all, high quality.

The chocolate houses tend to cluster like hazelnuts in the chic and newly wealthy *quartiers* of the Left Bank, so that you can visit most of them in a single afternoon. I began with one of the great originals, La Fontaine du Chocolat, a boutique in the rue Saint-Honoré owned since 1987 by Michel Cluizel – though M. Cluizel has now retired to the Normandy countryside to experiment with new recipes, leaving his daughter Cathérine to run the show. In the window, a three-tiered fountain of melted chocolate endlessly, voluptuously gushed, drawing children off the street as if by an invisible thread. I bought a tablette of rare *criollo* chocolate from the African island of São Tomé – a recent addition to Cluizel's *grand cru* range – and another whose cacao was entirely sourced from the Hacienda La Concepción in Barlovento. The bar's handsome orange and black packaging gave a small picture of a drying floor surrounded with a columned walkway in the colonial style. A product whose origins can be pinpointed to a particular place, like wines, seems to point to a possible future for the finest of fine chocolate. I picked open the bar's outer cardboard packet as I walked down the street, past the ranks of fashion shops and chic restaurants, and sniffed at the inner plastic sleeve as a whiff of rich, fruity chocolate aroma filtered out. I took a bite; the thin black shiny surface cracked under my teeth. This sensation is known as 'the snap' . Even in the less-than-perfect tasting conditions of the crowded rue Saint Honoré, I could tell this was a splendid piece of work, a grand orchestration of fresh fruit aromas – cherry, peach and plum – unfolding in waves against a dark sky of bitter caramel.

I seemed to be moving down a glittering corridor, a canyon lined with plate glass behind which were smug displays of clothes, food and jewellery. At no. 231 was a gleaming shop front that could have been another chic fashion emporium but was actually the HQ of Jean-Paul Hévin, genial master of the ganache and by now my favourite French chocolatier by a sizeable margin. Hévin is taking the *praliné*, the chocolate-coated filling supposedly invented by the Maréchal de Plessis-Praslin, Duke of Choiseul, to new heights of sophistication. He is a purist. Simplicity and lightness are his points of reference, even when working with ingredients which in other hands would all too easily turn sickly and overpowering.

There on display in the boutique was his chocolate frock, fresh from its triumph at the Salon: a long elegant cape made of chocolate strips encrusted with candy crystals, and a short skirt with a broad belt whose smooth brown surface gave it the uncanny appearance of fine leather. The outfit was accessorised with a handbag made of chocolate lace handpainted with silver leaf, and – the crowning glory – a cowboy stetson apparently inspired by Madonna's recent Country & Western look, studded with sugar diamonds and piped around the brim with something that looked very like chocolate mousse.

In the light of Hévin's Gallicly serious approach to the art of *chocolaterie*, these fripperies seem all the more bizarre. For as well as a virtuoso, he is equally a master of subtlety and restraint. He is less interested in novelty *per se* as in a return to the essentials: the fine tablette of black chocolate made from a top-quality cacao, the perfectly executed ganache. A small box in brown textured cardboard trimmed with blue, nothing flashy, goes against the grain of the branded chocolate box *de nos jours*, which tends to favour garish, attention-seeking colours and slippery-shiny surfaces. The accompanying booklet, austerely entitled *Les Chocolats*, is a document smaller than a credit card which unfolds like a concertina. It repays careful study, for the chocolates are not easy to identify by appearance alone, being simple blocks and squares minimally decorated with a stripe or two across the corner, a cross-hatching or stippling or other textural effect over the top. The chocolates are modestly sized, but each is a Pandora's box of sensations that billow and bloom in the mouth.

'There is one thing I can tell you,' says a well-to-do lady standing at the counter, giving me a conspiratorial smile as she nibbles a sample of Hévin's 'Carupano', described by its creator as an 'osmosis between the savour of honey and the caress of half-bitter chocolate'.

'Once you have tasted M. Hévin's chocolates, no other chocolate will do.'

There on the other side of the counter is the man himself, with a short peppery beard and glasses, wearing black from head to foot, giving him a faintly ecclesiastical look appropriate enough for a high priest. Hévin is a member of the most exclusive chocophile organisation in Paris, which is to say in all the world: the Club des Croqueurs de Chocolat, whose 150 members include fashion designer Sonia Rykiel (she is also their President) and baker of sublime sourdough loaves, Lionel Poilâne. To say that the Club takes chocolate seriously is to fall somewhat short of the mark. Every other month on a Wednesday morning at eleven o'clock precisely, the faithful convene in the great hall on the first floor of the Hotel Nikko on the quai de Grenelle. Meetings turn around a particular theme and always include a blind tasting, be it of black chocolate ice cream, milk chocolate *praliné*, caramel ganache or fine chocolate spreads *à la* Nutella – currently in vogue among the French. But there is also a polemical side to their deliberations. Since 1993 they have campaigned against what for true chocolate lovers is the Great Crime: the substitution for cacao butter of other oils of vegetable origin. Their cause has been well received in the corridors of Brussels and Strasbourg. The Club has even created a seal of quality – Chocolat Pur Beurre de Cacao – which it offers freely to those chocolatiers of whose work it approves. And over the course of time it has inspired other societies of a similar nature, notably the Club du Chocolat aux Palais, for membership of which only those who belong to the great institutions of the Republic – lawyers, judges, MPs, parliamentary attachés, diplomats and so forth – are eligible. If further proof were needed of the extraordinary nature of French chocophilia, try imagining an equivalent organisation in Britain or the United States.

For Jean-Paul Hévin, the use of non-cacao-derived fats in chocolate manufacture is not just a brazen piece of bad faith. To a chocolate worshipper such as himself it amounts almost to sacrilege.

'*C'est un scandale*,' he hisses at me across the counter, as if I personally am to blame for this state of affairs.

'My opinion is this: if we let them use these cheap fats, they will not stop there. They will want to substitute other inferior ingredients. Perhaps even a falsified, chemical version of cacao – who knows? We mustn't give in. Have you not seen in my little books, how it says "the chocolates of Jean-Paul Hévin are and will remain pure cacao butter chocolates"? *Voilà, c'est tout*. And if you ask any of my colleagues, they will surely say the same.'

Together with a handful of other artisans both in Paris and in the provinces, Hévin is at the cutting edge of chocolate-making as an art form, taking it in new and unexpected directions. His 'energetic' or 'dynamic' chocolates, a recent creation inspired perhaps by cacao's historical reputation as a stimulant, incorporate such unusual components as Kola nut, bandé wood and nutmeg. He gave me a brief tasting of some of his *pralinés*, the sweetly spicy '*bois bandé*' with its chocolate coating that seemed to fizz electrically in the mouth, the Trinidad flavoured with lime zest, the Manon with its lightly whipped, frothy ganache and delectable hint of caramel, and the Carupano with its famous osmosis of half-bitter chocolate and three honeys. (Quite why a single honey will not do is clearly not a question that mere mortals can answer.) I finished off this miniature banquet with a stunning truffle, one of the best I could remember tasting, made of a rich bittersweet ganache with a discernible tang of fresh cream, the little ball rolled in a power-fully flavoured cacao powder.

Parisian chocolate culture is indeed a wondrous flowering of excellence. There were times during my stay in the city when it seemed I ate little else. Chocolate flooded my senses, haunted my dreams. It was everywhere I looked; it was in everything I saw. My eyes were mesmerically drawn to the chocolate crepe, the éclair in the patisserie window, the whipped hot chocolate in the fancy tearoom. Chocolate leapt out of the menus at restaurants. At the New Wave bistro Les Bookinistes on the Left Bank I ate what seemed to me the most sensational *petit pot au chocolat* of all time, a velvety melange imbued with the smoky resonance and the exhilarating citrus freshness of Valrhona's Guanaja. Later that afternoon at Angelina's on the rue de Rivoli, I fought my way through the ranks of old ladies caked with make-up and smelling of rosewater, to partake of a splendid silky hot chocolate with a cup of whipped cream served on the side.

That same evening at Spoon, Alain Ducasse's modernist temple to the new world order in food, I had a sudden craving for pizza. Not a ordinary boring sort of pizza with a cheese and tomato topping. What I wanted was M. Ducasse's chocolate pizza. It arrived in triangular wedges, warm, the crisp biscuity chocolate base smeared messily with delicious dabs of melted chocolate. I ate it up in a trice, wiped my face as a mother wipes a child's, and clicked my fingers for the dessert menu.

Michel Chaudun's chocolate shop in the rue de l'Université is a corner site with a green awning and gold lettering. I stood outside the shop for a good while doing what the French call *lèches-vitrines* – literally 'licking the window'. The kitsch factor of that window display was mesmerising, but behind it I sensed a mischievous sense of humour. There was surely no way anyone could possibly be serious about these chocolate Eiffel Towers, mobile phones, horse brasses, baby bottles, carpentry tools and figurines of piglets in curious attitudes . . . or was there? M. Chaudun has another branch in Tokyo. Who knows: perhaps all this sugary whimsy is an attempt to reach out towards the notoriously babyish Japanese market.

I was mulling over the existential conundrum of a full-sized power tool complete with cable and plug, entirely made in chocolate, when a little man in a brown shirt darted out of the shop and asked me if I would like to come in. '*Voulez-vous entrer? . . .*' A shop is a public space and one can enter in one's own time, but there is something about being invited in off the street – especially when the invitation comes from the owner and presiding genius of the place – that puts the experience on a different level of importance.

For Chaudun, as for me, the love of chocolate has its roots in childhood. As we tasted our way through his celestial range of *pralinés*, he went off on an emotional digression into his memories of Easter egg hunts in the family garden and chocolate coins and packets of chocolate cigarettes. (I too remember those cigarettes – I believe the brand name was Hollywood – and the way we used to pose with them languidly as they rapidly melted in our hot little hands.) His reminiscences of the *pain au chocolat* and of *le chocolat chaud*, those crucial appurtenances of a traditional French childhood, were rapturous effusions of rose-tinted nostalgia.

'The *pain au chocolat* for me was a rarity, because at the time my parents could not afford it. We were three children, and it was just bread, butter and cacao powder, at four o'clock in the afternoon. We were sometimes given the real thing on Sunday mornings, and that was *un délice*. I have wonderful memories, too, of *le chocolat chaud*.' He seemed to take pleasure even in the sound of the words, relishing their sibilants and voluptuous vowel-sounds. 'I learned to love hot chocolate with its persistent aroma, tender and powerful at the same time. We were, *peut-être*, the last generation of schoolchildren to be offered a bowl of foaming, steaming hot chocolate when it was cold outside . . .'

Michel was a precocious child. At an age when most kids are stuffing themselves with milk chocolate, he had already graduated on to bitter black Nestlé or Menier bars. At the age of eight he was already making his first chocolate truffles, aided and abetted by a schoolmistress and a dinner lady. Clearly the culinary regime at French primary schools in the 1950s was a cut above the average. But this boy knew where he was going. At fourteen he was apprenticed to Michel Chasles at his chocolate shop in the Loire Valley. For twenty-two years he was a journeyman chocolatier, working with the great names in France, Switzerland and Germany. In 1986 he set up shop in the rue de l'Université, and the accolades came rolling in.

Chaudun handed me a typewritten list of his multiple prizes, medals, cups and certificates. A couple of details leapt from the page. His bust of Tutankhamun in chocolate covered in gold leaf had won him the *grand prix* of the city of Arpajon in 1968; and the following year another Tutankhamun, this time in white chocolate, had done the business in Tours. The gold medal in Trouville in 1979 brought him the prize of a trip to Greece – one of the least chocophile nations in Europe. I pictured him in tourist mode, climbing the Acropolis, or pink and uncomfortable on a beach. Rather like the cacao tree, and chocolate itself come to that, chocolate-makers don't usually thrive in direct sunlight.

Life in the shade is healthier and a good deal more comfortable. Unlike Hévin, Chaudun is not one for parading his creations under the spotlight. Not for him the publicity, nor the diffusion lines, nor the high-class tearoom, nor the mad adventures in chocolate *haute couture*. He has never even been to see his store on the Ginza in Tokyo, for instance, and had been conspicuous by his absence at the Salon du Chocolat. 'I have not the time . . .'

He picked up a basil *praliné* – made with fresh basil leaves – and popped it in his mouth, eyes twinkling, mouth chewing away hurriedly like some forest rodent. In his own quiet way Chaudun has had more influence on the French art of chocolate-making than many a hungrier, media-friendlier talent. When all is said and done, he is less a follower than a setter of trends. The current mania for crazy creative combinations can be traced back to his experiments in the mid-1980s, when the Club des Croqueurs de Chocolat, dazzled by Chaudun's invention of a chocolate bonbon perfumed with black truffles, bestowed on him the greatest honour in their power to give, the Diplôme d'Honneur. Before it was fashionable, he was working with black pepper and chilli and ginger and orange blossom.

'In my daily life, you know, I am always in search of new flavours. I have tried so many things; it is interesting. Some things don't function. Cassis, *c'est un désastre*. Strawberry: it is so difficult to find the point of intersection. Orange and chocolate, they can be friends. Lemon and chocolate, they are more like enemies.'

Sadly, the innovation of which he is most proud is the one for which he has received least credit. The genial idea of combining bitter chocolate with tiny pieces of crushed roasted cacao bean occurred to him in 1993. It was the kind of inspiration that could only have sprung from a creative mind like Chaudun's, dedicated to the passionate exploration of chocolate's possibilities. Yet Chaudun saw his idea shamelessly pilfered by the big chocolate companies, who all launched their *éclats de fèves* bars in the years that followed. He has a drawer in the shop reserved for samples of this peculiar gastronomic plagiarism, and pulls it open to show me.

Given his solitary artistry and the romantic halo hovering over his childhood memories, Michel Chaudun was never likely to be well disposed to the machinations of the global confectionery industry. As it is, he has nothing but contempt for them.

'The industry can't compete with us. How could it possibly compete with fine cacao beans, pure butter and cream?' he asks rhetorically. By 'us', of course, he means the handful of dedicated artisan chocolatiers like himself, for whom chocolate-making is not just a mere product, nor even a craft, but practically a branch of the fine arts.

'The only thing that matters these days is money, money, money,' he says firmly, busying himself at the counter, as if to wipe out disagreeable thoughts by applying himself to the day-to-day business of the shop. A batch of fresh caramel *pralinés* must be removed from their tray to a place where they can be seen and bought. He picks them up with a delicate movement of forefinger and thumb and deposits them, swiftly but meticulously, in neat rows, in the glass-fronted cabinet which he keeps at a constant 17 degrees.

The time has come for me to leave him to his work. But there is one more thing he wants me to try: his famous *pavés de la rue de l'Université*. Squares of chocolate ganache, shaped like the paving stones from which their name derives, dusted with chocolate powder, they are packed side by side in a little box with a brown wax seal and a black ribbon. He hands me one on a cocktail stick. It is a miniature bombshell of chocolate flavour – powerfully rich, yet leaving in its wake a delicious sensation of freshness.

Michel Chaudun observes me as I stand there by the door, still stupidly mumbling and murmuring with pleasure. After thirty years in the business, I suppose he must be used to watching people's reactions to his work. Perhaps, as with all artists, it is the pleasure you are able to produce in your audience that finally makes up for all the years of struggle.

'I see from your face, *monsieur*, that you are a true lover of chocolate. We are the same,' he tells me, *charmant* to the last.

'For me, you see, a world without chocolate would be a 'orrible place. It is a necessity for my wellbeing. It is the companion of my solitude and the cure for the sickness of love. It puts the smile on the lips, makes the eyes shine. It is a cure for the fear, the hunger, the bad feelings. It is a friend for every moment – it gives me inspiration. "Bitter as the pain it consoles, but sweeter than the love it inspires." I adore it! *Au revoir, monsieur! Au revoir!*'

PART FOUR

THE BIRTH OF
AN INDUSTRY

Sniffing out the 'chocolate towns' in
Birmingham and Pennsylvania

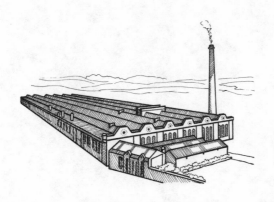

Gastronomic literature does not exactly abound with descriptions of Cadbury's chocolate. Has anyone ever bothered to sit down and write an appreciation of Dairy Milk, that central pillar of our British experience of food and eating? Not as far as I know. It is puzzling that this should be so, because it seems to me that Cadbury's milk chocolate is an intimate part of our Britishness, or, to put it another way, a British part of our intimacy; a corner of our psychological identity that is forever England, Scotland, Wales and Northern Ireland.

The reason why milk chocolate has such a powerful claim on our souls has to do with the plain physical fact that it melts at 35 degrees centigrade, a temperature just below that of the body. Under normal circumstances it remains a solid. But as soon as we place it in our mouths, it thaws and resolves itself into a dew, vanishing under the pressure of our tongues. Chocolate of the Dairy Milk or Galaxy sort, laden with sugar and fat, is not so much about flavour as physical sensation. Its pleasures belong to the oral phase, as Freud might have put it. This is why children adore milk chocolate above all other types, and why even for adults this kind of super-sweet toffee-tasting British confectionery continues to be rich with childhood associations. It offers a permanently available connection with our infant selves; a sentimental backtrack into the past.

England itself is chocolate-coloured. Or so I thought as I leant my head idly against the window of the cheapskate Silverlink train that rattled slowly north out of Euston, taking so long to cover the distance from London to Birmingham that you could have arrived in Paris and be sitting down to lunch in less time than it took to creep into New Street. On this winter day the landscape was a deep, luscious brown. It was gently curved and comforting to contemplate, like some kind of gorgeous homemade chocolate pudding, and the remains of last week's snow were dusted over the top of it like icing sugar.

I got off at Bournville, the dedicated station for Cadbury World. The station gives you an eyeful of the deep purple that has become the dedicated colour of the brand. If it were possible to copyright this shade Cadbury's would surely have done so, since nothing is more powerfully evocative of the 'Cadbury taste' than this bright ecclesiastical *purpura*, vaguely redolent as it is of power and exclusivity and luxury. The town is drenched in it, the Day-Glo livery of railings, benches, roadsigns and rubbish bins, making them leap out startlingly from the grey and green drabness of their suburban context.

The point of departure for industrial chocolate – of which, I think we can agree, Cadbury's represents a salient example – was the cottage industry of handmade chocolate in solid form, which gradually shaded, or melted, into factory production *per se*.

What made the difference was mechanisation. As early as 1795, J. S. Fry, the Bristol company, bought a Watts steam engine as a power source to replace the factory's original watermill; the puffing monster duly became one of the talked about marvels of the city. Across the Channel, François Pelletier found that the four horse-power steam mixer he acquired in 1819 allowed him to produce no less than 75kg in a morning's work. Bordeaux had 'a number of little factories with steam-powered machinery' by the early nineteenth century. Despite a certain resistance to the new technology, which was still somewhat unreliable (the machines kept breaking down, complained one Bayonne manufacturer), France was ahead, for a while, in the field of technical innovation. But as the Napoleonic Wars raged on and cacao supplies from the French colonies became scarcer, the British chocolate industry, which had access to beans from its own colonies, forged ahead.

Generally speaking, as a product, chocolate still left a great deal to be desired. The main problem was excessive cacao butter, which could account for as much as 55 per cent of the total weight, so that when the drink was allowed to cool even slightly, the grease floated to the surface. This unpleasant fact brought others in its wake. In late eighteenth-century England ground cacao was commonly mixed with potato starch, arrow-root, ground acorns, even powdered seashells in order to soak up the oil. Food adulteration, one of the curses of the age, was a permanent factor in the business of chocolate, as it was in almost every other foodstuff, from milk to bread. Powdered rust and brick dust were added for colour. 'Great quantities of cocoa nutshells and husks have been lately imported and after such importation are fabricated and worked up so as to imitate coffee or chocolate and then are vended and sold as such', claimed a report in 1731, during the reign of George II. But in 1851 a survey by the *Lancet* medical journal revealed that in an analysis of fifty commercial cocoa brands, no less than 90 per cent were adulterated – principally with starch and lead-based pigment.

When it was realised that cacao butter could be removed by the simple expedient of a hydraulic press, the door was at last open to a series of improvements. J. S. Fry is thought to have begun removing excess cacao butter as early as 1760, probably by simmering the cacao mass and skimming the fat from its sur-face, and other manufacturers across Europe had developed their own techniques – but the fame of Conraad van Houten has eclipsed them all. Van Houten was a doctor by trade who had been grinding his cacao in a watermill since 1815. When he discovered the technique that became known as Dutching, by which cacao powder was treated with alkaline salts so that you had only to add water for an instant chocolate drink, lighter in texture than the old-fashioned version and without the fat or foam, the modern era in chocolate history could be said to have begun. Wolfgang Schivelbusch characterises this moment as the Protestant volte face over centuries of Hispanic Catholic tradition, opening the door to the democratic habits of consumption that would revolutionise Western ways with chocolate.

The idea of the chocolate 'company town', constructed in fulfilment of some philanthropic social ideal, was also something new. The Menier factory at Noisiel on the Marne, which had reached such a size and magnificence by 1872 that it was known as 'la cathédrale', provided its 2000 workers with a library, an infirmary, a food shop where payment could be made with special tokens, and a pleasure garden. Model towns, like New Erswick, Seebohm Rowntree's creation three miles outside York, would become a feature of the late nineteenth-century industrial landscape. But the Cadbury dynasty's peculiar venture at Bournville remained the template, at least as far as the Anglo-Saxon world was concerned, for the way things could be done.

In the closing years of the eighteenth century Birmingham was a microcosm of the social change from rural and agricultural societies to urban and industrial ones. Richard Tapper Cadbury was born in Exeter in 1768 but relocated to Birmingham in 1794 in search of an opening in the dynamic new entrepreneurial scene of the Midlands. At first the family business was fabrics; but in 1824 his son John opened a shop next door at 93 Bull Street, specialising in coffee, tea and chocolate. On 1 March an article in the *Birmingham Gazette* declared: 'J. C. is desirous of introducing to particular notice Cocoa Nibs prepared by himself, an article affording a most nutritious beverage for breakfast.' Despite a slump in the rest of the world, cacao consumption in Britain was booming – from 122 tons in 1822 it jumped to 910 tons in 1840 – and after 1832 duty on imported cacao was substantially lowered. The time had come for chocolate's acceptance by a much wider social constituency.

In his new workshop in Crooked Lane, John Cadbury began to experiment with a range of new chocolate products, of which a dozen saw the light of day in 1842. The new brands included Broma, Spanish Chocolate, Churchman's Chocolate and other drinking chocolates in the form of powder, flakes, paste and nibs. Soluble Cocoa was advertised as 'light and nutritious in its nature, grateful to the palate, and in price within the reach of all classes'. 'French Eating Chocolate' was a remarkable novelty for the time and still a rarity.

The business went through a bad patch in the mid-nineteenth century, but the brothers Richard and George Cadbury were young men with energy and flair, and in the 1860s things began to pick up again. They brought in new lines: Iceland Moss, a mixture of cocoa and lichen believed to be healthy, was undoubtedly the most unusual. They hired their first commercial traveller, Dixon Hadaway. I have seen a photograph of this splendidly dapper Victorian gentleman in his top hat and long frock coat and his magnificent beard, who was expected to cover immense distances (his remit was Northampton to the very north of Scotland) by pony and trap. 'Eating chocolate' was still such an unfamiliar quantity in the provinces that the salesmen who invited shopkeepers to try the product would 'watch their faces lose their customary shape, as if they had taken vinegar or wormwood'.

Before long Cadbury's had 230 staff and had outgrown their factory at Bridge Street in Birmingham town centre. Bertha Fackrell, a worker in the so-called 'crème room' where a new range of chocolate-covered fruit-flavoured bars was made, complained of the discomfort and difficulties her work involved. She and her fellow workers were so 'cramped up', it was a wonder they were able to function at all. 'Sometimes when the boxers came for the work it was not ready for use, owing to the imperfect conveniences for cooling at that time, and that would settle work for that day . . . I remember once we girls putting

our work on to the windowsill to cool when someone acciden-
tally knocked the whole lot down into the yard below', she
recalled.

True to their Quaker upbringing, the brothers had always
had a thought for the welfare, physical and spiritual, of their
employees. Workers were given a half-day holiday on Saturdays;
some were paid for piecework, which effectively tripled their
earnings. Works tea parties were common. Every morning a
reading of some religious text took place in the stock room.
These rituals, said the clerk George Brice, 'gave the impression
of being more like the early morning prayers of a family than a
works meeting, and absentees were of rare occurrence'.

Chocolate's links with religion in ancient Mexico and
baroque Spain are peculiar enough, but the nineteenth century
gave them another surprising twist. Of all the biggest names in
British chocolate, four of them – Cadbury, Fry, Rowntree and
Terry – were companies founded by a nonconformist religious
sect that might have been expected to despise a substance that
had been associated for centuries with moral laxity. Why the
Quaker connection? In part it was a simple piece of business
sense: there was a gap in the market, and capitalism abhors a
vacuum. In a general sense, of course, the Lutheran revolution
of which nonconformism was a consequence had primed its fol-
lowers for business success (the famous 'work ethic') in a way
that Catholicism had not. It might of course be a tremendous
coincidence. But if there is a reason, it might be this. Like other
religious minorities in England (including, let us not forget, the
Catholics) it was not long ago that the Quakers had been
actively oppressed. Religious intolerance leads easily into other
kinds of social marginalisation, and even in the nineteenth century, access to many of the traditional trades and professions
was made difficult for practising Quakers. Cacao and chocolate,
however, occupied a part of the market which was still virgin
territory, with no social barriers and little existing competition.

As the founders of the Fry, Cadbury, Rowntree and Terry chocolate dynasties quickly realised, for once there would be no one to stand in the way of their business success or, for that matter, of their personal advancement.

In the rush for expansion and self-advancement during the economic upsurge of the early nineteenth century, in any case, chocolate's associations with sloth, lust and greed seem to have been conveniently forgotten. The new wave of Quaker chocolate manufacturers preferred to accentuate the positive: drinking chocolate was nutritious, tasty and convenient. If it was not yet cheap and universally available, it soon would be. Much of the impulse towards the industrialisation of chocolate manufacture springs from the conviction that chocolate was a highly nourishing food that would do the working class a power of good, if they could only afford it. Importantly for the paternalistic social conscience of the early industrialists, chocolate had another great blessing to bestow. At a time when large numbers of working people frequented beer halls and gin palaces and malnourishment among children had become a social scourge, chocolate was recognised as a wholesome alternative to liquor. 'Cocoa rooms' like Lockhart's in Leeds became a focus for the temperance movement. According to research by Seebohm Rowntree in the York of the late nineteenth century, more than a quarter of the population existed on a diet insufficient to maintain a day's work – the implication being that a good cup of hot cocoa or a bar of chocolate would boost their productivity no end. The Victorian authorities seemed to share his view. Among the daily diet recommended for orphan children by the Metropolitan Asylums Board in 1895, breakfast consisted of bread and butter (dripping on Fridays) washed down with a generous three-quarters of a pint of cocoa per child. For the Quakers, in short, chocolate seemed on the whole to be a force for good, and by extension the whole business of making and marketing the stuff could be justified on moral grounds.

Bournville Village is an important topos in the industrial history of Great Britain, in so much as it rehearsed early on the question of employees' personal welfare *vis-à-vis* the cut and thrust of the profit motive. The Cadburys had ambitious plans to improve their employees' quality of life beyond anything the first wave of factory workers could have expected. The new plant would be purpose built on 14.5 acres of land on open countryside four miles outside Birmingham, surrounded by farmland and trout streams. The new site was well served by communications, with the Worcester and Birmingham Canal and Midland Railway running close by. The name Bournville was chosen for its French associations, for French chocolates represented the quality and refinement to which Cadbury's products were supposed to aspire. Apart from the factory, which was the last word in modernity, the Bournville site would provide accommodation for workers in 'cottages', plus dining rooms (one each for men and women), gardens, a sports ground and a Musical Society. If the Cadbury family's first aim had been to build a profitable business, wrote Edward Cadbury in 1953, their second had always been 'to make Bournville a happy place. The provision of amenities, of good buildings, is of course a help, but a spirit of justice, of fellowship, of give-and-take, an atmosphere of cheerfulness, are more important than material surroundings.' Bertha Fackrell, for her part, was delighted with the move from Bridge Street to Bournville, for, she felt, 'everything that thoughtful kindness could do for our comfort was done'.

'Follow the finger signs' said a purple sign on the station platform; though you could just as well have followed your nose. Wherever you went in Bournville that smell was in the air, a fragrance as exquisite and evocative to the English nose as jasmine blossom.

I aimed for the heart of Bournville Village, a township created in the early years of the twentieth century. The neat little houses, built in the style of medieval almshouses, each had their own gardens at the back. Some had apple trees and plots of cabbages and leeks – just as George Cadbury had foreseen in 1895 when he insisted that each of 'his' families should be self-sufficient in fruit and vegetables. Diet and religion; both were fully catered for. The village church, a dour piece of Victorian Byzantine, was right opposite the entrance to the works, so that denizens of the factory could go straight from work to prayer, or vice versa.

The village green, speckled with yellow and purple crocuses, struck me as a fairly unconvincing stab at English ruralism, complete with a shopping parade in half-hearted Tudor style, all overhanging eaves and darkwood beams. The Bournville Baths, a grand Victorian edifice dating from 1904, must have marked a great step forward in the hygiene of the town. Bournville was certainly a healthier place in which to live and work than Birmingham itself, as would seem to be indicated by a much improved infant mortality rate: at the turn of the century, statistics showed that seven children in every thousand died prematurely in the Village, as compared with thirteen in the city centre.

The signs, and the smell, take you skirting round the factory, past the Cadbury Club for employees – by popular lore, the only place in this squeaky clean Utopia where a man can buy a drink – over the millstream, past the village green and into the vortex of Cadbury World, the visitors' centre that has leapfrogged Stratford and the Tower of London to become one of Britain's biggest tourist attractions.

Steering clear of the restaurant, which smelt of cheap frying oil and generic burgers, I headed for an exhibition which took you schematically, automatically, through the chocolate story from the Maya to your mouth. Ushered through the front door by a girl in a purple uniform who pressed a Twirl bar and a Caramel into my hand, I found myself in a plastic rainforest complete with moth-eaten parrots and squatting tribesmen with long hair, loinclothed and headdressed like Red Indians, as unrealistic as shop-window mannequins. In one scene a small dog, wearing an expression of infinite patience, awaited the sacrificial axe poised permanently like the sword of Damocles above its head. In another part of the forest, a squatting slave girl prepared chocolate in a *jicara*, clasping a wooden whisk which, as we know, was not a feature of Mexican kitchenware until the post-Conquest era.

Further on, there was a generic nineteenth-century street scene complete with clip-clop sound effects. On one side of the street was the neoclassical doorway of White's Chocolate House. On the other was a mock-up of the original Bull Street, with Richard Tapper Cadbury, Draper, next door to J. Cadbury, Tea Dealer. All versions of the Cadbury gospel mention the quality of the plate glass used in the first shop window, which was almost as admired by the good folk of Birmingham as the items to be glimpsed beyond it.

The chocolate aroma was stronger and stronger. I wondered whether it was being pumped into the atmosphere along with the sound effects. In spite of myself, under the barrage of *son et odeur*, I found that my mouth was beginning to water. Unwrapping my Twirl bar, I ate it all at once. A kind of second-generation Flake, it crumbled pleasantly under the teeth. But then the sweet fattiness kicked in, coating the interior of my mouth with a sticky layer that had the texture, and some of the taste, of lard. I walked briskly over to a demonstration area where a notice board answered some of the company's FAQs.

Q: Do the staff ever get fed up of eating chocolate?
A: Never. They are all chocoholics. Chocolate is a way of life.

Overwhelmed by demand, and increasingly worried about industrial espionage and the problem of hygiene, Cadbury's called a halt to factory tours in 1970. But enough of the process is still visible, both 'virtually' and in the flesh, to remind you what it was about the chocolate factory that caught the Western world's imagination in the first place.

No industrial process has ever exercised a greater imaginative appeal, or woven such a powerful myth around itself, as the process of chocolate-making. There is something about the chocolate factory that transcends the charmless pragmatism of factories in general. If, as a rule, the kind of factory that makes cars, or cooking pots or cardboard boxes, does not tend to offer a factory tour, this is because there is nothing intrinsically appealing or romantic as such about the manufacture of almost any mass-market product on an industrial scale. On the other hand, if consumers crave one thing more than to eat chocolate, it is to *see chocolate being made*. There is something about this process that, however mechanised and streamlined it might have become, still manages to trigger a range of primal emotions, from awe and childlike delight to a gluttonous revelling in sensory stimulus. The sight of all that thick velvety melted chocolate swirling endlessly in its giant tanks, its sublime transmogrification from bean to bar, and the deliquescent aroma that emerges from the factory and floods the nearby town, can turn the visit to a chocolate factory into a powerfully intoxicating experience.

Roald Dahl's *Charlie and the Chocolate Factory* is a kind of extended recounting of this modern myth. The factory and its products, remember, are the focus of all Charlie's existential longings; and the fact of living so close to Mr Willy Wonka's factory, in a two-room shack with his parents and four grandparents, and yet never having anything to eat but bread and margarine for breakfast, boiled potatoes and cabbage for lunch and cabbage soup for supper, becomes a metaphor for all his deprivations.

And it wasn't simply an ordinary enormous chocolate factory, either. It was the largest and most famous in the whole world! It was WONKA'S FACTORY, owned by a man called Mr Willy Wonka, the greatest inventor and maker of chocolates that there has ever been. And what a tremendous, marvellous place it was! It had huge iron gates leading into it, and a high wall surrounding it, and smoke belching from its chimneys, and strange whizzing sounds coming from deep inside it. And outside the walls, for half a mile around in every direction, the air was scented with the heavy rich smell of melting chocolate!

Twice a day, on his way to and from school, little Charlie Bucket had to walk right past the gates of the factory. And every time he went by, he would begin to walk very, very slowly, and he would hold his nose high in the air and take long, deep sniffs of the gorgeous choco-latey smell all around him. Oh, how he loved that smell! And oh, how he wished he could go inside the factory and see what it was like!

I stood, as mesmerised as the little Bucket boy, before a multi-media machine that revealed, at the touch of a screen, the secrets behind such talismanic British brands as the Crunchie – slablets of bright yellow honeycomb moving in stately pro-gression through curtains, torrents, cloudbursts of melted chocolate – and Fry's Turkish Delight, invented in 1914, acquired by Cadbury's in its buy out of Fry's in 1919, and one of the oldest surviving confectionery products of all. Needless to say, any resemblance to the kind of sweetmeat, delicately flavoured with rosewater and pistachios, that you might find in the bazaars of Istanbul, is purely coincidental. The video showed amazing scenes of a vile jelly, scarily bright pink, squirted while still warm on to a belt which then passed through a machine called the enrober, which finally coated the gruesome filling both above and below with its blessed dis-guise of milk chocolate. What I was watching was not simply the triumph of technology, but its curious marriage with sensuality. In a chocolate factory, physical stimulation is moulded, filled, coated, chilled and wrapped: by the application of speed, efficiency and ingenuity, our pleasure is measured out and parcelled up.

It was the Saturday before Christmas, and Chocolate World was rife with families with offspring whose excitement at their big day out had pushed some of them into a state of near-hysteria. There were Santas ho-ho-ho-ing at every doorway, doling out chocolate bars to wide-eyed, wide-mouthed kids who smeared their faces and strewed the floor with purple sparkly wrappers. Meanwhile the parents had long since given up trying to keep order, but moved about in a zombie-like daze, like stunned animals. The look in their eyes seemed to speak of a profound relief, in part, for at Chocolate World, suddenly and gratifyingly, there was no more pestering, no more of the beseeching whine that parents loathe beyond measure. What their children wanted was everywhere you looked. So far from having to beg for chocolate, they were actually having it thrust upon them.

For as long as they could fill their faces, everyone was happy. At an impromptu stall in the upstairs bagging room, mini pots of liquid chocolate were being handed out.

'All roit, see if you can get this down without lickin' yer lips,' said a big lady in a mob cap.

The adults' treat came later. A bank of video screens on the upper floor rehearsed a brief history of Cadbury's TV advertising. The viewers glanced at each other in a warm rush of self-recognition. More than political parties, more than strikes and speeches and crises and shortages, chocolate advertising brings us together as a generation. Its melodies are more evocative, more redolent of time past, than even that most potent transmitter of memory, the popular song. The video went by decades, placing the advertising in its historical context –

though the ads themselves told the truth more concisely than anything. The 1960s: an Indian paddling his canoe through a rushy swamp, to a hippy-dippy tune that went 'Only the crumbliest, flakiest chocolate/Tastes like chocolate never tasted before . . .' The 1970s, the classic era of wacky creativity, featured one of my particular favourites – the Pythonesque antics of 'Everyone's a Fruit and Nut case/Crazy for those Cadbury's nuts and raaaaai-sins', which even today make it impossible for a British person of my generation to hear the Dance of the Sugar Plum Fairy from Tchaikovsky's *Nutcracker Suite* without 'Everyone's a Fruit and Nut case' playing like a sample in their head. The 1980s were all glamour and sex. A lizard crawls across a ringing telephone, while a woman sits on a window seat *en déshabillé*, devouring a Flake as she gazes out into the unknown. If there has ever been a better evocation of chocolate's exotic, languid, sensual, forbidden-yet-available allure, I have yet to see it.

I fell into a reverie, pondering great matters. The mysterious destiny that shapes the ends of confectionery brands, so that for example Chocolate Buttons, which I loved as a child for their shape, which fitted into the hollow roof of your mouth and stuck there until they dissolved, have almost disappeared from the market, whereas the Creme Egg is still triumphantly visible in petrol stations and off-licences across the country. The Egg was invented in 1922 and is still mysteriously one of the company's biggest sellers, despite being, to my adult mind, an object so horrible that it amounts to an affront to civilisation itself. I find it hard to construe the pleasure that so many people seem to take in an artificially coloured yellow and white gunk, so sweet that you can feel your teeth protesting. When you bite into the thick containing wall of chocolate, this gunk oozes out in gelatinous strands that stick to your fingers and have you running for the nearest washbasin. To eat a whole Creme Egg – and it is hard to eat less than one, unless you throw part of it away – is to feel sick in soul and stomach for the rest of the day.

For there is pleasure, a complex and mysterious emotion, and there is the sheer sensory overload that this kind of candy is meant to provide. Perhaps it was the sugar hit of my earlier Twirl bar, but as I stepped aboard the purple buggy that was to take me on the Cadabra ride – 'a magical Cadbury journey' – I felt a mild dizziness and a hot flush around my neck that made me wonder whether somebody had spiked my drink, or whether I was suffering from the first symptoms of a bout of flu. The ride was an overdose of gaudy, hurdy-gurdy, sugary surrealism, as cartoon cacao beans cavorted in a myriad poses, among higgledy houses, in forest glades and up snowy mountains, my purple buggy trundling with agonising slowness through a hallucinatory vision of marketing hell. I stumbled off the ride, sweating and feverish, and jostled my way through what remained of Cadbury World, pushing rudely past the meandering, entranced Yuletide families, into the fresh air and dull colours of the real world.

Chocolate crept into British life along with two other peculiar novelties: coffee and tea.

At first the new drink was very much a poor relation of the first two. Coffee-houses were all the rage – at the start of the eighteenth century there may have been five hundred such places in London alone, or one coffee-house for every thousand inhabitants of the city. If chocolate was drunk in these places it was as a sideline to the main business of the house. Lorenzo Magalotti, whose twenty-year stint in London is recorded in his *Relazioni d'Inghilterra* (1668), gives the typical menu of the coffee-houses as 'not only coffee, but other drinks, like chocolate, tea, sherbet, cock ale, cider, and others, according to the season'. In some of these establishments you could buy chocolate powder along with a list of instructions for making the drink at home. The Grecian coffee-house in Devereux Court, Essex Street, off the Strand, even gave classes to its customers in the correct preparation of chocolate and tea, and advertised the fact in the periodicals of the day. It will be pleasing to the likes of Jean-Paul Hévin and Michel Chaudun that the very first chocolate sold publicly in England was probably served up by a Frenchman. A 1659 newspaper advertises the 'Chocolate, an excellent West India drink, sold in Queen's-Head-alley, in Bishopsgate-street, by a Frenchman, who did formerly sell it in Gracechurch-street and in Clement's-church-yard; being the first man who did sell it in England. There you may have it ready to drink . . .'

Coffee and tea, the great novelties of the day, had arrived in England trailing clouds of controversy. The coffee-houses, though hugely popular, gained a reputation in some quarters as hotbeds of idleness and political ferment, and were profoundly disapproved of by Charles II who tried (unsuccessfully) to suppress them in 1675. Tea, for its part, was accused of all manner of evils. A polemical *Essay on Tea, considered as Pernicious to Health, obstructing Industry and Impoverishing the Nation*, by James Hanway, brought down the wrath of no less an inveterate tea drinker than Doctor Johnson, who was known to take anything between thirty and forty cups a day.

Chocolate, by contrast, did not stir up anything like the same degree of passion. (Today, between chocolate and tea, one would be hard put to say which has the greater claim on our British souls.) Of the three new drinks it is by far the least powerful as a stimulant, containing on average ten to eighteen times less caffeine by volume than coffee and four to ten times less than tea. It therefore tended to be seen rather as a soothing than an exciting preparation. It was also associated more closely with the female sex than coffee or tea were: the coffee-houses were exclusively male establishments, and coffee may have been thought an inappropriate drink for ladies. The following lines are taken from a lewd poem entitled *A Curious History of the Nature & Quality of Chocolate*, by James Wadsworth, which was handed round in pamphlet form among the coffee-house rakes of the Restoration:

> 'Twill make Old women Young and Fresh
> Create New Motions of the Flesh
> And cause them long for you know what,
> If they but taste of Chocolate.

As usual, it was the medical properties of the drink that most exercised contemporary intellects – though, again as usual, there was little agreement on which particular maladies it might be expected to cure. Doctor Richard Brookes, in his *Natural History of Chocolate* (1724), gives a glowing report of the nutritive powers of the drink, citing a case which had recently come to his notice. 'There died recently in Martinique a Councillor of about a hundred years of age. He subsisted for thirty years on nothing other than chocolate and some biscuits. Occasionally he would take a little soup to eat, but at no time meat, fish, or other nourishment. Yet he was so fit that, at the age of 85 years he could still mount his horse without stirrups.'

The noted doctor and physician to Charles II, Henry Stubbes, famously believed an ounce of chocolate contained more fat and nourishment than a pound of meat. He also had an unshakeable belief in its powers as an aphrodisiac – that particular myth, created by the earliest Spanish conquistadores, was still alive and kicking, and is not entirely dead even in our own day – which he expressed in a quaint piece of literary quackery that would surely have appealed to the Marquis de Sade. It has been quoted often by historians of chocolate, but I make no apology for quoting it again. 'The great Use of Chocolate in Venery, and for Supplying the Testicles with a

Balsam, or a Sap, is so ingeniously made out by one of our learned Countrymen already, that I dare not presume to add any Thing after so accomplished a pen', writes Stubbes in his *Natural History of Coffee, Thee, Chocolate, and Tobacco* (1682). We know that, when preparing the drink for the king, he usually added a double dose of cacao. Given the reputation of Charles II as a philanderer, perhaps the good doctor felt that an additional supply of Balsam, or Sap, might be required by the royal testicles.

There is no doubt that chocolate was still a drink destined mainly for the elite, as it had been since the time of the Maya, and with which the vast majority of the population would have been unfamiliar. The Spanish authority Antonio Colmenero de Ledesma, whose 1644 treatise on coffee, tea and chocolate was widely read throughout Europe, reports that it is 'much used in England, as Diet and Phisick with the Gentry'. It quickly became a popular drink at spas like Bath, Buxton, Cheltenham and Tunbridge Wells, those topoi of aristocratic fashion throughout most of recent English history. At Epsom, according to the late seventeenth-century diarist Celia Fiennes, it was customary to be served a cup of chocolate and a plate of caraway sweetmeats after taking the waters.

While pressure on the government by the East India Company brought the price of tea down to levels which the ordinary consumer could afford – and the reduction of duties on tea in 1784 finally triggered a boom in tea-drinking, to the detriment of coffee and chocolate – high import taxes on cacao continued to make chocolate an expensive and exclusive pleasure. The duty levied on cacao imports was ten shillings per hundredweight, and on made chocolate two shillings and threepence; and the new drink was no cheaper on the other side of the Channel. In France in 1768, 'the great sometimes partake of it, old people often, but the common people never'. In Belgium the urban poor preferred coffee to chocolate, although they did partake of a poor man's chocolate ironically known as 'little coffee', a milky infusion of ground roasted cocoa shells with sugar and cinnamon.

As sipped in a coffee-house in the early years of the eighteenth century, what would this novel refreshment have tasted like? We have precious little information as to recipes, and one gets no sense from the literature of the period that chocolate consumers in England loved the drink with the all-consuming sybaritic passion of their French counterparts – to say nothing of their descendants, the chocoholics of the twenty-first century. The spice and piquancy typical of the chocolate drink in former times was now giving way to a mild, bland richness of which the major protagonist, increasingly, was sugar. Cane sugar had become more common in England since Catherine of Braganza sailed from Portugal in 1662 to be married to Charles II in a ship laden with sacks of sugar as ballast. The years 1640–80 had seen a boom in sugar production in the Caribbean, and by the turn of the century sugar was shipped in quantity from English-owned plantations in Trinidad and Jamaica. Stubbes recommends adding a glug of sherry to each cup of chocolate – an echo of the German aristocratic practice of first dissolving the ground cacao in wine. Eggs were also a common ingredient, which would have added to the richness of the drink and perhaps improved its texture.

But the major novelty was the addition of milk. Colmenero de Ledesma knew of the English liking for chocolate made with milk and eggs, instead of water, but disapproved of it. Though it was 'more dainty', he believed it to be 'less wholesome'. In his *Cook's and Confectioner's Dictionary* of 1727 John Nott gives a recipe for milk chocolate which, minus a couple of ingredients, comes close to the kind of hot chocolate modern Britons might sip from a mug on a rainy afternoon. 'Take a quart of milk, chocolate without sugar 4ozs, fine sugar as much, fine flour or starch half a quarter of oz., a little salt, mix them, dissolve them and boil.' Sir Hans Sloane, the great physician and botanist (1660–1753), author of a series of works on the native plant species of the West Indies, founder of the British Museum, immortalised in London's Sloane Square, is often claimed as the only begetter of the milk chocolate recipe. Sloane is known to have recommended his patent mixture, consisting of an ounce of chocolate dissolved in a pint of hot milk, for its 'lightness on the stomach and its great use in consumptive cases'. In an intriguing pre-echo of much later practices, he also thought it a healthy drink for children.

Given that, in the words of one historian of British food, the milk sold in urban centres during the first half of the eighteenth century was 'almost indescribably bad . . . nearly sour, and in a condition which would have driven a modern dairy bacteriologist frantic', one wonders whether the health benefits were really as great as all that. Yet it seems to me that the addition of milk makes for a watershed in the history of chocolate. In terms of taste and texture, replacing water with milk prepared the English palate for what was to be the great love of its life: milk chocolate for eating, with the creamy sweetness that soothes rather than excites.

The process by which a substance which for at least 2000 years had been taken as a drink – and as a spicy, unsweetened drink at that – changed its nature to become a solid food, is one of the more peculiar phenomena in culinary history. Of course chocolate had been known in dry, solid form for centuries, at least since cakes or blocks formed part of Aztec military rations. As soon as sugar became a part of the recipe, it is perfectly possible that these cakes were nibbled at from time to time. On the whole, however, they were merely a convenient way of preserving the toasted, ground, seasoned cacao beans until such time as a drink of chocolate was required. In any case, the great change from drink to food is impossible to pinpoint in time and place. It was such a long-drawn-out process that even in the nineteenth century chocolate was not yet automatically associated with eating rather than drinking. The elderly Goethe, on holiday in the Austrian resort of Karlsbad in the 1820s, bought a box of chocolates as a present for his nineteen-year-old friend Ulrike von Levetzow. Included with the gift – which he sent, bizarrely, along with a load of geological samples – was a note which translates as follows: 'Enjoy this whenever it suits your mood. Not as a drink but as a much-loved food!'

Quite why it should have happened at all is hard to account for, but the change in the nature of chocolate as a substance brought with it inevitable changes in what might be called in modern marketing terms 'consumer behaviour'. Gradually chocolate broke free of its links by custom or tradition to particular times of day, and in fact became dissociated from the domestic routine. Eating chocolate did not necessarily have to be consumed while sitting at a table; it was an entirely portable product that needed no preparation beyond unwrapping. (Good news for an emerging mercantile economy that put more and more pressure on time.) What it offered to the palate was a far more powerful dose and intensity of flavour. Whereas drinking chocolate provides a range of physical sensations – the warmth or thirst-quenching cold of the liquid itself, not to mention the feel of the porcelain cup, the sweet aroma of the steam as it rises, and so on – the point about eating chocolate is that the physicality of these sensations is dramatically restricted and now concentrated almost entirely around the palate.

Chocolate as solid has a very different social meaning from chocolate as liquid. From the Maya onwards, whether in the domestic or public context, the chocolate drink was predominantly a communal experience, taken in company. Eating chocolate, however, is much more of an individual than a collective act. The box of truffles can be handed round, the Toblerone broken off into peaks, or the Kit-Kat shared out among a group – though the latter is rarer than you might think, at least in my experience. But the pleasure of chocolate, flowing in waves from the mouth to the brain, remains essentially a personal, private matter. Chocolate as drink was a collective rite; chocolate as food is an intimate communion.

There is nothing so foreign as another country's confectionery culture, and for a European chocolate-lover, the United States might as well be Mars – the planet, that is, not the bar.

American chocolate is a world apart. It is the great exception to the rule that when America decides to sell its symbols, the rest of the world falls over itself in the rush to buy them. But since its home market alone is the biggest in the world, it has never worried unduly about having so little market share abroad.

Rumours, and they are no more than rumours, have reached us on this side of the Atlantic. Some of us have heard of the Hershey's Kiss and the Hershey bar, that quintessential piece of Americana, but few of us have ever tasted them. If M&Ms are a little more familiar to Britons, it is only because to a Brit they appear to be an upstart imitation of Smarties. (In fact M&Ms were originally inspired by Forrest Mars' trip to the battlefields of the Spanish Civil War, where he saw soldiers eating chocolate lentils encased in sugar candy; thus they pre-date our national version.) As for Reese's Peanut Butter Cups, Mr Goodbar, Tootsie Rolls, the Heath bar, and the rest of the universe of American chocolate products, without the dense fabric of brand history and our own memories woven around them, they say nothing to us; they are merely empty signifiers, devoid of meaning.

Hershey, Philadelphia – the place, not the bar – is a small town set among the rich pasture land of central Pennsylvania with a population of around 20,000, half of whom are employed by the Hershey empire in one way or another. I drove there in a couple of hours from Philadelphia airport, booking in to a bed and breakfast at which I was the only guest, apart from a couple from New Jersey who had nipped over for a show at the Hershey Theatre and decided to stay the night. The B&B had once been a lodging house for orphan boys. It overlooked the railway line that brought in raw materials for the chocolate factory. At night the freight trains loaded with sugar and nuts and sacks of cacao beans announced their arrival with a deep, melancholy whoop that echoed around the sleeping town.

The relationship Americans have with Hershey – the brand, the bar, the name – goes beyond mere enjoyment. It is an intimate reminder of their own identity, up there with apple pie, Big Macs and peanut butter and jelly sandwiches. At breakfast on my first morning the Steinbacks, my fellow guests, were only too keen to corroborate this view.

'What does Hershey mean to us?' said Bill emphatically, flooding his waffle with another dose of syrup. 'It's what you think of when someone says "candy". It kind of just *is* candy. You grow up with it. As kids, it's, like, part of your life. And I've been a fan ever since. Ain't that true, Marge?'

'Uh-huh, I should say so, Bill. Hershey's Kiss, now, personally, that means so much to me, because when I was a little girl growing up in Atlantic City, those little candies were special to me. My Mom, whenever she'd come back from shopping, she'd give us all a Kiss. And there was nothing in the world that tasted so scrummy to me. Sometimes I'd save up those Kisses till I had two or three, then eat them up all at once to get an extra big mouthful,' said Marge, giggling at the memory.

For those beyond the borders of the United States, when we refer to the Hershey's Kiss we are talking about a drop-shaped morsel of milk chocolate, more or less conical in shape, wrapped in silver foil with a strip of tissue paper (the company calls it a 'plume') emerging from the tip upon which is printed the brand name. On a good day no fewer than thirty-three million of these items might be produced at Hershey Central.

The conversation turned to the 'Hershey taste', the unique and unusual flavour which Americans love and which Europeans, notoriously, find repulsive.

The previous evening on my way in from Philly I had bought a Hershey bar from a gas station on the Interstate 76. In order to contribute to the debate, I fetched it from my bedroom, ripped away the maroon and silver wrapper, and nibbled a couple of chunks, trying my best to repress any lurking cultural prejudices. It was certainly quite unlike any other milk chocolate I'd ever tasted before. Whereas the chocolates I grew up on, notably Galaxy and Cadbury's Dairy Milk, were mostly bland and more or less generic, Hershey's has a taste you can't ignore: a piquant background flavour of something faintly sour, cheesy, or overripe – what chocolate experts call a 'barnyard' taste. This is the taste that, according to Joel Glenn Brenner in her book on Mars and Hershey, *The Chocolate Wars* (1999), causes foreign reps at meetings to spit out the stuff in disgust. There is even a whispered suggestion on the part of some European chocophiles that Milton Hershey's heavy cigar habit had actually crippled his sense of taste, making all his experiments in milk chocolate more or less a stab in the dark. Brenner quotes Hans Scher, President of the Cocoa Merchants' Association, who believes that 'Milton Hershey completely ruined the American palate with his sour, gritty chocolate. He had no idea what he was doing . . . Who in their right mind would set out to produce such a sour chocolate? There is no way Mr Hershey did this on purpose; it had to be a mistake.'

'Can I get you some more coffee there?' said Tammy, my landlady at the B&B, pouring me another cup of thin brown liquid and sitting down to join the fun. Tammy was an Adlerian psychologist by trade, as I was to find out later, and turned out to have some interesting theories about Milton Hershey's contribution to the collective psychological health of the community he had created.

'I do know some folks have a problem with Hershey's chocolate,' she explained almost apologetically. 'I've heard people complain that it's not so nice, that the texture's waxy, the taste kinda harsh; a little, like, sharp. But that's just comparing it with, you know, gour*met* chocolate.

'To me it's, like, Milton Hershey wanted to make a chocolate that *everyone* could enjoy, not just the fancy eaters.'

'Well, I don't see anything wrong with it,' retorted Bill. 'What's more, I'm not aware of anyone else who does.' He sounded a little gruff, as though the notion that the Hershey bar might not be a paragon of perfection had offended some deeply held American shibboleth.

Hershey, PA, was described in its tourist literature as 'quaint', which made you half-expect half-timbered houses and cobbled streets. In fact it was a pretty enough, sleepy sort of small American town, interspersed with woodlands and manicured meadows, though surrounded with the same greasy layer of shopping malls and drive-in junk food restaurants that no American town is entirely free from. There was none of the breezy cool of the East Coast cities; this was the sticks. Lunch in Hershey was at midday, dinner at six. Alcohol seemed to be frowned upon altogether. There were more churches than bars; I counted a dozen places of worship without looking too hard, including the original Derry Church (founded in 1726) around which this model town took root. After dark in Hershey there was little to do, unless you fancied taking in a movie at the Cocoaplex cinema. I cruised aimlessly around town in my big rental car, crisscrossing the quiet suburban streets with their neat clapboard houses painted grey, pea-green or cream yellow, their neat lawns edged with a trimming of late snow, their columned porches hung with American flags.

In the deserted dark of the evening, in the dreadful witching hour between American dinnertime and early bed, I drove up a long driveway towards the corporate headquarters of the Hershey Foods Corporation, the most powerful and secretive chocolate company in the United States. The Corporation's offices, silent in the street lamps' artificial moonlight, were a series of bunkers, a post-modern fortress. There was something vaguely threatening about their blank, baleful presence.

From my vantage point up here on the hill, I could see the whole town laid out neatly below me, with the vast chocolate factory at its heart, all two million square feet of it, the domed and turreted shapes of its silos giving it something of the air of a great Gothic cathedral. The immensity of those silos, thought to contain more than forty-five million kilos of cacao beans, is only rivalled historically by Montezuma's royal warehouse in Tenochtitlan.

Though the working day was over, the night shift had begun, and the factory continued its rattle and hum. Lorries came and went in its loading bays. Plumes of smoke emerged from its chimneys and drifted off at angles into the night sky, like the factory smoke in an L. S. Lowry painting. The air all about the town was full of a particular smell – not quite the sweet chocolatey fragrance of myth, Roald Dahl and Cadbury's Bournville factory, but a toasty, acrid reek that wrinkled the nostrils. I remembered the drying floor at Chuao, and the bitter, roasty smell that filled the village, and wondered whether tonight's task might be toasting cacao beans.

The chocolate factory is the hub of the town in every sense, employing at least half of Hershey's 20,000 residents in one capacity or another. The company runs a visitors' centre, a roller-coaster theme park, a zoo, various hotels, a hockey team, five golf courses and a practically endless list of facilities and utilities. There is indeed an element of truth in the town's hyperbolic description of itself as The Sweetest Place On Earth™.

The chocolate connection certainly ran deep. The town's two main streets, lit by lamps in the mushroom shapes of the Hershey's Kiss, were signposted Chocolate Avenue and Cocoa Avenue, while its residential streets bore cocoa-related names like Caracas, Java, Grenada and Ceylon. Dessert menus all over town offered pies, cheesecakes, mousses and muffins, all made with the best-known local product. You could stay at the Cocoa Motel, and when the time came to work off a few calories, the Cocoa Court fitness centre would clearly be the place to do so. Yet I soon began to pick up a powerful *genius loci* that had less to do with chocolate in the strictest sense and more to do with one of the most remarkable personalities of the American twentieth century.

Milton Snavely Hershey (1857–1945) was the only child of a Pennsylvania farming family which could trace its lineage back to 1717, when Swiss immigrant Christian Hirschi left his home village in the Bernese Oberland and settled in Derry Township, PA. The Hirschi/Hershey family were members of the nonconformist Mennonite church founded by Dutchman Menno Simons (1496–1561), one of Pennsylvania's tapestry of fundamentalist Protestant sects (another being the Amish, who still have their base in nearby Lancaster County). Though Milton Hershey's mother Fannie was a devout Mennonite, she was to be the last of the line. Milton himself had no particular affiliation, and when the time came to thinking about a church for his model Chocolate Town, cheerfully gave out bits of land to a rainbow of denominations, from United Brethren and Derry Presbyterians to Lutherans and Catholics.

As a teenager he was apprenticed to a candy-maker and spent the first two decades of his career pursuing various (ad)ventures in the local confectionery industry, all of which failed. There followed a period of journeyings in Europe, notably a return to his roots in Switzerland, where he made a surreptitious study of the use of milk in chocolate and cheese –

thoroughly confusing both techniques, according to the contemporary *mauvaises langues* who find in his chocolate a suggestion of rancid Emmental.

At the 1893 Columbian Exposition in Chicago, at a stall belonging to J. M. Lehmann, the Dresden-based manufacturer, Hershey was impressed by a display of the latest in chocolate machinery, and bought everything he saw. The following year he founded the Hershey Chocolate Company, poached workers from the Walter Baker Company in Massachusetts, and began producing a series of weird-sounding chocolate novelties – Lobsters, Vassar Gems, Chrysanthemums and Bicycle Tablets were just some of them – before moving upmarket into proper bars with fancy French names like Le Roi du Chocolat and Le Chat Noir.

Though he had since hit the jackpot with the Lancaster Caramel Company, which had branches in Philadelphia and Manhattan, Hershey's imagination was already operating on a far larger scale. In January 1903 he sold the caramel business for a million dollars and immediately bought a thousand acres of land in his home village of Derry Church, intending to build a brand new factory in the heart of the Pennsylvania countryside. It would be a fine-looking building, for Hershey, like Willy Wonka, couldn't abide ugliness in factories.

His big idea was to make and market a milk chocolate bar that would do away once and for all with chocolate's image of exclusiveness and mystery. Mass produced and competitively priced, it would be an entirely democratic product, within easy reach of every single man, woman and child in America – a kind of edible equivalent of the Model 'T' car, with Hershey as chocolate's Henry Ford.

The plan must have seemed to Hershey's contemporaries like the very extreme of madness; yet it was buoyed up by sound reasoning. The sheer grandiosity and ambition of his idea required unlimited space, and that kind of space was not to be found in the urban context, even in 1903. Communications were not a problem: the railway link was already in place, and a tram service would connect the factory with the outlying townships of Lebanon, Elizabethtown and Palmyra. Perhaps the major advantage in business terms was the area's rich dairy industry, which, he reasoned, would come to supply the milk for his Hershey bar. In that supposition he was right, and nowadays the staggering figure of 700,000 quarts of milk arrives at the factory on a daily basis from the surrounding farms.

The factory would be surrounded by a model town, complete in every detail. There would be housing for his workers. There would be schools, shops, hospitals, banks, churches and leisure facilities of every conceivable kind. It would be an instant community, planted in the heart of the country. Other industrialists, including Cadbury in Britain, had had similar dreams before, and dozens of American companies were subsequently inspired by his example, notably Du Pont in Wilmington, Delaware, and Deere & Co. in Moline, Illinois. But no one before or since has taken the concept quite so far. At the heart of the plan was a dream of Utopia. Hershey's eponymous town would have no 'taverns, piggeries, glue, soap, lamp-black factories, no blacksmith shops' – none of the squalid realities of modern city life. There would be culture, bracing exercise and plenty of fresh air. Seen in the light of Adlerian psychology – and I owe this insight to Tammy, my landlady – the Hershey factory and town were a genuine expression of their progenitor's interest in the promotion of mental wellbeing.

One of the first tasks he faced as the fabric of the town took shape was to give it a name. Suggestions were invited, with a prize of $100 for the winner, and hundreds came in. Given the extreme ineptness of most of the suggestions, however – they included Beansdale, Cocoahirsh, Chococoa City, Etabit, Ulikit, Hersheycoco, Hustletown, Qualitytells, St Henry, St Milton and

Thrift – it is hardly surprising the place ended up simply as Hershey.

I spent a morning poking about the nooks and crannies of the town. In an urban landscape magicked out of thin air there was plenty of room for architectural fantasy, and I stumbled on some glorious pieces of pastiche – the Hotel Hershey, a neo-Mediterranean villa on a hillside overlooking the town, and the gold-slathered pseudo-Byzantine interior of the Hershey Theatre, both built in 1933 during a successful attempt by Hershey to fight off the effects of the Depression on his town by means of an artificial construction boom.

Though some of the town's best original buildings have been demolished or disfigured, enough are still intact to give a fine idea of the scale and idealism of the project. The department store, which offered a butcher's and grocery, a hair salon, a bicycle shop and a furniture department (the furniture built by the Hershey Lumber Co.) was still there on the corner of Cocoa and Chocolate Avenue, though its near neighbour, the Cocoa Inn, social centre of the town with its Oyster Bar and Soda Fountain, was long gone. The Ice Palace, a huge covered ice rink, was now the town's museum. And the Highpoint Mansion, the imposing country house Milton Hershey built for himself and his wife Catharine, had been turned into an office building. I parked the car outside the neoclassical columns of the front porch and walked around the grounds. From the sash windows of his bedroom Mr Hershey would have had a privileged view of the factory, which is just a few hundred yards away beyond the garden. Its two brick chimneys spell out his name in vertical letters, just in case he needed reminding that everything he saw was his. But just beyond the house in the other direction was Derry Church, founded in 1726, where he and his parents worshipped as a child. (As at Bournville, it was clearly thought important that the church should stand within easy reach of the factory and vice versa.) And down in a sylvan glade, also just within sight of the house, was a further element in the emotional topography of this place: a tiny wooden hut, the former one-room schoolhouse where Hershey was once a pupil. The little clapboard house, pretty in its rural surroundings, was so ancient a construction by American standards, and so crucial a site in the hagiography of the town's Great Man, that it gave out a palpable aura of sanctity.

Perhaps it was his own education, so scanty and incomplete, that led Hershey to place so much emphasis on it in later life.

The most remarkable and enduring legacy of this man is generally agreed to be the Milton Hershey School. Like Willy Wonka, who had 'no children of my own, no family at all', Milton and his wife were unable to have children, and decided to put their parental energies into the care of orphans. In 1909 they founded the Hershey Industrial School for orphan Christian boys. At the beginning pupils actually worked on the dairy farms, each child being required to milk three cows before school. After Catharine's early death Milton became increasingly attached to the school, and when he eventually died in 1945 he bequeathed his entire fortune, including a controlling share of the company, to the Hershey Trust which now runs the school and, by extension, effectively rules the roost in the town. The Milton Hershey School is now one of the richest educational foundations in the US. With a budget of several billion dollars a year, it has almost more money than it knows what to do with. Its 1200 pupils – not just male orphans, nowadays, but girls and boys from underprivileged backgrounds – have at their disposal a range of facilities that would be the envy of all but the most expensive private university, an Olympic sized pool, etc, etc, not to mention a pupil–teacher ratio of 9:1 and an annual grant of $35,000 per child.

I took another morning to explore the campus, which has become a major must-see on the Hershey tourist trail. Most tourists head straight for the Homestead, the simple Pennsylvania

Dutch farmhouse where Hershey was born which is now, inevitably, a sort of shrine to his memory. The other great attraction here is Founder's Hall, a domed construction on a massive scale which can be seen for miles around. No school assembly room that I know comes anywhere near this one for size and splendour. The entrance hall is a massive rotunda whose roof forms a cupola – the biggest in the Western hemisphere and the second largest in the world, apparently, after St Peter's in Rome – though I'm sure I've heard that said of a number of buildings. The whole thing is faced in white marble from top to bottom, and the slightest sound fills the space with echoes. A bronze statue of Hershey with one of 'his boys' stands in pride of place, with a plaque which reads solemnly: 'His deeds are his monument. His life is our inspiration.' In truth, Founder's Hall feels more like a mausoleum than an assembly room.

It was hard to believe, as I gazed up at the flags hanging round the roof and the Christmas tree as high as a house, groaning with three tons of tinsel, and the ultra-modern full-sized theatre adjacent to the Hall, as well equipped as anything on Broadway, where the entire school meets for a compulsory ecumenical service on Sunday mornings, but all this was paid for in large measure by the sale of Hershey's Kisses.

In the Heritage Room at the side of the Hall was an exhibition of photographs relating to the school and its glorious founder. On one wall were colourful action shots of kids in all shades of black, white, yellow and red, happily doing stuff with plants and animals. Along the other side was a historical gallery. Here was a portrait of Milton's mother Fannie, the Mennonite matron, her hair severely parted from forehead to crown, glaring at the camera. She outlived her husband by many years, and Milton eventually installed her in a small house opposite the factory. She had always taken an active part in her son's business ventures and continued to hand wrap her own quota of

Kisses, there in her front room, until the day she died.

Evidently Fannie never quite saw eye to eye with her daughter-in-law; indeed, the two of them never exchanged another word after Fannie, helping to unpack Catharine's trousseau, asked the young woman if she had ever been 'in the theatre'. Being a Catholic, Catharine Sweeney was at a disadvantage as far as Fannie was concerned. But it was easy to see from some of these pictures that there were other elements of her personality that must have displeased the old lady. A posed portrait taken in Nice in 1910, during one of Milton and Catharine's European grand tours, showed her as an Edwardian beauty in a broad-brimmed feathery hat and clutching a fox fur muffler, very much a follower of fashion. At her side stands her beau – besuited, moustachioed, quite the gentleman, yet there is a softness in his gaze and his hands are stuffed casually into his pockets.

If the personality cult around the man has not blurred the true nature of his character, Milton Hershey was a rare example of the tycoon who was also a modest and good-hearted person. By all accounts he took a keen interest in the welfare of all Hershey residents, but particularly in that of 'his boys'. 'You knew he cared about you and loved you. When you saw him you just knew it,' said one alumnus of the Milton Hershey School. Other sources tell how, after Catharine's early death in 1915, Milton would invite schoolboys up to the mansion on New Year's Eve to serenade him with his favourite song, 'My Hero', from the operetta *The Chocolate Soldier*.

At the local historical society the director, Kathy Lewis, was Hershey born and bred. Her father was a trusted Hershey employee of the chocolate company's accounts department, and in 1911 even travelled to Cuba, where Mr Hershey had set up a sugar refinery with a small-scale 'model' community attached to it. Given all her Hershey connections, what, I wondered, were her impressions of the man himself?

'I was just a little girl at the time, of course, but my personal impression is of generosity. I remember these great Christmas parties Mr Hershey laid on for us in the Arena. We all got a big bag of Hershey's Kisses as a take-home gift. I suppose he was what you might call a benevolent dictator. He got what he wanted, but he got it mainly by being nice to people. My main impression is that he was loyal to his people and his people were extremely loyal to him.'

Kathy was a dental hygienist by profession who helped run the Historical Society in her spare time.

'Hershey's a good place for dentists,' she said matter-of-factly, omitting to explain whether this was due to the amount of chocolate consumed, or to some other ontological advantage of the place.

She ushered me around the little museum she and her colleagues had created, a pleasing clutter of mementos charting in minutest detail the social reality of Chocolate Town from its very beginnings in the primeval swamps of the early twentieth century. There was even a dose of pre-history: a glass cabinet with flint arrowheads and the usual shards of pottery and inchoate lumps of stone, relics of the Indian tribes that roamed the forests hereabouts. But the rest was archaeology, too, in a way. At the back was an old wooden counter rescued from the post office at Vian, one of four tiny rural communities existing in Derry Township before the return of the prodigal Hershey. Beside it, a metal box carried around by sellers of 'Icebergs': these were bars of ice cream coated with milk chocolate, essentially an early choc ice.

The walls were crammed with black and white photographs, each with its charge of nostalgia. A crowd of schoolboys at Highpoint, their grinning faces barely visible as they hid among the calla lilies in the front garden. A scene from the zoo, a little girl in a frilly frock hugging a baby deer. 'Now who do you think that is?' chuckled Kathy, eventually pointing at herself.

What must it have been like to have been raised in such a picture-perfect world?

'Well, it was extraordinary,' she breathed. 'You had everything you needed. There was a department store where you could buy clothes, hardware, china, furniture . . . There was an art deco ballroom with huge chandeliers, hung with satin, where you could go dancing. Harry James, Betty Grable, Glenn Miller, there were always big names coming through town. There was an ice rink and a huge swimming pool and a park where the rides were free.' She pointed out the exhibit of a ladies' bathing suit, an ungainly black garment with legs like pantaloons that came down to the knees, which could be rented at the pool. 'All our sports grounds were immaculate. One time I went to Carlisle with the hockey team on an away game. I remember thinking, "My goodness, this field is still under construction!" Because ours was so much better.

'What else can I tell you? There was zero crime in those days. The town had one policeman. Just one! Everyone knew everyone, and everything was OK. This was a wonderland. When I think about it now, I realise we had no idea we were so privileged.'

For a worker in the factory, life was not, perhaps, such a permanent experience of bliss, although the delights of Hershey living may have taken the edge off its physical hardships. Lawrence Pellegrini senior was one of many Italian immigrants in the town. During the 1940s, according to an interview I found among hundreds of oral testimonies transcribed for posterity and stored in the vaults of the Hershey Community Archives, Pellegrini first worked in a labour gang unloading sacks of cacao from the boxcars that came in on the railroad. From there he moved to a job in the roasting room, and from there to the so-called 'Longitude' department. This great hall with its immense horizontal conching machines inspired awe in the thousands of visitors who streamed through it, because it was the place that more than any other seemed to typify the chocolate factory: heavy machinery pumping away in vats of melted chocolate, bashing away at those grittily resistant cacao particles to create the velvety smoothness that the modern chocoholic both desires and expects.

Pellegrini's accounts make hair-raising reading, and it is not surprising this information is under lock and key, for some of the practices at the Hershey Chocolate Company in the 1930s would be criminal offences today. According to this worker, the sweepings from the floor were fed right back into the system, and there is even a suggestion from his account that animal fats were being surreptitiously used in some chocolate products. As for health and safety, conditions at the factory plainly left a great deal to be desired. During his time as a cleaner, Pellegrini recalled:

'I cleaned what they call the haulers and the roasters. You had to crawl in the roasters with a vacuum, and vacuum it all out, and every now and then you'd have a fire, because the shells would catch fire, and you had to watch it, because it went in this big container, where it blew them in, and it would catch fire and they'd have to put it out. They'd douse it. But, yeah, there was a lot of embers in there. You'd crawl in there. They were actually like ovens, big ovens. They had, like, doors that you crawled in there with a hose and sucked all this stuff out. Oh, my.'

In the Longitude department Pellegrini was put to work at some unspecified and complicated task involving buckets, spatulas and scrapers. The heat in the great conching room was intense, so that anyone working in there would be 'all sweated'. Whatever he was doing – and it's not easy to understand from his description – it sounds as though he was taking his life in his hands to do it.

'You just had to time it perfect. As that arm went back, you went in. As that arm went back, you just went in and dump it and dip it out, dip it out. Then you took a scraper, a pretty nice-

sized scraper . . . Sometimes you went, like, from a dark chocolate to a light chocolate, so you had to clean them out pretty
good, and that was dangerous, really. Oh. Today I don't think
they'd allow it. You even had to go behind the arm, you had this
big arm that went back, and every once in a while you couldn't
get out. You'd pull your hand out, the bucket would be there,
and it would just mash the bucket. A few guys got their arms
caught in there. Like I say, it was dangerous. But it was all in
timing. You just had to time it right . . .'

In the old days the factory tour at Hershey was one of the high-
lights of any visit to the town. But the ever greater competition
in the industry, particularly from Mars, imposed a greater need
for secrecy to protect not only the company's brands but the
sophisticated industrial technology that went into their making.
('All the other chocolate-makers, you see, had begun to grow
jealous of the wonderful sweets that Mr Wonka was making,
and they started sending in spies to steal his secret recipes', as
Grandpa Joe explains to Charlie Bucket.) Add to this an
increasing emphasis on safety, and in 1973 the factory doors
clanged shut on anyone not directly involved with whatever
went on inside.

Paradoxically, of course, the fact that it was now forbidden to
witness the process only served to heighten its mystique, and
the demand for some kind of 'chocolate experience' was greater
than ever.

The answer was a virtual 'factory tour'. Chocolate World at
Hershey is the American version of our own Cadbury World,
but, being American, it is considerably bigger, slicker, brighter
and brasher.

The Chocolate World Café, for example, is no dreary self-
service caff like the one at Bournville, but a fully fledged

restaurant where waitresses come up and do their American thing, all smiles and 'specials' and pens poised to take your order. From the menu I wavered between the Chocolate-Dipped Banana Split and the Reese's Peanut Butter Pie, before eventually throwing caution to the wind with the Chocolate Overload, a magnificently excessive pig-out featuring chunks of fudge brownie mixed with various ice creams, this melange smothered with a hot fudge sauce, ladled with whipped cream and the entire confection decorated, or rather 'sealed', with a Hershey Kiss. I ate half of this monster and staggered off to the souvenir store, an emporium of hypermarket proportions which was also, in a sense, a kind of living museum of Americana.

I prowled the aisles somewhat shakily, notebook in hand, feeling like an anthropologist undertaking fieldwork in some remote community in which a European had not set foot for many years. Never mind globalisation – the world is still so full of foreignness, and tastes in candy set up cultural barriers as rigid as religion. In the global village, there is not just a single sweetshop.

The names alone produced a frisson of cultural *Verfremdung*. How was it possible, with the rise of the Internet and satellite television, that we in Britain had not heard of Pay Day, Milk Duds, Fifth Avenue and Watchamacallits? The sheer strangeness of some of these brand names – like Almond Joy, or the coconut and dark chocolate things called Mounds ('indescribably delicious') – reminded me of some Americans I once met in London, who fell about in hysterical laughter whenever anyone mentioned Boots the Chemist.

I noticed an all-American family in the opposite aisle and tuned in to their conversation.

'OK, I'm gonna pick up some Jolly Ranchers for Becky, they've got some big bags in here. What about your sister – isn't she a Krackel fan?'

'Yeah. Go for it. Get her that big box of Krackels. Hey, Dad, remember these?'

'What's that?'

'Skor bars. They were way cool.'

'Can't say I remember that one.'

'It was kind of like a Heath bar, only with less taffy.'

It took me a few seconds to remember that 'taffy' is American for 'toffee'. The rest of the conversation might just as well have been in Konkani, for all that I understood of it.

In its earliest days as a chocolate culture, the United States of America was in the unique position of being a cacao 'receiving' country that followed the fashions of Europe, despite being right next door to the source of the raw materials. For at least a century after the chocolate fashion took root in the colonies of the East Coast, cacao was actually imported from Europe and arrived in the ports of Salem, Marblehead and Newport, Rhode Island, having crossed the Atlantic twice. The Dutch in Nieuw Amsterdam were an exception, since their cacao came from Surinam.

American chocolate history began as it did in Europe, with an emphasis on medicinal values rather than taste. In 1712 a Boston apothecary was already advertising cacao for sale. James Baker was a physician in Dorchester, Massachusetts. But Baker seems to have seen ground cacao as a money-maker. At first he merely rented space in Mr Hannon's water-powered grist mill at Milton Lower Mills on the Neponset River, clients either buying the cacao ready ground or bringing in their own beans for grinding. By 1777 Hannon's Best Chocolate was confidently advertised as follows, with the added bonus of a money-back guarantee: 'Warranted pure, and ground exceeding fine. Where may be had any Quantity, from 50wt. to a ton, for Cash or

Cocoa, at his Mills in Milton. NB If the Chocolate does not prove good, the Money will be returned.'

In 1768 there were four chocolate makers in Philadephia, a city of 40,000 souls. Mister Welch's cocoa mill in Boston was producing a ton a day by 1794. Thomas Jefferson's ringing endorsement of the new drink was a brave prediction, though it proved to be entirely mistaken: 'The superiority of chocolate, both for health and nourishment, will soon give it the same preference over tea and coffee in America which it has in Spain.' The nineteenth century saw a triumphant arrival on the West Coast, where there was not only serious money about, thanks to the gold rush, but a hungry market for all things sophisticated and European. Etienne Guittard and Domingo Ghirardelli, the two great names in California chocolate, were both European adventurers, French and Italian respectively, who arrived in search of gold but eventually moved into what turned out to be an even more lucrative business. Guittard, who had brought with him from France a supply of chocolate to be used as barter, eventually set himself up in San Francisco as a wholesale chocolate manufacturer in 1868. As for Ghirardelli, he arrived in 1849 but quickly became disappointed with the pickings to be had from mining, and finally opened a general store near Sacramento selling chocolate and provisions, relocating to San Francisco in 1852. The Ghirardelli Manufactory and Soda Fountain on Ghirardelli Square, with its slightly preposterous neo-Tuscan clock tower and its original 1895 equipment still going strong, is now an official landmark of the city, as popular with tourists as Fisherman's Wharf or Alcatraz. Since 1998, however, the oldest continuously operating chocolate manufacturer in America is owned by Lindt & Sprüngli, the venerable Swiss choc company (and bountiful bestower of Milk Chocolate Animals) which beats it in age by just seven years.

If the cultural centres of US candy are New England and the

West Coast, its industrial powerhouse has always been the Midwest. Even now a third of American confectionery production is based in Chicago, where the big names are Brach's, Curtiss, Tootsie Roll, Ferrara Pan Candy Company, and, last but not least, the mighty Mars. In the Hershey Public Library I enjoyed my studious reading of a book by 'candy historian' Ray Broekel, which charts the development of the all-American candy bar from its earliest incarnation in the Baby Ruth bar (1920), the Butterfinger (1926), to the Reese's Peanut Butter Cup, a concoction of salty peanut butter in a sweet chocolate casing which continues to be America's third biggest selling brand. The real boom came about in the 1930s, with a slew of extraordinary names that have lost any significance they might have had in their brief glory days, like Oh Henry!, Big Hearted Al, Oh Mabel, Guess What, That's Mine and Fat Emma. The candy bar industry experienced a positively baroque flowering during the Depression years, when, as Broekel explains, chocolate came to stand for the kind of nourishment that many Americans weren't getting from the food on their plates. Thus, apart from the morale-boosting Smile-a-While, Chuckles, Smirkles and Pep Up, a bizarre new genre grew up. Choc bars began to bear names like Idaho Spud, Idaho Russet, Idaho Toasted Taters – would someone please explain the association of chocolate with *potatoes*? – and even Chicken Spanish, Chicken Bone and Chicken Dinner.

While all this marketing creativity was taking place, Forrest Mars, future CEO of the world's most powerful chocolate company, was to be found in exile in Britain, where he was working away on his recipe for success, living in such poverty, in a bedsit in Slough, that his wife and child had been forced to return to the States. The Mars bar was invented on an August Bank Holiday in 1932, when Forrest and his team were slaving in the summer heat in a tiny room that doubled as a laboratory. The new bar, with its inspired combination of caramel, sweet milk chocolate and that other layer of whipped malted fondant, was virtually guaranteed to appeal to the English palate. The brown paper wrapper bore the legend: 'It is more than a sweet, it is a food: the eggs, the large amount of milk and butter, the malted milk, all combine to form a nutritious tonic' – an assertion reminiscent of the clerical debates of the seventeenth century as to whether chocolate could be described as a food, and if so whether it broke the fast. The Mars bar took its place in a market hitherto poorly provided for in terms of gooey chocolate and caramel bars: at threepence it was more expensive than existing brands like Penny Pegs, Penny Puffins and Nora Block, but was three times the size of any of them. Forrest must have been doing something right, for in just one year he sold two million of the new bars. Before the decade was out it had not only become the best loved choc bar in Britain, but made Mars into the third biggest chocolate producer in the country (after Cadbury and Rowntree).

Back in America in the early 1930s, when the Depression threatened the continued existence of his earthly paradise, Milton Hershey embarked on a series of construction projects in order to keep the town's economy on the boil. The most remarkable of these grand projects, and the flagship of the town today, was the Hotel Hershey. On his visits to Europe in the 1900s, MSH had kept notebooks in which he jotted down details of design and decoration. An early design of 1909, subsequently abandoned, was inspired by the Heliopolis Hotel in Cairo. Then Hershey unearthed a postcard of some grand Mediterranean hotel (unidentified), instructing his architects to base their plans around it.

Construction began in 1932. Despite the unpromising economic backdrop of the time, there was to be no expense spared. The total cost would be two million dollars. When his mother objected to the project's extravagance, Hershey retorted: 'Other men have their yachts to play with. Well, the hotel is my yacht.' When it finally opened on 26 May 1933, a local newspaper declared: 'Somewhat belying the simplicity of taste for which the "Chocolate King" is noted, the hotel is characterised by great luxury of detail and elegance of appointment.' To look at now, the Hotel Hershey is a gorgeous pile of thirties kitsch, an American folly. At its heart is the Fountain Lobby, a central patio apparently inspired by the Alhambra, though an inhabitant of Granada would be horrified by the comparison. Around the sides runs an arched walkway in textured 'whitewash-look' picked out with mosaic tiles, its walls hung with canopies. At the centre of the courtyard a fountain plashes, while an upper gallery allows for a sedate *passeggiata* under a painted Mediterranean sky. It all brings to mind the Hollywood set for some swashbuckling Hispanic epic. You almost expect Errol Flynn to come swinging past on a chandelier. In the 1940s, it is said, there were canaries in cages all around the balcony, and a parlour maid whose sole responsibility was the care and feeding of the birds.

Off the patio on an upper level is the Castilian Room, a Spanish-style ballroom with dark beams and massive oak doors and wrought-iron sconces. Downstairs is the famous Circular Dining Room – circular, it is said, thanks to Hershey's anti-elitist beliefs ('in some places, if you don't tip well, they put you in a corner. I don't want any corners'), with its views out over a Tuscan garden with fountains and cupolas and a box hedge pruned into the letters HH.

The hotel is somewhat chocolate-themed, as you might expect, though thankfully does not push things too far. The Iberian Lounge, an old-fashioned hotel bar in a dark baronial style, all oak beams and leather armchairs, offered a sickly brown concoction that rejoiced in the name of a Chocolate Martini. In the Circular Dining room you could eat – and I needed no encouragement to do so – a three-course dinner of 'cocoa-seared' scallops (if this sounds alarming, they were not so much sweet as pleasantly spicy) followed by braised veal osso bucco with polenta and a bittersweet chocolate sauce, and chocolate soup for pudding.

When I retired to bed that night I found a card on my pillow wishing me a good night's sleep, with four Hershey's Kisses holding down the corners. I have never quite understood the tendency of hotels to leave items of confectionery on your pillow – one grand country house hotel in England used to leave a whole Terry's Chocolate Orange – as if there were some deep-rooted medical connection between sugar intake and a good night's sleep.

Apart from the fact that I had just brushed my teeth, I didn't really feel like eating any more chocolate just now. Adding the Kisses to my sizeable stash, I examined the card. According to the symbols someone had circled with a ballpoint pen, it would be cold and rainy tomorrow. On the back of the card was an invitation to 'rejuvenate mind, body and soul' with the chocolate-flavoured treatments at the hotel's brand-new spa. With all that cold and rain, it sounded like an invitation I could usefully accept. Before turning in for the night I rang down to Reception and booked myself in for the following day.

Thus it was that Jeff, a reassuringly brisk masseur from Atlanta, Georgia, requested I lie down, relax and submit to a double session of choc therapy – preceded by an energetic going-over with something that looked very like a clothes-brush 'to help with exfoliation'.

While waiting in the foyer I had been reading up on the spa, and knew all about its gracious interior, specially designed to reflect Milton and Catharine Hershey's love of nature's beauty, and its promised use of chocolate 'not just as another treat to eat, but a necessary ingredient for innovative, relaxing spa services'. Since the problem of what to wear, or what not to wear, is often a vexing one on these occasions, I was relieved to discover that staff at the spa would 'never compromise your modesty. All of our Spa Therapists are highly trained in draping techniques to ensure your comfort at all times.'

First came the Cocoa Bean Scrub. A pale unguent speckled with dark brown spots – cacao butter whipped into an emulsion with crushed roasted cacao pods – was smeared and massaged all over me. It looked a little, but did not taste at all, like slightly melted vanilla chocolate-chip ice cream. It smelt fragrant and faintly soapy and there was a burnt-toasty sourness about its fragrance that I couldn't quite put my finger on. Jeff got to work, explaining that the point of the scrub was to exfoliate, moisturise, and feed my skin with all the vitamins of cacao.

There was some half-hearted barbershop chat. ('Have you been to the States before?') The spa is just three and a half hours from New York City. Jeff told me: 'After 11 September, people came like you wouldn't believe.' What were they seeking? Spiritual comfort food, I supposed, in the form of a Whipped Cocoa Bath followed by a Cocoa Latte Frothing Exfoliation ...

Then came the wrap. The Chocolate Fondue Wrap. Jeff produced a bowl of dark brown gunk, a mixture of moor mud and ground cacao, and applied it to my body in a thick layer. It looked like chocolate pudding, or the kind of rich dark sauce you might have poured from a jug in some 1970s restaurant scenario. I was becoming a human profiterole. But the fondue smelt, not sweet like chocolate, but sour and smoky and roasty and fermenty. Suddenly I was able to place that smell. I remembered it – it had lodged in a corner of my brain – from the drying floors of Mexico and Venezuela.

Smeared with this stuff, with my hands crossed over my chest like a medieval saint, I was wrapped in an aluminium space blanket and left to cook. I tried to ignore the New Age muzak – how odd and irritating it is, this cross between elevator music and mood-elevator music – and made an effort to bring about in myself an appropriate state of mental calm.

As the heat rose inside my carapace, strange things began to happen. I felt smeary and sticky, but curiously relaxed. The mud and chocolate mixture began to penetrate my gaping pores, and I felt as if I was slipping down a long dark slope into an agreeable state of half-slumber. The tropical heat and the dappled half-light filtered through my eyelids; a series of indecipherable aromas curled up into my brain.

Before I drifted into sleep I had the strangest impression – an illusion of extraordinary clarity, almost a hallucination. I was back in the cacao groves of Mexico, wandering on winding paths that led deeper and deeper into the jungle, when there among the forest appeared a great stone head, hieratic and tranquil. But as I looked closer, it was clear that the face in front of me was not that of Buddha or Quetzalcoatl, but of another man accorded superhuman powers, at least by the natives of central Pennsylvania. It was none other than Mister Milton Hershey, purveyor of happiness to the United States, moustachioed and genial, carved in stone and smiling.

PART FIVE

MODERN TIMES

From the London boardroom to your kitchen –
The selling of chocolate

The history of chocolate in the last century, like the history of any other comestible item you care to mention, was all about scale, efficiency and quantity of product. Earlier generations of makers and consumers would have been amazed, and possibly more than a little disgusted, by the gargantuan amounts of chocolate needed to satisfy a world whose hunger for the stuff appeared to know no limits.

The templates, the basic formulae, were already in place. By the beginning of the century most if not all of the big-name chocolate companies of today were already up and running. What had started as a pharmacy selling ground cacao for medicinal use, or perhaps as a water-powered mill barely converted from its former production of animal feed, was now a factory filled with state-of-the-art machinery. Any businessman with a modicum of shrewdness had realised some time before that chocolate was neither a passing fad nor a minority taste, but might in time make for a soaringly profitable business.

Not everything was plain sailing. Quality, in particular, was not what it might be. An urban myth circulating in the 1920s held that it was common practice in chocolate factories for workers to hand over their shoes as they clocked off for the night. The shoes were then scraped clean and any chocolate bits adhering to them returned to the vats.

If the hygiene wasn't always up to scratch, neither was the product itself. The Edwardian era in Britain saw some new products reach the market which not only sound revolting but were in at least one case actually lethal. 'Chocolate Chumps' were described by one contemporary writer as 'half the size of a rolling pin, a nauseous thing thickly lathered with brown paraffin wax'. Twelve-year-old Jessie Blake from Birmingham was reported to have died, one imagines in dreadful pain, from peritonitis, two days after eating one of these objects. Since 'Chocolate Chumps' were believed to be made mainly from 'grocer's sweepings', in other words a mixture of soap, sawdust, wax and soda, this sounds to me like a tragedy waiting to happen.

Thankfully there were still people in the business prepared to put their ingenuity to better use. In 1912 Jean Neuhaus, a Swiss resident in Belgium, invented a chocolate shell that could be filled with anything the chocolate-maker wished, from almond paste to nougat and ganache. The praline was born, and with it the greatness of the Belgian chocolate industry. Since Lindt's discovery of so-called 'fondant' chocolate it was now possible to pour chocolate into moulds and, more importantly, to extract the finished shape with a simple tap on the mould. The chocolate Easter egg had been around since 1875, but the new moulding technology made it a very much easier proposition. By Easter 1893 Cadbury's already offered a range of eggs, the more expensive of them packaged in silk and satin. Fry's catalogue for Easter 1924 shows eleven different chocolate eggs, plus a range of other animals much more varied and imaginative than anything on today's sweetshop shelves, including hens, pigs, fish, elephants, bears, and, in an interesting throwback to the pagan origins of Easter, a leaping hare.

Many of the brands we have come to know and love have their origin in the first decades of the twentieth century. The birth of Toblerone, courtesy of Theodor Tobler of Berne in 1908, is surrounded by clouds of unknowing. What on earth can have been the origin of its triangular shape? It is whispered abroad that Tobler was secretly a mason and that the triangle therefore reflects some symbolism of ancient Egyptian origin, incomprehensible to those of us not attuned to it. As a theory, it reminds me of the one that claims to prove a connection between tobacco giant Philip Morris and the Ku Klux Klan from the geometric designs on the Marlboro cigarette packet (and, spookily enough, the Suchard Tobler company is actually a subsidiary of Philip Morris). Another explanation, only slightly more plausible, is that Theodor Tobler was inspired to give the Toblerone its distinctive shape after a night at the Folies Bergère in Paris, where the show culminated in a human pyramid formed of scantily clad girls. Forcing us to consider a third possibility, which is that the triangle represents the mountain of Cervin – despite the fact that the Alpine peak in question did not begin to appear on the packaging until a few years later . . .

The walnut whip, a totemic brand for Britons of my generation, dates from 1910. Originally made by William Duncan's factory in Edinburgh, not many people know that it formerly contained two walnuts, one within and one on top. When Duncan's was bought out by Nestlé, machinations by the accountancy department ensured that the walnut in the centre mysteriously disappeared, leaving only that dubious 'whip' for filling.

But it was the 1920s and 1930s that were the glory days, the *cinquecento* of the classic Anglo-Saxon brands. Cadbury's Flake dates from 1920, and the Fruit & Nut bar from 1928. Then came Black Magic (1933), Aero and Kit-Kat (1935), Rolos and Smarties (1937).

This was also the era of the great Mars brands. Milky Way was to become the product on which the fortunes of the company were made, after Frank Mars, patriarch of the firm, launched it on an unsuspecting Minnesota public in 1923. Mars' son Forrest had some ideas of his own, however, first of which was the Mars bar, born in England in August 1932. The bar is admired by industry people even today for its virtuoso combination of two technically 'difficult' elements: soft caramel, which was hard to produce and had a short shelf life, and a chewy nougat which managed to remain light and airy rather than hard and sticky. A further piece of technical wizardry, by which a malt and sugar mixture was expanded under vacuum conditions into an airy nothingness and then coated with milk chocolate, suffered an initial setback in the UK on account of Forrest's choice of name. Energy Balls, as they were initially known, were shortly afterwards rechristened Maltesers.

Notwithstanding this surge of creativity in the field of products, recipes and techniques, it might almost be said that the real innovations of the century were as much in packaging, advertising and promotion – the field of marketing, in short – as in production *per se*. As increased competition turned up the heat on the market and established brands were jostled by new arrivals, inventiveness was at a premium. The French drinking chocolate brand Banania put its trademark – a grinning negro accompanied by the slogan 'y'a bon' – on to school blotting pads and exercise book covers in an early attempt to capture the minds of children and transform them magically into lifelong consumers. Confectionery trade magazines in the 1930s suggested to sweet shop owners that they place a card in their shop window that read:

MONDAY: Maid rejects youth
TUESDAY: Youth contemplates suicide
WEDNESDAY: Youth thinks suicide cowardly
THURSDAY: Youth sees and buys Slater's chocolates
FRIDAY: Maid sees youth and eats Slater's chocolates
SATURDAY: Youth promises maid a weekly pound of
    Slater's chocolates, and maid marries him.

Rowntree's spent £227,000 on promoting their new Black Magic box, with an extraordinarily daring minimalist art deco design to the box, and were rewarded with initial sales of 3.5 million boxes. Market research prior to the 1933 launch of the famous black box was some of the most ambitious ever undertaken. According to Nicholas Whittaker in his history of confectionery, *Sweet Talk* (1998), 'Development of the assortment involved a survey of over seven thousand people – dealers as well as consumers "of all classes" – some of these, so it was rumoured, being guests at a "very superior garden party". As part of the evaluation (supervised by a team of shrinks from the National Institute of Industrial Psychologists) guinea pigs were given "units" in numbered wraps of tissue.'

The new wave of chocolate advertising no longer majored on sylvan scenes, pink-cheeked kids and demure maidens. The deal was to persuade customers that the product in question was not just a frivolous indulgence, nor even a solemnly medicinal contribution to your physical health, but a reflection of your own natural sense of style. The Needler's Company began selling 'novelty' chocolate boxes that seem unbearably tacky to today's jaundiced eyes, yet were clearly intended as *objets d'art* that would reflect the user's innate class. The 'Ripple' Water Set of six glasses and a jug packed with chocolates – 'what could be more natural?' – was at least useful, where the Galleon Flower Holder – 'a wonderfully realistic antique galleon, beautifully made in Staffordshire semi-porcelain. Special holes for flowers. Large hole at the back for emptying and cleaning' – was not.

As the market grew, so it matured. Chocolate, especially if it came from France or Switzerland, offered an elegance and sophistication to which the basic national candy could not aspire. British chocolate assortments with names like Geneva, Biarritz, Matterhorn and Riviera duly cashed in on the growing appetite for continental chic. Hollywood stars were photographed in provocative poses picking idly at chocolate boxes. The scene in George Cukor's film *Dinner at Eight* (1935), in which Jean Harlow sits up in bed sulkily devouring an enormous box, was a remarkable throwback to the eighteenth-century image of chocolate served in the boudoir to a woman *en déshabillé*. It all helped to reinforce the image of glamour and exclusivity. 'Girls used to be happy with bullseyes or strippet balls. Now it must be expensive chocolates,' complained one London beau.

If in general chocolate was gradually transforming itself into what would now be called a 'lifestyle product', there were some areas of society in which the emphasis remained on solidly traditional values. Chocolate use by the military, during wartime, and in Polar and other expeditions, brought back to the forefront a much earlier historical debate. The importance of chocolate lay not in its identity as a luxury, as an aphrodisiac, as a slimming aid, or as a branch of the culinary arts, but as an invigorating and fortifying substance that also happened to be a portable, affordable and easily digestible form of nutrition.

The military connection can be traced all the way back through Napoleon, who drank chocolate on the eve of battle as he pored over his maps, to the Aztec armies who were given chunks of it to nibble on. Since the mid-nineteenth century the British Army, like the Royal Navy, had been a major purchaser of chocolate for drinking. Troops on the front line during the Crimean War were given one and half ounces of chocolate per day, which seems a mean ration even given the straitened circumstances. In 1900 Queen Victoria ordered 100,000 tins each containing a half-pound slab of eating chocolate (the tins were to have been filled with cocoa powder, before it was realised that conditions on the front were much worse than anyone had imagined, and that some troops had no drinking water) to be sent to her loyal soldiers in South Africa. At home a range of new products hit the market, bearing jingoistic names like Kimberley Relievers, Baden-Powell Shells, Mafeking Creams and Bullets for the Boers.

With the First World War under way there was a further outbreak of confectionery patriotism, typified by John Bull Caramels, Duchess Chocolates, Tally-Ho Mixture, and Colonial Assortment. It was all meant to stiffen our upper lips, but there was plenty of debate over the morality of chocolate production and consumption in time of war. The nub of the question was whether chocolate was to be considered a vital source of energy for a needy nation, or a waste of resources that could be much better used in other ways. One factory, it was reported, got through seventy thousand gallons of milk a week, until an Act of Parliament put a stop to the use of milk, condensed or fresh, in the making of chocolate.

The industry itself was in a parlous state. The supply of ingredients was often interrupted and sometimes dried up altogether. Sweet shop owners complained of unfair competition from music halls and theatres where chocolates were sold from slot machines in seat backs, and from demobbed servicemen who plied their wares in the street with boards that read: BY BUYING THE CHOCOLATE OFFERED, YOU WILL BE DOING YOUR BIT, AS THEY HAVE DONE THEIRS.

When it came to the crunch, or the snap, there were few foods that combined so neatly the virtues of convenience and high vitamin content. That was the subtext of newspaper reports on the great expeditions of the twentieth century, which always took care to mention the presence of chocolate among the explorers' supplies. Shackleton, Scott and Amundsen all took cacao powder and chocolate bars on their trips to the South Pole. After Alcock and Brown's sixteen-hour flight across the Atlantic in 1919, the first such crossing by plane, it was revealed that their inflight catering had consisted largely of Fry's Vinello bars. 'It was our chief solid food on the journey', said J. W. Alcock. As a publicity coup for Fry's, there could be few better.

Despite the inter-War flowering of luxury and glamour as part of the general perception of what chocolate could be, the Second World War once again brought the old nutritional questions to the fore.

The Hershey factory in the States developed a field ration

bar whose 4oz weight was packed with six hundred calories, or just enough for a subsistence diet on the battlefield. Half a million of these so-called Ration D bars were produced. The company recommended they be 'eaten slowly (in about half an hour)'. Despite tasting 'no better than a boiled potato' according to one opinion, the bars became a means of exchange in wartime Europe, and GIs were known to have swapped Hershey bars for cigarettes and bottles of wine.

In 1938 an admirer was reported to have sent Neville Chamberlain a box of Nestlé's Home Made chocolate assortment to congratulate him on his (apparently) successful appeasement of Mr Hitler. But when war finally broke out the chocolate box, a luxury item if ever there was one, went underground for a while. The important thing now was to make sure the nation was properly nourished. And under the aegis of Lord Woolton, Minister of Food, there is no doubt that it was better nourished than at any time before or since.

There were shortages of almost everything. For the industry, the most severe was the shortage of sugar. Suddenly there were other more pressing uses for what limited amounts of sugar still reached the English ports. Half a million tons of it were requisitioned by the War Office for making synthetic rubber, while the government suggested manufacturers use substitute sweeteners derived from indigenous fruits like plums and apples. The Use of Milk (Restriction) Order of 1941 was the cause of grave problems, logically enough, for makers of milk chocolate.

Factories were forcibly converted into munitions warehouses or made to manufacture other products needed for the war. From 1939 to 1945 the Jameson's chocolate factory in Tottenham turned out emergency food parcels, while Cadbury's in Birmingham found itself assembling gas masks and filling rocket cases with explosive. Chocolate and military hardware sometimes made for a dangerous mixture. Terry's of York, who were bravely trying to combine their usual business with the manufacture of aircraft propellers, were forced to pay £800 compensation to a man who had found a razor blade in one of their chocolates. This was not the worst that could happen, however. Mackintosh's Norfolk factory, which had been making Rolos and Quality Street, burned down completely after an air raid in April 1942.

The chocolate industry took the blows on the chin. Determined to stay afloat, companies placed advertisements on the one hand apologising for shortages, and on the other eulogising the nutritional virtues of their brands. A particularly skilful piece of publicity, artlessly combining self-justification and hard sell, came from Fry's of Bristol – by now a wholly owned subsidiary of Cadbury's – who must have been feeling the pinch since they had just seen their factory commandeered as a design workshop for the Bristol Aeroplane Works.

'After the bombardment of Coventry, a van loaded with Fry's chocolate and armed with a special permit was one of the first food consignments to reach the stricken city' ran the text of an advert in the *Picture Post* on 3 May 1941. 'Similar deliveries were rushed to Southampton, Portsmouth, Bristol, Manchester and Liverpool to help tide over the first difficult days after heavy bombing. Another front line call on supplies [of confectionery] is from shopkeepers who have been bombed, for damaged or lost stock is immediately replaced. In addition to all this, a third of Fry's output is earmarked for the forces, munition workers and civil defence services. The rest (and it is still two-thirds of Fry's total production) goes to shops, but so many people now realise that chocolate is a really valuable food that there is not always enough to go round. So please don't blame the shopkeeper, and remember all the vital wartime jobs that Fry's chocolate is doing.'

'Cadbury asks you not to blame the shopkeeper when you cannot get the kind of chocolate you want', echoed Fry's great rival, now its master. 'It is not his fault. He is doing his best to be fair to all.' Elsewhere they were prepared just to announce baldly: 'Cadbury's Milk Chocolate is a Food!' The stress was on no-nonsense food values. An advert in the *News Chronicle* for 2 May 1945 might be thought to have gone a little too far in this direction. I quote: 'Two good reasons for using Mars bars – they add extra food value to the war time diet and they save sugar and stretch the sweet ration.' The company then gave a bizarre recipe for Mars Potato Buns, the ingredients for which were to include fat, dried egg, raw potato, dried fruit 'if liked', flour, baking powder, salt and one melted Mars bar.

The nutritional effects of the war on the British diet were dramatic. Thanks to rationing, the average weekly intake of sugar was to be reduced from the pre-war level of 6 or 7oz to less than 3oz. Coupons from books RB11 and RB11a, issued in July 1942, could be used to buy a maximum of 2oz of sweets and chocolate per week – though the limit oscillated between 2 and 5oz throughout the war and rarely fell below 4oz. Confectionery rationing was lifted on 24 April 1949, to universal relief – in an access of highly publicised generosity Mars sent out 7000 Mars bars to Dr Barnardo's children's homes – only to be reimposed two months later and only definitively removed in February 1952. Even then, happy days were not quite here again, whatever the song might have suggested. An outbreak of 'swollen shoot' disease in the plantations of West Africa pushed cacao prices through the roof, with a ton now costing more than six times what it had before the war. High cacao prices were to be a constant factor during the next three decades, which may explain the 1960s explosion of new chocolate bars filled with nuts, toffee, caramel, dried fruit, puffed rice – anything, in short, but chocolate itself.

For it was the 1960s and 1970s that saw the real boom. As children growing up in the late 1960s, we saw it all from the consumer perspective – from the other side of the sweet counter, so to speak. To have a few pence in your pocket was to hold the key to a marvellous world of colour and flavour. Callow youths though we were, when it came to confectionery we knew what was available, what it tasted like and how much it cost. Most days after school my brother, sister and I would toddle up the lane to the village for our regular bagful of sweets. The shopkeeper knew our tastes so well that, like old geezers in the pub, we only had to ask for 'the usual'.

If one could examine them now, the contents of our paper bags would reveal a kind of archaeology of late-twentieth-century British confectionery history. The bulk of our purchases, the equivalent of those endless bits of pottery dredged up by archaeological digs, was made up of traditional goodies like liquorice allsorts, sherbet fountains, gobstoppers, lollies, pastilles, bubblegum, Smarties, Spangles, and penny chews. We were conscious that chocolate bars *per se* represented a cut above these workaday candies, and duly treated them with a little more respect.

No other food has chocolate's indelible links to childhood memory. The brands I liked are as clear to me as if they were here in front of me; I remember not only their taste, but the colour and design of their packaging, even the TV advertisements that sold them to me. Twix, Crunchie, and Marathon, as it then was (like many of my generation I have still not recovered from the psychic shock of its change of name to Snickers). There was Milky Bar, and the freckle-faced Milky Bar Kid who was strong and tough, and only the best was good enough . . . Curly-Wurly, a trellis of toffee strands covered in chocolate (mothers detested them, since the chocolate flaked off the toffee as soon as you bit into it) . . . For anyone born in the early 1960s in Britain, these are cultural shibboleths. Curious, too, how the memory fishes up brands that either died years ago or whose popularity has faded, like Rowntree's Nutty – as I remember, a chewy kind of caramel confection encrusted with peanuts; Munchies – a tube of square biscuity chocolates, quite delicious; and Cadbury's Aztec – a caramel and nougat bar launched with great fanfare in 1968 and quietly killed off ten years later. The wrapper had a deep purple background with white lettering in a funky 1970s typeface. Even now the death of the Aztec bar, like the sudden death of the Aztec empire in 1521, continues to preoccupy a whole generation of English intellectuals.

Over all these blue remembered brand names, however, there hovers a memory more powerful than any. A name that, three decades later, is still able to conjure in my mind a mild Pavlovian reaction of excitement. For me as a child, it was to all those other chocs as Krug is to other champagne: something rare and unique and worthy of the greatest possible respect. This was a choc that was not to be casually dispatched as I skipped home, dodging the puddles in the lane, but savoured in pious tranquillity.

The reader will understand, therefore, in what state of mind I found myself as I made my way from Kilchberg railway station, in a suburb of Zurich, towards the headquarters of the Chocoladenfabriken Lindt & Sprüngli (Schweiz) AG.

I was expecting the smell. I left the station with my nostrils twitching in anticipation, and I'd barely gone a few hundred metres when it hit me. A chocolate-factory smell – they all have it. But this one had something faintly different about it, something extra-special. Pushing aside the images that had suddenly crowded my mind, images of days on the beach at Frinton-on-Sea with my grandmother, the chocolate half-melting in its box in the heat of an English August, I struggled to analyse that smell in a professional manner. There was a sweetness and a warmth to it, and a dairy smell like fresh cream, and the deeper chocolate fragrance, and a general impression of freshness that you don't get from the smell of shop-bought chocolate. You could have led me blindfold along that street, and I still would have known where I was going. I have come to the conclusion the clue, and the difference, lies in the faintest whiff of sweet tobacco smoke – or is it the smoky-sweet aroma that rises from caramelising sugar that is on the point of burning? Or a mixture or cross between the two?

It is the Lindt smell, anyway, which is of course intimately connected to the Lindt taste. And the Lindt taste is like the Hershey taste or the Cadbury taste – though in my opinion qualitatively superior to both – in the sense that it is slightly different from that of any other milk chocolate, and that no one can explain exactly how or why.

Clearly it has something to do with the conching. But then it would. The conching machine lies at the heart of any milk chocolate production process, but here it has an even greater importance than usual. Not just because Lindt is conched for longer than other milk chocolate, giving it a greater creaminess and depth of flavour, but because conching itself is a technique invented by the founder. It was a red-hot trade secret for twenty years, and was probably the main reason Johann Rudolf Sprüngli was prepared to pay 1.5 million Swiss francs for the business – a vast sum in 1899. There is a sense, therefore, in which the conching machine is the symbol and soul of the Chocoladenfabriken Lindt & Sprüngli.

You can still see one of the early machines in an exhibition of Lindt memorabilia within the factory. It is a small and primitive contraption, relying on a belt-driven wheel which pushes a roller back and forth, but essentially the procedure has not changed. The idea is to push the chocolate paste to and fro in the trough, making it slap against the sides and over the top of the roller. This not only grinds the cacao particles to an infinitesimal fineness, but also aerates the chocolate, allowing the complex aromas to be released, and creates friction and heat, causing the bitter and acidic elements produced during the cacao's fermentation to evaporate. The so-called '1879 formula' enables chocolate to be poured and moulded with far greater ease. It also gives the product a wonderful silky sheen. Prior to Lindt's discovery chocolate was of a coarse, heavy texture, and actually had to be chewed before it could be swallowed. Now it would melt in the mouth with an explosion of rich caramel flavour.

As often happens with momentous discoveries, a certain amount of mythology has grown up around *chocolat fondant*, as it came to be christened. One version of the story has it that Rodolphe Lindt, who was running a small water-powered factory in a former spice mill down by the river in Berne, left the old grinder on when he left for the weekend, returning to find that after seventy-two hours of continuous churning a magical transformation had taken place. Contemporary accounts describe Lindt as a debonair, eccentric figure, a *bon viveur* who was more interested in hunting and the fine arts than in exploiting his business ideas to the full. For ten years *fondant* remained a speciality product, supplied only to a few keen local connoisseurs. Among Lindt's first loyal customers were the young ladies of the finishing schools in Berne and Neuchâtel, who clearly knew a fine piece of *delikatessen* when they saw it.

I was met in the foyer by a PR lady who would be my faithful companion for the whole morning, patiently answering my dumbest questions, furnishing me with piles of printed information and, finally, loading me up with bags and bags of factory samples. Katia led me straight into the Presentation Theatre, sat me down and showed me a film illustrating the progress of the company from its origins in the Sprüngli family *chocolaterie* in Zurich in the 1840s to its current status as the biggest independently owned chocolate company in Switzerland.

'You like to try?' whispered Katia, handing me a large box of *Pralinés Connaisseurs* as the historical bit ended and the high-tech bit began. Together we worked our way through the box as the images of machinery in balletic motion flashed mesmerically across the screen. Boxes like the one on my lap, packed by computers defter and faster than any human fingers. Brittle chocolate spheres rotated in a tunnel to coat the inside with thick chocolate puree (these are known as Lindor Balls). The making of Kirsch Sticks, mother of all liqueur chocolates, by means of a ferociously difficult process that works from the inside out, the liquid filling first encrusted with sugar then coated with chocolate. All of this to the loud accompaniment of Strauss waltzes. As a demonstration of Lindt's technological prowess, it was an impressive piece of cinema.

Being a PR person, Katia was used to having to persuade. With me, however, it soon became obvious that there was no more persuading to be done. So that instead of her being the cajoling PR and me the sceptical journalist, we spent an agreeable morning chatting about the past and present of Lindt milk chocolate, while simultaneously managing to consume a sizeable amount of the stuff.

The Kilchberg factory, she told me, was built on a greenfield site in 1900 by Johann Rudolf Sprüngli-Schifferli, scion of the Zurich Sprünglis who had just paid a fortune for the Lindt business in Berne.

The factory, situated by the lake to take advantage of its icy waters for cooling machinery, now employs people of fifty nationalities. An invented language called Fabrikano or Spaniano or Spitalian, a conglomeration of Spanish and Swiss-German with elements of Serbo-Croat, Italian and Turkish, is spoken on the factory floor.

Katia cleared her throat, smoothed down her shirt and said in a loud voice, as if she was reciting poetry: '*Zovani co prima altre masine puce tise sila*. I think it means something like, Giovanni, go and clean the other machine first – leave this one alone.'

Until the appointment of Ernst Tanner as chairman of the board in 1994 there had always been a Sprüngli in charge at Kilchberg. But Tanner has declined to reinvent this 'good Swiss chocolate company', as he calls it, as an anonymous mega-corporation. It has never had a big company mentality and didn't go in for acquisitions until very recently, when it took over Caffarel in Italy and Ghirardelli in the USA. To all intents and purposes it is still a family business – like nine out of ten Swiss businesses of any kind.

The structure of the company, which has wholly-owned subsidiaries all over the world, allows for a flexible approach to the vagaries of national taste. The Chocolate Animals, my childhood weakness, have been discontinued in most countries but are still made, by an extraordinary act of selfless charity on Lindt's part, for the UK market. In some ways Britain represents a puzzle for them. We have such strange fondnesses – for the combination of chocolate and mint, which no continental can quite fathom – and such a cast-iron loyalty to the National Chocolate Taste represented by Dairy Milk and Galaxy, that Lindt hasn't had an easy time finding a foothold.

The company has been through all manner of trials and tribulations. On the train ride back to Zurich, ignoring the picturesque views of woods and water, I read all about them in a Lindt-produced account of its own history, modestly entitled '150 Years of Delight'. From 1919 to 1946 sales were at a virtual standstill. Foreign markets dwindled under the influence of recession, global protectionism and finally world war. What saved the company was the domestic market, which grew slowly even during the war years despite the scarcity and expense of ingredients such as cacao, vanilla, and almonds. (Cacao went up in price by 150 per cent in 1936.) Wrappers from 1938 and 1939 show patriotic and sentimental Swiss scenes, no doubt intended to bolster the national ego at a time of agonising international tension.

In 1944 Lindt & Sprüngli celebrated the beginning of its 100th anniversary year. Its annual report for that year shows the company putting a brave face on what was a truly desperate international situation and being thankful for small mercies, such as the continued neutrality of Switzerland. Biased though I am in a way, I find it a positively moving document – which is a lot more than you can say for most company reports.

But our joy in celebrating this rare and splendid occasion must be muted for we are in the sixth year of a dreadful war, waged with a ferocity and lack of mercy that is unprecedented. When we look beyond our borders to the north, south, east or west we see endless deprivation and appalling misery and amid this ocean of horrors sits our own country, peaceful and intact . . . Despite all the difficulties we are doing our utmost to maintain the reputation for quality of our brands. It is gratifying that the public is asking in the shops for our chocolates in preference to other brands; sadly we are a long way from being able to produce enough to satisfy this demand. We hope that the day is no longer too distant when the many devotees of our brands will again be able to buy our highly prized chocolate bars, particularly the Lindt varieties, in every outlet and in whatever quantities they desire.

Two years later the tone of the report was much more upbeat.

Dear Customers. 1946 brought us the end of chocolate rationing. All of us hoped that we would soon be able to enjoy chocolate whenever and wherever we wanted. There was some rush! Today we are selling much more chocolate than in the pre-war years. Our factory is working at full steam. It simply cannot produce any more than it does, because we lack the necessary staff and because there is a shortage of packaging material. Also, we do not

want in any way to compromise on the excellent quality
of our chocolate. Let us hope that the new year brings
normality somewhat closer.

The end of war brought a swift upturn in the fortunes of the
firm. Exports immediately began to take off. The 1950s saw an
extraordinary increase in turnover and profits, and 1960 was the
best ever year in the history of the company. At the height of
the boom the personnel needs were so great that executives
went on regular recruitment trips to the hard-up villages of
southern Italy in search of nimble-fingered young girls for the
packing rooms. The girls arrived in Kilchberg under the watch-
ful eye of three Italian nuns who were with them night and day,
making sure they went to Mass and were in bed by nine.

The Lindt & Sprüngli Chocolate Process (LSCP), a complete scientific rethink of conching which refined the whole
technique, bringing the time down from seventy-two hours to
just nine while actually improving the chocolate quality, was
triumphantly introduced in 1972. Productivity at the factory
soared, from 2.5kg per person per year in 1900 to 15 tons a
hundred years later.

It was a happy ending; but then the good people at
Chocoladenfabriken Lindt & Sprüngli always knew that things
would come right in the end. Sensible and hardworking, and
full of the conviction that their milk chocolate was the best in
the world, they plodded on. The Swiss have always believed in
the value of efficiency and hard work as a way of keeping the
dark forces at bay, the chaotic uncontrollable forces of passion
and unreason. Quite apart from that, in the words of another
piece of Lindt literature, 'An unshakeable belief in the victory of
good over evil is plain in the history of the company.' How
could they not succeed, when there was so much in their
favour? Sweetness would eventually triumph over bitterness,
they knew, and there would be Chocolate Animals for all.

Everyone has played those silly parlour games that consist of
listing all the famous Swiss people you can think of and all the
famous Swiss things. The list of people is longer than you think
and actually becomes rather impressive as it goes on, what with
Rousseau and Le Corbusier and Klee and Giacometti. As for
the list of famous things, it starts out with the usual clichés –
cuckoo clocks, private banking – and ends up rather surprisingly
interesting. Let's see; there are watches, diamonds, drug companies, finishing schools, fondue, needle parks, the Alps, the
Saint Bernard dog which thoughtfully dispenses liquor to
stranded mountaineers ... What about the Swiss army
penknife, a great invention if ever there was one? And no more
worthy vehicle for national pride can be conceived, in my opinion, than the Vacherin des Monts d'Or, reigning emperor
among glorious smelly cheeses.

But if there is one thing that Switzerland is famous for
throughout the world, it is chocolate. Or rather chocolate and
the chocolate industry, since what it is famous for is as much
the dynamism and streamlined efficiency of its manufacturing
and marketing as for the quality of the products themselves.
The Swiss did not exactly invent milk chocolate. Their historical achievement, however, is to have developed a kind of
mass-produced milk chocolate which is so very creamy and
velvet-smooth that it actually melts in the mouth, and then to
have convinced the world that this kind of milk chocolate represents some kind of paragon, some kind of ideal to which all
other makers of milk chocolate must necessarily aspire. The
fact that this is in fact true, at least in my opinion, does not
lessen the scale of the achievement.

The modern chocolate industry is characterised more than
anything by economies of scale. The Swiss industry produces a

colossal 130,000 tons of chocolate every year. Of that figure just under half is exported, but that still means a massive amount of chocolate stays in Switzerland, to be scoffed by the Swiss. These people are the world's biggest chocolate-lovers by quite a long way. They are said to get through an amazing 11.9kg per head per year, which works out at around a quarter of a kilo per week, roughly the equivalent of two normal-sized flat bars of milk chocolate for every man, woman and child. It is rumoured that factories in Switzerland have 'chocolate breaks' as other countries have coffee breaks, in which workers are invited to recharge their batteries with a slab or two.

Yet these figures hide a curious conundrum. For such enthusiastic consumers the Swiss are terribly discreet about their chocophilia. Walking the streets of Geneva or Zurich, it is rare indeed to see anyone munching, or even purchasing, a chocolate bar – a case of inconspicuous consumption, perhaps. Swiss housewives are supposed to buy their chocolate practically in bulk, but despite hanging around supermarket checkouts in the major Swiss cities for hours at a time, I have found no evidence of it. There is little chocolate presence in the kiosks, the garages, the newspaper shops, unless you count the ubiquitous Mars, Kit-Kat, and M&Ms. But the strangest thing is that the Swiss in general are not a nation of fatties – on the contrary, they seem remarkably slim and trim as they potter about their business in their no-nonsense Swiss way. Though plain chocolate is not necessarily fattening, milk chocolate necessarily is, especially when consumed with the enthusiasm of the Swiss. So what exactly is going on? Perhaps they are secretly burning off the extra calories on compulsory treadmills installed by the Confederation in every Swiss sitting room. Or perhaps the fat is burned off automatically by the cold.

The connection between chocolate and climate has been insufficiently explored. There is definitely something about cold climates and high altitudes that makes a mouthful of creamy milk chocolate seem like a good idea. Temperature plays an active part: the chocolate snaps and cracks in the cold, yet the sensation in the mouth is of warmth and wellbeing. When the outside world seems determined to freeze everything solid, there is something empowering about your tongue's ability to reverse the situation.

I walked down the rue de Rive one February afternoon, breathing great gulps of cold clean air. At the end of the street, almost close enough to touch, were craggy mountains daubed with snow against a backdrop of blue. On a clear winter's day with the sunlight sparkling on the snow, the entire Swiss countryside is one big advertisement for chocolate. Seized by a sudden craving, I ducked into the *chocolaterie* Du Rhône (est. 1875), just one of Geneva's many small establishments catering for that element of the national taste which cares equally for quality *and* quantity.

It was a dark, luxurious interior composed of black and white lacquer and mirrors. At the back were a few small tables where elegant Genevoise ladies whispered to each other over cups of the house speciality, a rich and unctuous hot chocolate. Settling into this somewhat stifling atmosphere I ordered a cup of chocolate – it came with a glass of cold water, in the time-honoured fashion – followed by a piece of fine chocolate encrusted with fruit and nuts, and a truffle or two. The chocolate drink was strong and pungent, though barely sweet. Its flavour was still rolling round my mouth as I stepped back into the darkening streets. But by the time I got back to the flat, after a brief detour along the shores of the lake, it was no more than an aromatic shadow on my mind.

'I must say, living in Switzerland has really changed my eating habits,' said my friend Georgia as she set about making supper for the kids. When I knew Georgia in London she was a Galaxy girl – the type of young woman who will cheerfully buy in a load of milk chocolate and several sackfuls of crisps, to be washed down with Diet Coke as she sprawls on a sofa with a girlfriend or two to chat the night away.

'I've started doing a real Swiss thing. On the way home from wherever I've been, I nip into a chocolate shop and buy a few little things. I buy a chocolate ladybird for one child, a chocolate bunny for the other and a truffle for me. The shop wraps it up all nicely, and we open them up when we get home in the evening.

'With our tea,' she added with a wry smile, flipping a fish-finger. 'There are some things that never change.'

In a café in the old town, around the corner from the Auditoire where Calvin preached his grim sermons, I met with the city's most important chocolate personage: the President of that august Swiss body, the Club des Passionnés du Chocolat. She arrived lugging two huge bags which she dumped on a chair beside her. Madame Falony-Leiber was a well-preserved elderly lady, hair in a neat bob, dressed in a little tweed jacket decorated with sparkly brooches and smelling rather strongly of some expensive floral scent.

'*Les Suisses ont un grand amour pour le chocolat, certaine-ment,*' she said sagely.

'*Mais . . .*' She wiggled her hand in the air as if to suggest that all was not quite as it seemed.

'Of course, you know that the Swiss are ever so traditional. Their chocolate for me is much too fatty, much too sweet,' she confided.

'More like Belgian chocolates?' I ventured to say. 'I agree with you. I'm not too keen on the Belgians either.'

'But I myself am Belgian!' she beamed.

I have to admit to being disappointed. Not because she turned out to be Belgian, simply because I had hoped she was Swiss. For reasons I find hard to explain without offending someone, I could not help feeling it would have been nice to meet a friendly lady with her charming, open-hearted man-ners, and for her to have been Swiss.

Despite this upset, I soon took to Madame Falony-Leiber. I liked the way she was liable to pronounce solemnly on a certain truffle, a certain tablette, as if they were matters of tremendous importance, and then break into a merry little laugh, as if none of it really mattered a fig.

A confirmed Francophile, she wrinkled her nose in displeasure at the mention of Swiss industrial chocolate, particularly the German-Swiss sub-genre.

'*Il est trop gras, trop sucré,*' she stage-whispered, grimacing as if at some dreadful outrage. (I chose not to tell her about my Lindt fetish, fearing this might prejudice once and for all her opinion of me.)

She whipped out one of her enormous scrapbooks, struggling to arrange it on the teeny café table, and flipped through a series of menus, visiting cards and other mementos brought back from visits of the Club des Passionnés to various European chocolate hot spots. The majority seemed to be photographs of dinners held at posh hotels in Brussels, Lyon, Paris and Geneva. The flamboyant creations of famous chefs, including foie gras with chocolate sauce, pigeon with a chocolate-flavoured stuffing, and several staggering architectural desserts, were photographed by flash and had an oddly shiny, clinical look against the bright white plates, like laboratory samples. The club had lately been to Bernachon in Lyon, one of the four or five artisans in France still making chocolate from cacao beans roasted and ground on the premises. Madame glowed with pleasure at the memory.

'*Oh, c'était merveilleux!*' she said, her eyes glittering.

We knocked back our coffee – mankind cannot live on chocolate alone – and Madame took me on a whirlwind tour of the city's *chocolateries*, of which there were a great number. On the rue de Rive alone there were three: Du Rhône, the Chocolaterie Auer and La Bonbonnière, a proper old-fashioned choc shop with crimson flock wallpaper, where I bought a whole cacao pod moulded in chocolate tied up with a pink ribbon, and a bottle of Maury wine – believed by a certain class of French gourmet to be the only wine that really 'goes' with chocolate. Up to the old town, and Chocolats Canonica: down to the lakeside, and Zeller, with its famous *moules du lac* – Lake Geneva mussels. None of this seemed to interest Madame, who was impatient to arrive at the only establishment in town which she truly thought worthy of praise: Chocolats Micheli, owned and run for the last thirty-five years by Pierre Poncioni. Here we sat and sampled M. Poncioni's delicious double cream ganache-centred *pralinés* and listened to the story of his long struggle against the dominion of the big Swiss brands and the big Swiss love of sweet milk chocolate.

'I have four little children. I make them a special chocolate for drinking. But they don't like it! They prefer Nesquik! It's terrible!' he lamented, striking his brow in mock-desperation.

The Swiss came late to chocolate. When Goethe came on holiday in 1797 he was so unsure of being able to find a source of drinking chocolate that he brought his own supply. But they have been making up for lost time ever since. In 1890 total exports of chocolate amounted to 600,000kg. By 1914 this figure had rocketed to 17 million kilos. Within twenty years Switzerland had risen to a position of extraordinary dominance in the world; at the start of the First World War Swiss products accounted for an extraordinary 55 per cent of the global chocolate market. As the century progressed, meanwhile, domestic consumption soared from a kilogram a year per person in 1905 to the current world record of almost 12kg. And now, of course, they are the world's undisputed chocolate superpower.

The Swiss have few serious heroes apart from William Tell, and even he is none too convincing. But the men who founded the Swiss chocolate industry, known locally as the 'pioneers', have more than a touch of the heroic about them. The initial impulse came from Italy, where many Swiss emigrated in the nineteenth century in search of work. As a young man François-Louis Cailler, originally from Vevey, was employed for two years at Caffarel in Turin, originators of the *gianduja*. On his return to Switzerland in 1819 Cailler founded the country's first chocolate factory at Corsier, Vevey – just around the corner, today, from the HQ of the mighty multinational originally founded by Henri Nestlé.

Like the apostles, there were twelve of them. Some of their names ring all sorts of bells in the mind of the chocophile – big clanky cowbells, I imagine them to be, around the necks of doe-eyed dairy cows. There was Philippe Suchard, who set up his factory in Serrières in 1826; Johann Jakob Tobler, who begat Theodor, who begat the Toblerone; Daniel Peter, who developed the technique of combining milk with chocolate in 1875; and perhaps the greatest visionary genius of them all, Rodolphe Lindt. For most of the nineteenth century chocolate was, as one Swiss writer puts it, 'a brittle, rough-surfaced and somewhat bitter substance which was laboriously pressed into moulds by hand'. In his water-driven mill below the cathedral at Berne, Lindt made two discoveries which would revolutionise the chocolate industry: the 'conching' technique which creates a hyper-smooth texture and haunting, faintly caramelly flavour, and the addition of cacao butter back into the mix, which helps give the chocolate its melting, luscious viscosity. Armed with these two crucial processes, the Swiss chocolate industry was poised to begin its conquest. What Lindt understood, as none of his contemporaries had, was that the eventual global apotheosis of milk chocolate would have almost more to do with texture – that refined silkiness, solid turning to fluid on the tongue – than with taste as such.

But there is another name more familiar than any of these, a brand-name that is now applied equally to a vast corporation with its tentacles in every corner of the world. It is a name that casts a chill in the hearts of radicals and hippies everywhere. Yet to business folk its slick global functioning, its brilliantly contrived corporate identity, are worthy of total admiration. Nestlé is to Switzerland what Coca-Cola is to the United States of America: not just a product, nor even a range of products, but a name that has become symbolic of the Swiss way of doing things.

There are some things that can't be kept secret, and one is that Nestlé employs 224,541 people and owns 479 factories, making it the largest food company in the world. The list of its brands is as long as your arm. It either makes, or owns other companies that make, such well-known chocs as Kit-Kat, Milky Bar, Lion, Aero, Smarties, After Eight, Quality Street. It is the world's biggest user of cacao, buying up a tenth of total world production. The confectionery side of things has always been secondary at Nestlé, however, given that the company's main interest from the beginning was milk powder and its possibilities as a substitute for mother's milk. Chocolate now jostles for space among the food-related brands the company has made its own thanks to an aggressive programme of acquisitions, from Carnation in 1985 to Perugina-Buitoni in 1988, Perrier in 1992 and Spillers Petfoods in 1998. Now you can feed your baby, yourself and your dog, without leaving the Nestlé 'family'. (It is also a major shareholder in L'Oréal cosmetics. Now we know where all that excess cocoa butter ends up . . .)

The roots of this monstrous organism lie in the most unlikely terrain. The town of Vevey, like most Swiss towns, is picturesque, immaculately clean and terminally sleepy. I took a train there on a Monday morning, the railway line sweeping in an arc around the lake shore, among vineyards in terraces racked up against the hillside like the cheap seats at the opera.

For such an unremarkable looking place, Vevey boasts a

number of remarkable historical associations. Originally it was perhaps its very sleepiness that attracted the famous foreign residents it is so proud of, generally exiles in their twilight years, veterans of artistic or political ferment who were tired of the struggle and craved a little R&R – with the additional attraction of a restful tax regime. Graham Greene and Charlie Chaplin are both buried in the town cemetery. Victor Hugo (he liked the 'cleanliness'), Lord Byron, Dostoyevsky, Henry James, Gustave Courbet, Oskar Kokoschka, Stravinsky, Hemingway, Nabokov and Noël Coward – not a bad collection – all spent agreeable seasons here. Down on the lake front towards Montreux stands a statue of Freddie Mercury, punching the air in high-camp rock 'n' roll style. Freddie recorded various albums here and stayed on, finding peace and contentment in the last painful years of his life.

But I was in search of a much less flamboyant figure whose impact on contemporary lives, nonetheless, may have been greater even than Freddie's. I found the place behind the station, just above and beyond the platform underpass.

It was here, at no. 14 rue des Bosquets, that the legend took shape. Daniel Peter, scion of an old Alsace family, finished his apprenticeship with a candle-maker in 1852 and founded the Société Frères Peter with his brother Julien. The small factory they bought in the rue des Bosquets formerly belonged to Cailler, then by far the biggest chocolate company in Switzerland. Daniel Peter fell in love with Louise Fanny, daughter of Alexandre Cailler, and married her in 1863, cementing the family ties by founding a joint venture, Peter-Cailler et Compagnie.

It was increasingly clear to Peter that, if he wanted to make money in the new high-tech industries, the business to be in was not candles – the paraffin lamp had almost put an end to their everyday use as lighting, anyway – but food. Industrially manufactured foods, as he wrote in a memoir thirty years later, 'are destroyed every day and the need for them is renewed continually, without being susceptible, as many other [products are], to the fantasies of fashion. One has seen, it is true, certain food specialities enjoy a great success for a period of time, only to be supplanted, rightly or wrongly, by others. It will not be thus, I believe, with chocolate.'

It took Peter a while to find his niche in the market, but the niche turned out to be on his doorstep. When his baby daughter Rose developed an intolerance to mother's milk, he turned to a friend and neighbour at no. 17 rue des Bosquets. Henri Nestlé, a German pharmacist originally from Frankfurt, had begun marketing a so-called 'milk flour', and was already exporting eight hundred boxes a day to Paris, London and America. If his daughter could not take real milk, perhaps Nestlé's substitute might solve the problem.

Apart from its benefits to his daughter's health, there was an additional advantage to this concentrated powdered milk. Previous attempts to make milk chocolate had failed mainly because the water in the milk refused to form a stable emulsion with the cacao butter. Peter quickly realised that Nestlé's formula, combined with cacao solids and cacao butter in the right proportion, could be the product that would make his fortune. He would christen the brand Gala Peter and sell it as healthy, nutritious, good for children. The packaging for his first bar bore slogans that set the tone for the marketing of Nestlé's products as well as his own: Gala Peter was 'very nutritive', 'very digestive', *peu sucré*; in short, it was 'the healthiest of all chocolates'. The mergers soon began: first with Kohler, then with Cailler, and finally (in 1905) with the already globalised Nestlé. Synergy, in today's weird business lexicon, was assured.

Advertising would become a pillar of Peter's business practice. 'Gala Peter: the first milk chocolate in the world' says the legend attached to a classic early ad. But the beautifully painted image says rather more. Two robust countrywomen, pink-cheeked and radiant with health, stand on the green sward of a mountainside. One holds a small scythe, the other a long rake over her shoulder. The image exalts the hardworking Swiss woman and her place in the traditional rural order of things. But it cannot help but remind us of the surprising fact that Swiss women, whatever their capacity for work, did not get the vote until 1971.

The year of Peter's invention was 1875. It said so on the plaque on the house in the rue des Bosquets. '*Dans cette maison a été créé en 1875 le premier chocolat au lait du monde.*' I made a little mental genuflection. What was surprising about the house that bore the plaque, however, was its strangely dilapidated state. The external walls, a grimy shade of French mustard yellow, had not been painted for years. I pulled open the dark green shutters and tried in vain to peer through the windows; the glass was caked in dust. As one of the great Swiss historical sites, which this assuredly is, it perhaps deserves a little more respect, if not a total transformation into museum, gift shop and tearoom.

If the Nestlé company has little interest in celebrating its past, this may be because it is too busy forging ahead into the future. From the town square I turned down the Avenue Nestlé, which seemed like a reasonable avenue to take, and within a few minutes a large and shiny modern building hove into view. A giant, gleaming, modernistic castle – a slick piece of contemporary architecture in one of the most extraordinary settings of any corporate HQ in the world, just a hundred metres from the lapping waves of Lake Geneva, surrounded by lawned and landscaped gardens, with a wall of snow-streaked, cloud-capped mountains in the near distance. The industrial era is drawing to a close in the Western world, and the pride that companies once deposited in their state-of-the-art new factories now seems to have transferred itself to their head offices.

I sat in the enormous, echoing foyer among the few carefully chosen items of modern furniture, feeling a dozen cameras turn their beady eyes on me. If Nestlé HQ – known rather menacingly as The Centre – has ever been besieged by grungy protesters furious at the company's activities in the Third World, as one might half-expect, its cast-iron security arrangements would surely have stopped them in their tracks. Even I, in a long coat and woolly gloves, felt scruffy and out of place as the glistening multi-national Nestlé employees clicked by in their patent leather shoes.

It did not feel like the kind of workplace I remembered from my office days, in which you sat at your desk from nine to five with nothing more interesting to look at than a dusty ficus. But then the twenty-first-century workplace in all its casual fabulosity has made the idea of coming to the office just to *work* seem something of an anomaly. The modern-day corporate office is more like your home – a space in which to live, learn, work, and simply, you know, *be*. I picked up a glossy in-house magazine, *People Building Brands*, and read with an amazement tinged with nausea the testimonies of ecstatic employees describing The Centre as a 'serene, tranquil respite from our rushed and hurried lives' and 'a very free world' . . . 'Whenever I come back to the building from overseas trips, it's like returning to the nest. I feel happy. It's like coming home,' said Gerard Pré, head of packaging and development strategy. Other Nestléites were prepared to go further, comparing the act of going to work to a religious experience. 'It's like visiting the Vatican. So solemn, so awe-inspiring.' 'It makes me feel like a pilgrim going to Mecca.'

There was no denying the HQ, a kind of palimpsest building redesigned by Richter et Dahl Rocha around the original 1960 classic by Tschumi, was a splendid piece of work; but there was an odd kind of anonymity at its heart. From the building's public spaces, apart from the Nestlé logo (a bird in a nest, feeding its young) behind the reception desk, there was no telling what kind of business this might be. It could just as easily have been a bank, a pharmaceutical company or an advertising agency as a purveyor of food and drink. This vacuum is typical of the post-modern company which does not so much produce objects as philosophical entities. It is of little consequence, ultimately, whether the product is a perfume or a chocolate bar, a bottle of water or a tin of dog food. Because what is interesting is the brand, not the product. The product on its own has no *raison d'être*, no presence in the marketplace, until Nestlé has woven a shimmering layer of meaning around it.

Back at the station, I grabbed a Kit-Kat and ate it in my usual ritual fashion, splitting the foil wrapper with a thumbnail and biting down on the bar without snapping in two, thereby contravening the implicit law that states that Kit-Kat, the brand, is made for sharing. It took an intellectual effort to realise that this humble snack, one of the biggest-selling choco-late bars in the whole damn world and the biggest of all in the UK, belonged in body and spirit to the branding cathedral of The Centre. It tasted the same as it had always tasted, of course, whether in the UK or in Switzerland or the States – the worka-day choc with the feelgood crispy bit inside, the chocolate itself made a little sour in my mouth by the memory of all that creepy corporate nonsense.

For the chocolate-lover the city of Zurich offers two special attractions, connected historically but profoundly different in character. The one that is not the Lindt & Sprüngli factory is the famous Sprüngli café and chocolate shop on Paradeplatz, where the Sprüngli clan took their first steps in the business of *confis-erie*. This is the mother ship, or the mother shop, the deep root of the venerable chocolate tree from which this family business sprang.

I walked to Paradeplatz amid a miasma of whirling snow. The Sprüngli story can be said to have begun in 1845, when David Sprüngli-Schwarz and his son Rudolf Sprüngli-Ammann opened a water-powered chocolate mill in Horgen, a fishing village outside Zurich. The Paradeplatz shop was opened in 1859. Neumarkt, as the square was then known, was a risky choice of site, being next door to the dubious Kratz area with its bars and brothels. But a contemporary engraving shows it as a spacious, posh sort of establishment where ladies could sit and sip their hot chocolate, fanning themselves daintily, while their chosen sweetmeats were packed up for them in beribboned boxes.

The great *confiserie* now occupies a whole block, what with the café and a posh restaurant upstairs, and a mail-order service for out-of-towners. This being one of Zurich's greatest institutions, along with the *Neue Zürcher Zeitung* and the Zurich Bank, there is a constant stream of visitors through the front doors. To stand by the doors and watch the crowds come in – to hear their barely suppressed, delighted gasps, to see the sly smile that lights up on their faces and feel the charge of pleasure that hovers in the air as they begin to roam greedily around the room – is an education in itself. For a foreigner the wonder of Sprüngli lies mainly in its glorious Germanic patisserie, its *gugelhopfs* and *luxembergli* (tiny macaroons sandwiched together burger-style), and *Zürcher leckerli*, dense squares of ground hazelnuts and chocolate perfumed with sandalwood and vanilla. But the chocolates are not to be sniffed at either. There were carefully made truffles and *pralinés* and mendiants of all kinds, and a brand-new range of *pavés* made from Venezuelan *criollo* cacao, pushing all the right fashionable buttons of rarity and exoticism.

The café at the Sprüngli on Paradeplatz was where I realised once and for all that hot chocolate and a cold climate go together like a horse and carriage. Outside the window the flakes of snow were not falling, but being swept upwards by a howling wind. To be inside was to be ensconced in a warm fug of *Gemütlichkeit* and *Schlagsahne*. The decoration, sixties-snug in shades of brown and cream and maroon, the walls hung with copper chocolate moulds, was spot-on. Ladies in furs and gents in green Germanic hunting hats and coats, sat at the bar like walk-on parts in some early Lubitsch movie – though some of these customers were more like the stars themselves. One old thing, brittle and haughty, wearing a black fur-trimmed coat and a velvet bandanna cinched over the skull, with eyebrows plucked and painted and face a deathly pale, hobbled over the threshold in high heels looking like Gloria Swanson in her last days.

She folded her black leather gloves and flopped them softly on the counter next to me. I had seen her walk past the window, hunched against the cold, and then walk back a step or two and pause momentarily before the door. I guessed at that moment what was on her mind: a warming *Heisschokolade*, strong and sweet enough to remove the chill from soul and body.

I had already ordered mine and was halfway through it – a slim-waisted cup of intensely flavoured chocolate whipped to a creamy froth, with a surface sprinkle of chocolate flakes that melted and could then be slurped up in a sweet gooey slick. This was served with a square of Sprüngli's very own bitter-sweet Surfin-Chocolade – nothing to do with Surfin' USA, and everything to do with super-fine quality. I slipped it into the cup when no one was looking and stirred in the rapidly melting blob for a final mega chocolate hit. Of all the hot chocolates I had tasted anywhere in the world, from Harrogate to Oaxaca, this one came closest to perfection.

'*Ist gut, ja?*' croaked Gloria Swanson, her lips twisting into a smile.

Look about you – in the shops, in the supermarkets, the late-night garages, the factory canteens, the hospital kiosks of the United Kingdom. It is omnipresent. In the corner shop: rank upon rank of bars, tablets, bags, boxes; chocolate in a myriad forms, crumbly, chewy, crunchy, brittle, filled with caramel, toffee, nuts, dried fruit, alcohol, syrups, even bubbles of air. Chocolate has taken on a diabolical, Protean creativity.

There is a subtext to the history of chocolate which you could, if you wished, elucidate in Marxist terms. Chocolate follows closely the historical development of capitalism. It begins as an artisan commodity for the exclusive use of the religious and aristocratic castes. During the colonial era it maintains its connections with religion, thanks to its zealous promotion among the monastic orders. At the same time it filters into the upper reaches of the class system. In Europe it becomes an extreme luxury, monopolised by the bourgeoisie and unavailable to the working classes – a symbol of the decadent *ancien régime*, in fact. It is the Industrial Revolution that finally gives chocolate to the people in solid form, though at the cost of enslaving them in the factories necessary to produce it.

But the final triumph of chocolate, like the final triumph of capitalism, takes place in the late twentieth century. Chocolate is not only at the cutting edge of the Western consumer revolution – Mars and Cadbury were two of the first companies to set up shop in post-communist Russia – but a symbol of the market's uncanny ability to create desires, needs and irresistible urges to buy, where none existed before. Eating chocolate is the first luxury in history aimed at the masses rather than at the elite. In the leisure-driven society of the twenty-first century, which craves pleasure and sensation over any other aspect of food, including nutritional value, it is in its element.

Rampant late capitalism, and the weird new economy that Naomi Klein describes in *No Logo* (2000), have effected the strangest transformation. Chocolate, the substance, has become very much less important than the marketing of chocolate; the brand, the halo of intertwined concepts and values and meanings that hovers over the product, just as the signifier hovers over the signified, is now more important than the product itself. Klein writes: 'The old paradigm had it that all marketing was selling a product. In the new model, however, the product always takes a back seat to the real product, the brand, and the selling of the brand acquires an extra component that can only be described as spiritual.' This is just what has happened with chocolate: the spells of technology and branding have magicked it into an 'experience' in which style is considerably more important than substance.

The substance is not really chocolate, in any case, but a cheapened, denatured version of chocolate. I call it 'choc'. It is a flavouring, or a flavoured thing, a stuff used to cover and conceal and perk up other sweet 'foods' such as cakes, bars, biscuits, candies, ice creams, drinks, mousses, yogurts . . . Choc is the brown-coloured flavouring, in the same way that pink means raspberry and orange orange – a substitute or shorthand that has served for so long as the real thing that as far as our minds and palates are concerned it has come to have a certain legitimacy of its own.

Choc is one of the modern world's great signifiers of pleasure. Children will eat the most repulsive foods – carrots, for example – if they are flavoured with it. Even for adults, choc sets off a trigger in the mind that says luxury, exoticism, privilege and wonder. As Margaret Visser writes in *The Rituals of Dinner* (1991), this may have something to do with its colour. 'There is a tendency, also, to associate very dark food, such as coffee, chocolate, truffles, caviar, and ceps, as well as plum cake, with excitement and luxury. We feel obscurely that such strange dark stuff must be meaningful and ancient.'

Choc is a social point of reference around which we hover, turning to it, idly or torturedly or greedily, from time to time. The relationship is complex and puzzling. We adore and crave it; we love the sense of hedonistic excess it implies. We are happy to be 'chocoholics', yet agonise over chocolate's imagined tendency to make us fat, spotty and miserable. We impose sanctions on ourselves only to break them, thereby increasing the pleasurable release and, ultimately, the guilt.

A ground-floor office, around the corner from St John's Gate in Clerkenwell, a beguiling scrap of medieval London soaring away now into wondrous fashionableness and some of the highest rents in any world city. The Playroom is a design company, though it is inaccurate to call them merely that. They cover all bases. When the client comes to them with a vague or half-formed idea, they tell him what he wants and why. From then on, what they offer is a kind of seduction by attractive and fashionable young people full of zippingly creative intelligence, of duller older people who are mostly preoccupied with marketing truisms and corporate line-toeing.

You walk off the street into the Playroom, almost directly into a space where girls and guys as crisp and cool as lettuce leaves sit at a series of coloured i-Macs, the ones where your eye is drawn through the translucent plastic into an alarming void – the nothingness at the heart of the modern machine. When you walk in, some of them look up and say Hi! My school friend, owner of the Playroom, flies in from a meeting and introduces me: 'OK, this is Paul, everybody', and then flies out again. And everybody says Hi! again. Though, this time, some don't look up from their screens.

Today we have naming of products. We sit, the namers, around a large white post-modern boardroom table. A lady has come to talk to us from a market research company, though it would be inaccurate to describe the Big Frog merely as a market research company when what they do is of much higher band-width. What we do is, we assess consumers' attitudes and behaviours, and when companies come to us, we can guide their marketing from a consumer standpoint, Celia tells me later. We tell them what people need and what they don't need, where brands fit in, and how they can be 'engineered'.

A chart is handed round; there are words and lines and interconnections, charting the emotional landscape of the new product. In fact there are two new brands in the offing: one a chocolate bar aimed at the twenty-five to forty male market – a 'gutfill' product, in the industry's peculiar term-inology – and a range of naughty-but-nice choc products, including bar, cake, biscuit, ice cream, mousse and drink, all grouped under the same brand-name and aimed, with deadly accuracy, at the housewife of thirty to fifty belonging to social groups B, C and D.

The chart was produced by a company called the Church, an outfit so celestially groovy that it has no precise job description but is known to specialise in devising the conceptual and philo-sophical bases of brands. It has bubbles connected to other bubbles labelled Spiritual Growth, Meditation, Time For Me, Relax. The general theme is solitary sybaritism: this is my space, my time, a moment I dedicate to me and to nobody else – so there!

What extraordinary inroads the New Age has made into the machinery of contemporary capitalism! Accountancy firms have chill-out rooms with fish-tanks and Enya on the CD player. Merchant banks have yoga classes, massage at your desk. For the first time since the Middle Ages objects are being sold to us on the basis of their spiritual qualities: such-and-such a shampoo doesn't just clean your hair, it also soothes your soul. And this new chocolate product that we are discussing and

defining doesn't so much nourish, satisfy and stimulate eroti-
cally as elevate its consumer to a higher spiritual plane.

Nirvana? Well, that might be interesting for a start. Aura?
Yes, that's good. There are three hundred other brands called
Aura – does this matter? There is a theory that it doesn't, that
one set of brand values somehow feeds off and supports the
other. I begin to write down terms or concepts or meaningless
syllables as they float across my mind. Many of them seem to
suggest a superficially Eastern quality of quiet interiority. Tai.
Chi. Karma. Sari. Sayonara.

This is a high-indulgence brand positioning, an accompanying text suggests. The values of this brand are crucial, but we
must also bear in mind the importance of 'the eat'. The language of modern marketing is a jargon so repulsive that even
reading it silently makes me feel queasy. The meaning of 'the
eat' is, I suppose, the eating experience. For housewives in our
target market appear to enjoy more than anything a 'slow,
savoured eat'.

Celia gives us a run-down of the results of the 'focus group'
she has organised, convening ten women to talk about their
reaction to the proposed new brand. Housework, children, hus-
bands, and a tight financial budget are the major ingredients of
these people's lives.

Women have always been chocolate's keenest customers.
Today in Britain, they buy 66 per cent of all confectionery. José
de Acosta in 1590 described chocolate as 'a valued drink which
the Indians offer to the lords who come or pass through their
land. And the Spanish men – and even more the Spanish
women – are addicted to the black chocolate.' But the alliance
that women have since forged with chocolate is passionate,
mysterious, and, on occasion, distorted and bizarre. According to
feminist writer Cat Cox, in *Chocolate Unwrapped: The Politics of
Pleasure* (1993), chocolate is a major 'binge food' used by
women with compulsive eating problems. This is because,

claims Cox, industrial chocolate provides not only a powerful dose of calories in the form of refined sugar and vegetable fats, but seems also to offer a measure of emotional nourishment to consumers who have been taught all their lives to associate chocolate with love, caring and protection. A woman I know tells a story about her moment of glory in a low-budget film for which she played the violin in the soundtrack. After the premiere, flushed with success, she was standing beside the director when an important film producer told him the movie was great, but that he should 'sack the violinist'. Mortified with embarrassment and shame, she headed for home – but not without stopping off at a late-night garage. 'I bought seven Kit-Kats and sat on the sofa and ate them all one after another,' she recalls.

Among the focus group are several women who say their lives revolve around chocolate; it is the most important thing in their lives; they could not live without it. 'If tomorrow I was told I couldn't have my daily Wispa, I tell you I'd be gutted. Life just wouldn't be worth living,' says one.

Women in this context get pleasure from time, space, selfishness (there is no sharing involved here) and volume – the sheer quantity of stuff they can ingest. Some of the stories Celia tells are priceless. 'What I like is to get hold of a massive bag of Buttons, a bloody great grab-bag, and just sit there and work my way through them' is one memorable testimony.

The women say there are special little routines connected with their chocolate eating. One of them waits until the children have left for school, and, before she starts the housework, sits down at the kitchen table and eats a Flake, deliberately letting the crumbs fall around her in a symbolic act of wild abandon. Another unwraps her Wispa in a long spiral, leaving it naked and unashamed, before cutting it into four pieces and eating each piece at a time, allowing the chocolate to melt in her mouth. Here it is again – the groundswell of ritual behaviour that runs all the way through the history of chocolate. The difference is in scale and solemnity: the Aztecs employed it in grand public rites. What these modern consumers are using it for are sad little private ceremonies.

After the meeting Celia and I sit in a Camberwell café and ponder the chimera we are attempting to create. When it finally sees the light of day, it will take its place in a historical parade stretching back deep into the twentieth century. Confectionery brands, we agree, may involve a more deep-rooted memory than that offered by any other cultural experience in the marketplace. Drifter, Star Bar and mint-flavoured Aero are triggers for nostalgia. Men still buy Milk Tray because they believe in the romantic traditional values of the brand; their womenfolk are still perfectly aware that, far from going to any death-defying lengths to obtain the box, they have probably just picked it up at the kiosk at Waterloo.

The conversation turns to Great Brands Of Our Time and of the recent past.

'What about After Eights? Now *there* was a brilliant piece of marketing – the way it came to signify middle-classness. The black silky envelope: a stroke of genius. And what about the Creme Egg? Amazing. Imagine if I did a focus group on that. "Listen guys, this is the idea. It's an egg; chocolate filled with sweet coloured goo." They'd say: "That's disgusting. Salmonella!"' says Celia wryly.

'Part of what I do is to look at chocolate use. It's a bit like that film *Chocolat*. She basically interfaced with her customers. She said: "I knew he'd like sugared almonds, he was hard on the outside."

'People actually use chocolate in an incredible variety of ways. One woman says, "If I have a shit day, I eat chocolate." Another woman tells me about the way she gets in snacks and a bottle of wine on the way home. Her boyfriend will already have had a burger, so they'll have a glass of wine and she'll sit in front of a soppy movie, gorging herself on Galaxy.

'I talk to teenage girls, all size eights, and they're eating four to five chocolate bars a day. What they're doing is swapping "indulgence" for food. Chocolate is a placebo: it just makes you feel good. What's happening is that people are swapping nourishment as such for the "eating experience". And the manufacturers know that, and they tailor their marketing accordingly.'

All of this goes much further into the dark recesses of our history and future as a species, than I would have expected from a conversation about chocolate bars. But what we are talking about is an entirely new historical phenomenon: the distancing and estrangement (to use an old-fashioned term, the *alienation*) of human beings from the food they eat, and by extension, from the reality of the world around them. Against the backdrop of a gradual deconstruction of our old set-in-stone conception of dishes, mealtimes, the weekly routine of fish on Friday, roast on Sunday, the chocolate industry has led the way in the invention of a new kind of experience: un-food. Something edible but context-free, its sources and origins untraceable, possessing no apparent connection with either land or culture – a forcible slamming together of contrived sensory triggers and 'brand values', the metaphysical trappings that alone make one choc bar different from all the rest.

Celia puts down her coffee cup and stares into space. In the busy London street beyond the window, lunchtime office workers stride past, some munching hurriedly as they go.

'I don't know. To me there is a real sadness about chocolate as a product all along the line,' she says. 'At one end you've got those exploited workers in the Ivory Coast. At the other end you've got lonely Western women like the ones in my focus groups, seeking solace through fat and sugar and the lure of the brand. The food we eat traditionally provided a window on culture and nature and climate and situated us in relationship to all of that. Now everything has changed. And it's not food values, or nutrition, or even things like taste and texture, that are at stake any more. We are heading into hell.'

Things are changing – Celia is right about that. It is 2002 – five hundred years to the year, let us not forget, since Columbus set eyes on those mysterious 'almonds' – and there is madness in the air. The food industry has gone crazy and seems hell-bent on sending the rest of the same way. How else do you account for a product like multi-flavoured oven chips, the latest offering from Heinz? One of these new chips off the old block is coloured bright blue; the others are flavoured with sour cream and chives, cinnamon and sugar (this sounds particularly nasty) . . . and chocolate. Cocoa Crispers, as they are called, have sent nutritionists, already worried by the shocking diet of American children, into a fury. 'Kids don't know about nutrition, so to design food solely to satisfy what they like to eat is nutritional suicide. We're already in the middle of an epidemic of childhood obesity. I think it's time the food industry had some accountability,' said Barbara Rolls of Pennsylvania State University.

It is not just children who are getting the habit. 'Chocoholism' has become a generalised phenomenon. To be addicted to chocolate, or to imagine oneself as such, is not something anyone these days need feel guilty about. On the contrary it is something to be proud of, albeit in a jocular sort of way. The Internet swarms with dedicated chocoholic sites, 990 of them in total, not to mention the 2,930,000 web page matches summoned up by typing in the single word 'chocolate'.

Chocolate is the One True Passion,
Chocoholics Unite,
Complete Chocolate,

Chocolate Paradyce,
Chocolate Alliance,
Chocolate Guide,
Chocolate Craze,
The Chocolate Lovers' Page,
The Chocolate Lovers' Haven,
Chococlub,
Chocoland,
Virtual Chocolate,
are just the first twelve that came up on my screen.

To profess to love chocolate, to *adore* it, truly, madly, deeply, would seem nowadays to be almost a prerequisite for fame. Apart from being the only vice that is still safe to admit to, chocophilia is a useful gambit in interviews, conferring on the star a sugary image tempered by a titillating suggestion of immorality – nice, but naughty. In a single trawl through the newspapers I came up with Britney Spears saying, as she was presented with a huge heart-shaped hunk of candy: 'Chocolate for me is just like an orgasm.' A few pages later, here was Spanish ballerina Tamara Rojo: 'It's the thing I would miss more than anything on a desert island.' And in the sticky heat of the *Sun*, there was more melting and swooning. Juliette Binoche was asked by her interviewer whether she agreed with the 75 per cent of British women who would rather have chocolate than sex. She replied that she finds it better to have both at the same time: 'messy but interesting'. The motive for this disclosure was that the film *Chocolat*, in which Binoche starred, had just opened. Personally I saw the film as a sickly-sweet paean to the comforting, feelgood properties of milk chocolate, the cinematic equivalent of a bunch of girls on a sofa with a tin of Quality Street. 'A gorgeous movie' was the *Sun*'s opinion. 'A must-see for romantics and chocoholics alike.'

When I turned on the TV that evening a large Scots lady was

being interviewed about her imminent departure to a desert
island in order to attempt to lose some weight.

'When I moved down here I had very few friends. Actually I
had no friends,' she said ruefully. 'So what I used to do, I'd get
down to the local supermarket and stock up with goodies, and
sit in front of the telly and eat my way through 'em.'

You didn't need to be a qualified nutritionist to realise where
her weight problems stemmed from. Anyway, the time had
now come for her to see whether those extra kilos 'came off'.

Would she suffer from any particular deprivations on the
desert island, asked the presenter.

'Aye. Chocolate.'

Sly smiles from the sofa. 'Ah-ha. Bit of a chocolate fan, are
we?'

'Ooh, yes.'

'Well, you won't be getting any of that on the island, I can
assure you. We'll have searchlights and patrols . . .'

The large Scots lady understood that her favourite pleasure,
as well as the cause of her displeasure with herself, would
shortly have to be curtailed.

'Och, but I still have half a box of Milk Tray left over from
Christmas. If I can finish that off before I get on the boat, I
should be able to stay the course.'

I am late for a meeting and the Tube is stuck in a tunnel. I
stand there sweating under the neon, the silence broken only
by rustles of newspaper and the creaking of the train's under-
carriage. Strangers are all around me; I can feel their body
heat, hear their breathing. I shut my eyes and think of green
meadows, sparkling mountains, struggling to fend off the
encroaching panic.

I race up to the office and sit for a minute to catch my breath in the designed haven of the foyer, losing myself in the video screens. It is a pop video with the sound turned down, a glib narrative of escapism, a glittering sea, underwater shots of a lean blonde body intercutting with scenes of a colourless office where the same blonde girl is putting files in their place on shelves.

The office, this office, is overcrowded and has the dirty plastic smell of hot computers. My vision wanders. Through the glass wall I can see a woman unwrap a small bar of Galaxy and take a delicate bite, carefully folding over the top of the packet and placing it in a drawer.

What chocolate offers to the city dweller is just what city living seems to demand – an instant antidote to stress, a comforting reminder of the existence of your own body and its possibilities, a glimpse of interior vistas to shore up against the cooped-up, regimented, problematic reality of daily urban life.

Chocolate consumption in the Western world is at an all-time high, and continues to rise at a rate of 3 per cent a year. The vast majority of global choc is still consumed in Europe and North America, though the corporations currently have their beady eyes on 'emerging markets' like Japan, China and Brazil. The British, possessors of the world's sweetest tooth, still spend more on chocolate than any other nation and devour more than 8kg a head per year, mostly in the form of Kit-Kats, Mars bars, Snickers and other snacks. (The fact that, as Britons, we each consume 2lb of refined sugar per week – compare this to 2oz a week at the start of the Second World War – may go some way towards explaining why 48 per cent of our children suffer from tooth decay.) The confectionery industry is an enormous generator of statistics, some of which boggle the mind. Here is one that strikes me as intriguing: eighty-four million Cadbury's

Flake bars are bought each year in the UK, fifty-six million of them by women.

Cacao and chocolate are the raw and the cooked. What comes to mind is a dualistic, almost Manichean world, or rather two separate worlds living in almost total ignorance of each other. How many Western consumers have more than the faintest clue about cacao, its provenance and process? Meanwhile Latin America consumes 7 per cent of the cacao it produces; Africa, just 3 per cent. Chocolate and cacao is high-tech versus low-tech. Production-line workers versus peasant farmers. The twenty-first century versus the nineteenth.

Like most modern industries, chocolate is dominated by ever fewer and bigger corporations. Seventeen companies now account for over half of the worldwide market. Nestlé, nasty big daddy of them all, owns Rowntree and Perugina. Suchard, which owns Côte d'Or and Van Houten, was gobbled up in 1983 by Kraft-Jacobs, which in turn is owned by tobacco barons Philip Morris. Poulain, as resonant a name to the French as Cadbury is to the British – and it is no mere coincidence that the character in recent cinema history who most obviously represents French style and *joie de vivre* should be called Amélie Poulain – ironically belongs to the people from Birmingham. Godiva, a mythical name in Belgian chocolate as well as in English folklore, is owned by Campbell's Soup. Far from being a single bijou Brussels boutique, as I had always vaguely imagined it to be, Godiva is a big fat American firm with factories in Tokyo and New York, selling its big fat cream-drenched truffles in more than 1400 outlets including just about every department store and upscale shopping mall and airport in the West.

Even further up the business ladder, breathing the rarefied air of commodity capitalism, are a few giant companies the chocolate-user in the street knows nothing about, yet which collectively exercise a swingeing influence over the global marketplace. The fat cats of cacao 'processing' are Cargill; ED&F Man/Grace Cocoa, under the umbrella of faceless food multinational Archer Daniels Midland; and Barry-Callebaut, responsible for 11 per cent of the total world production of cacao. The latter, fruit of yet another monster merger, supplies 40 per cent of all the *couverture* used by European chefs, chocolatiers and chocolate manufacturers at a certain level of quality.

This kind of consolidation gives an air of stability and continuance to an industry which moves on into the future with all the unstoppable momentum of an oil tanker. Below the waterline, however, lie all kinds of unseen currents. In fact the single word that best describes the workings of the cacao trade, as opposed to those of the chocolate trade, is 'instability'.

In the world of cacao agriculture, nothing can ever be taken for granted. The uncertainty starts with the weather. Every two to seven years a phenomenon known as the El Niño Southern Oscillation, characterised by rising sea surface temperatures in the Pacific, leads to drought and falling cacao production in Indonesia, Malaysia and Papua New Guinea. It continues with the unpredictable behaviour of the cacao tree itself, which is unproductive for the first four years of life, then becomes an easy target for insect damage, drought and disease. Cacao crops are especially at risk from black pod and swollen shoot virus in West Africa, and from the fearful 'witches' broom' in Brazil, which has slashed production in that country from 400,000 tons in 1987 to 220,000 tons in the year 2000.

When the cacao beans finally reach the market, they do so by means of the exchanges in London and New York. Prices fluctuate wildly and irrationally. Because world cacao production is currently increasing at a slightly slower rate than consumption, for example, the market has perceived a shortage and massively overreacted – as markets do. From July 2001 to February 2002, the price per ton has risen from £788 to £1130. When prices are low, farmers suffer. When they are high, the chocolate companies naturally do whatever they can to reduce costs – which usually means reducing the amount of cacao solids in their products (many mass-market chocs now contain as little as 20 per cent).

Over the last hundred years, for such a problematic crop, *Theobroma cacao* has had a remarkably successful innings. If the focus of cultivation in the nineteenth century was South America, in the twentieth century it has shifted definitively to West Africa. Cacao arrived from Brazil on the island of Principe in 1822. The variety in question was the hardy and relatively high yielding *forastero* type known as *amelonado*, from the roundish melon-like shape of its pod, which subsequently became by far the most planted variety in West Africa. But it was during the 1870s, from the beach-head of Principe and São Tomé, that cacao began its conquest of the mainland. Cacao seeds were first planted in the Ivory Coast in 1870, in Nigeria in 1874 and in the Gold Coast (now Ghana) in 1879 – the same year, you will recall, in which Daniel Peter was busy inventing a new kind of milk chocolate in Switzerland. Where it first took off as a crop was in Ghana. For most of the twentieth century until the mid-1970s this was the world's biggest producer by some way, accounting for a third of total production. One in four Ghanaians still earn their living directly from cacao cultivation, which covers around a half of all the available agricultural land and constitutes a vital source of foreign exchange. The greatest boom zone of all, however, has been the Ivory Coast: Côte d'Ivoire, as it prefers to be known. The scale of the operation here boggles the mind. Six hundred thousand farms are worked by a million people – more than 15 per cent of the rural population – producing more than a million tons per year, or 42 per cent of the world production of cacao.

Export earnings have helped turn Côte d'Ivoire and Ghana into two of the continent's most prosperous countries. Abidjan and Accra, the capitals, are glittering high-rise cities, their nightclubs and hotel bars filled with besuited young cacao executives and their wives in flashy African fashion gear. Even so, there are inbuilt barriers to the wider prosperity of these relatively fortunate West African nations. As Cat Cox points out in *Chocolate Unwrapped*, cacao producing countries are at a severe financial disadvantage compared to those Western economies that process the raw material. In a typical year in the 1990s Côte d'Ivoire earned seven billion dollars from its export of 700,000 tons of cacao. In the same year, Holland – traditionally a centre for 'grindings' – imported just 258,000 tons of beans, but made five billion dollars from its own export sales of cacao products.

The fact is that the cacao business is riddled with injustices from top to bottom. Television programmes have exposed these injustices, none more powerfully than a documentary entitled *Slavery*, shown on Channel 4 in Britain on 28 September 2000. The programme focused on three surviving forms of slave labour in the modern world: child rug-makers in northern Bihar, India; imprisoned and maltreated domestic workers in the US and Britain; and cacao plantation labourers in Côte d'Ivoire. Research carried out by the makers of the documentary suggested that as many as 90 per cent of all the cacao farms in the West African country used slave labour.

It made for harrowing viewing. A young man named Drissa, forced to work for eighteen hours a day on little or no food, had been beaten so severely that the bones of his ribcage were actually visible. The maggots that had hatched in his wounds, though disgusting to see, had probably saved him from gangrene. Drissa had this poignant message for the chocolate consumers of Europe: 'They enjoy something that I suffered to make. I worked hard for them, but saw no benefit. When they eat chocolate, they are eating my flesh.' In the wake of the Channel 4 documentary the pressure group Anti Slavery issued a statement which effectively stigmatised the whole business of mass-market chocolate manufacture: 'Because of the way the chocolate industry buys its cocoa it is not possible to ensure that slave or other forms of illegal exploitation have not been used in its production.'

It was not within the scope of the programme to tell viewers that the persistence of slavery has been an integral part of the cacao industry for much of its history, from the days of the *encomienda* system to the black slaves on the Caribbean haciendas of the colonial era. When, in 1901, rumours reached Britain that cacao workers on São Tomé and Principe were in fact indentured labourers from Angola, William Cadbury of Cadbury's formed a coalition of European chocolate-makers and travelled to the islands to discuss the matter with plantation owners. 'In one of your best managed estates,' he told them, 'the doctor states that most of the mortality is from two diseases – anaemia and dysentery; complaints that are easily developed by people in a depressed mental condition. It is also admitted that the highest death rate is among the newly arrived labourers, and this is exactly what one would expect when we know that these people are forcibly taken from their homes for work across the sea, without any hope of return.'

As its dirty secrets are progressively revealed, the industry is under growing pressure to reveal its hand. We now know, for example, that in seven countries of the European Union up to 5 per cent of natural cacao butter may be substituted by cheaper vegetable fats, and that legislation to make compulsory the denomination 'vegelate' to describe such 'vegetable oil candies' was only avoided by a whisker. We know that in Brazil and some parts of South-East Asia, farmers habitually spray their trees with chemicals such as endosulfan, malathion, mancozeb and the notorious herbicide glyphosate, marketed by Monsanto as Roundup. Cadbury's recently admitted that tiny amounts of the insecticide Lindane may be present in their chocolate, and though they say there is no possible risk to human health, a 1998 report for the EU found that it was not possible to set a safe level for Lindane and recommended it be banned across Europe. We know that experiments funded by the American Cocoa Research Institute (ACRI) are under way at the University of Pennsylvania to produce a genetically modified cacao tree whose beans would be already sweet, requiring much less added sugar. Imagine what a dream this would be for dieters. Imagine, too, what a goldmine for the industry.

But there is little room for dreams in the modern-day cacao business. The massive expansion of cacao cultivation through West Africa, and now into South-East Asia, has tended to mask the painfully slow rate of technical change. Plantations still follow the traditional model: tiny plots of between one and three acres run by subsistence farmers whose independence and lack of resources have made it difficult to introduce new planting techniques and to combat disease. Ageing plantations – the cacao tree has around thirty or forty years of economic life, after which it must be replanted – are cared for by ageing farmers. This is a particular problem in Trinidad, where the shortage of young farmers is putting the future of the entire sector in jeopardy. Wages everywhere are heartbreakingly low. A worker on a cacao estate in Bahia, Brazil, commonly earns $25 per month. When a Ghanaian cacao farmer recently visited the offices of London-based fair-trade company Twin Trading, the conversation turned to the financial thumbscrews placed on cacao farmers by the chocolate industry. 'A rough back-of-the-envelope calculation, based on the current cocoa price of about £1100 a ton, shows that if Asamoah's cocoa were used in the leading 200g milk chocolate bar in Britain he could expect just 0.5p from the 90p retail price.'

Perhaps the greatest problem the industry faces in the long term, however, is the threat of ecological meltdown. The pattern of development in cacao-growing countries in the twentieth century has been similar wherever it has taken place. Old-growth tropical forest is first exploited for timber, and then planted with cacao. Shade trees, called in Central America 'mothers of cacao', without which *Theobroma* is both less productive and more susceptible to disease, are often dispensed with. Without the shelter of the leaf canopy, tropical rains pound down, scrubbing valuable nutrients out of the soil. Intensive cultivation requires far greater quantities of expensive pesticides and herbicides, putting even greater strain on what little forest wildlife remains. As forests in the tropical zone are eventually depleted and yields continue to fall through disease and poor management, we could begin to see a global shortage of cacao. Galvanised into action, the big chocolate companies are starting to talk about sustainability. In a rare show of solidarity, representatives from Nestlé, Hershey, Cadbury and Mars met up at a summit in Panama in the spring of 1997. Their conclusions were clear: shade-grown, environmentally sound cacao, though a difficult ideal, offers the best hope for the future. As Allen Young, author of *The Chocolate Tree* and a researcher into sustainable cacao cultivation, told the *New York Times*: 'We've got an organism here that's basically evolved over millions of years in tropical wet forest. Let's test the concept, which is new, of putting the rain forest to work and returning cacao to its natural habitat.' What Young doesn't say is that the idea of growing cacao as an integrated part of the tropical forest ecosystem is actually as old as the pyramids of Izapa. What is true, as he implies, is that a change of attitude on the part of the chocolate establishment is suddenly making those ancient, 'primitive' growing practices seem rather a sophisticated modern idea.

'It's a drug. As soon as I start to read, or listen to music . . . I give myself a shot of cacao within ten minutes,' says Sonia Rykiel, President of those Jedi knights of chocolate, the Club des

Croqueurs de Chocolat. The point being that for centuries chocolate was valued mainly for its medicinal properties, and appears to be recovering something of that role.

The twentieth century has mirrored the obsessions of earlier centuries with chocolate's properties and whether these were to be seen as desirable or unfortunate. Was it fattening *per se*, or could it actually contribute to weight loss? Was it indigestible? Was it an aphrodisiac? Was its effect on the constitution generally positive or negative? As we have seen, these were questions that had been asked ever since the first European contact with *cacahuatl*, but they had never received very satisfactory answers – until the last few decades of the last century, when news began to filter from the laboratories, the scientific journals and the university faculties of nutrition. The fact that a good deal of this research is actually funded by the chocolate multinationals, who then have a licence to crow about how good chocolate is for you, may give us cause to doubt their findings, or then again it may not.

Equally, recent scientific discoveries have tended rather to bolster long-held beliefs about chocolate than to disprove them. The Anonymous Conquistador, who swore by the energy-giving powers of the chocolate drink, might have been amused to read an article in the US magazine *Health* to the effect that a standard milk chocolate bar has eleven times more protein, ten times more calcium, seven times more phosphorus, five times more riboflavin (vitamin B) and eight times more potassium than an apple. Those who believed that chocolate did not cause the user to put on weight – rather the opposite – might find a crumb of comfort in the theory that stearic acid, present in chocolate, is transformed by the body into 'good' unsaturated, rather than 'bad' saturated fat. Katharine Hepburn, whose chocolate brownies are by her own admission 'sensational', was interviewed by *Good Housekeeping* magazine on the occasion of her seventieth birthday. Pointing to her lissom waistline, she declared: 'What you see before you, my friend, is the result of a lifetime of chocolate. A pound a day, often.'

Those historical commentators who found it gave them a feeling of wellbeing – like the great Doctor Stubbes, who believed the 'Indian nectar' to be a cure for 'hypochondrial melancholy' – would certainly feel vindicated by recent research into certain chemicals contained in chocolate, albeit in barely perceptible amounts, which are thought to have an anti-depressant or euphoric effect. One of these chemicals, theobromine, is a close relative of caffeine with a mildly stimulant effect on the nervous system. Another is a substance related to anandamine (from the Sanskrit *ananda*, meaning bliss), a brain chemical which mimics the effects on the brain of smoking hashish or marijuana. A third is phenylethylamine (PEA), believed to increase bodily levels of seratonin and dopamine, the neurotransmitters that make us feel good. If there is any foundation at all in the reputation of chocolate as an aphrodisiac, it may be in PEA that we should look for it. Studies undertaken by two New York parapsychologists, Michael Liebowitz and Donald Klein, have given a sheen of scientific respectability to a phenomenon we have all known about for years. The lovesick women chosen for their study had one remarkable thing in common: they all consumed abnormally large amounts of chocolate. Could this be, they conjectured, because the presence of PEA reproduces in the brain the ecstatic, amphetaminic rush of being in love?

It's a nice thought. The bad news as far as this theory is concerned is that both cheese and salami contain much greater amounts of PEA than chocolate, and you don't catch many lovesick women pigging out on cheese and salami sandwiches. As Jeffrey Steingarten drily remarks: 'There is a growing consensus, I think, that most women eat sweets, and especially chocolate, when they feel blue because this makes them happy . . . Put another way, people crave chocolate because it brings them generous amounts of sensual and aesthetic pleasure. It cheers them up. The secret chemical ingredient in chocolate is chocolate. That's all it is.'

'Eating chocolate helps cut high blood pressure' ran a headline in the *Daily Telegraph*, while chocophiles the length of Britain felt their pulses rise in excitement. Research into the lifestyles of an Indian tribe living on a group of islands off the coast of Panama had revealed that those who remained on the islands suffered much less from high blood pressure than those who emigrated to the mainland. When the research team began to look into the differences in diet between the two groups, they found that the island dwellers drank an average of five cups of chocolate per day, whereas those on the mainland had mostly kicked the habit. The effect on blood pressure is explained by flavonols, a group of chemicals contained in cacao (also in green tea, apples, blueberries, cranberries and red wine) which raise levels of nitric oxide in the body and thus prevent oxidation of the blood cells. An earlier study, sponsored by Mars Inc., had already come to similar conclusions about the importance of flavonols. But just when it seemed the evidence was overwhelming, it was left to the Director of Medical Information of the British Heart Foundation to point out an unpalatable but obvious fact that seemed to have been forgotten. 'Yes, chocolate does contain flavonols, but most chocolate bars contain high doses of sugar and saturated fat which raise cholesterol, cause obesity and lead to heart diseases.'

But of course: the health benefits of chocolate, if there are any, could only come from proper chocolate, made with a high proportion of cacao solids, relatively little sugar and no alien fats. They could hardly accrue from common or garden massproduced milk choc, which has very little of the good stuff and rather a lot of the bad. In all these learned scientific papers, the word 'chocolate' is discussed as if it were all the same thing,

Galaxy, Guanaja, Hershey's and Michel Cluizel's Premier Cru
d'Hacienda La Concepción.

If there is one thing chocophiles are finally beginning to
learn, it is that there is chocolate and there is chocolate. As
Winston and Julia realise in Orwell's *1984*, there is the chocolate we are fed to keep us docile by the powers that be, which
is 'dull brown crumbly stuff that tasted . . . like the smoke of a
rubbish fire', and there is the real thing, 'dark and shiny', rich
and satisfying and more than a little clandestine. This rare and
special food is what Winston and Julia choose to eat – signifi-
cantly enough, bearing in mind chocolate's ancient reputation
as an aphrodisiac – before they tumble into bed.

Down among the swamps of industrial vegelate, something is
stirring. A new generation is learning that chocolate is not
merely flavoured sugar and fat dressed up in the emperor's
new clothes of 'brand values', but a delicacy worthy of the
same respect we habitually give to fine wines.

The revolution began in France, but it is spreading slowly,
like a pool of melted *couverture*, across the chocolate-hungry
Western world. In Britain, thus far, it is has failed to take root
with very much vigour. There are few of the young professional chocolatiers with modern ideas, dedicated and wildly
creative, that I encountered across the Channel. The exception
might conceivably be Gérard Ronay, ex-pupil of Jean-Paul
Hévin, Robert Linxe, Christian Constant, Bernachon in Lyon
and Wittamer in Brussels. Ronay's chocolates may make use of
radically unFrench flavours like gooseberry, fresh mint, tomato
and geranium, but he is still, like it or not, a Frenchman. When
it comes down to it, the best English chocolatier of her generation, despite her French-sounding Christian name, may well be
Chantal Coady of Rococo.

Chantal's chocolate shop is a much-loved south-west London institution. It can be found at the lower end of the King's Road, Chelsea, at the point where the road kinks left in the direction of the river. This neighbourhood, known as World's End, was the solar plexus of pop culture in the late 1970s, and a few vestiges of that maverick spirit still remain. As a child at convent school (chocolate and Catholicism – they go way back) Chantal was denied chocolate, and therefore craved it. When she opened Rococo in 1983, fresh out of Camberwell School of Arts, she had spiky white hair and the punky attitude that says if there's something that needs doing, it might be a good idea just to get on and do it yourself.

What was needed was a wake-up call to British chocophiles, snoozing in lethargic ignorance. In those days there was little demand for bitter chocolate; Bournville plain, with a cacao-mass content of 36 per cent and a sugar content so high that any true chocolate flavour it might have had is simply obliterated, was as far as it went. Fans of the real thing were forced to scour the shelves of expensive delis in search of 'cooking chocolate' – so called because it was considered much too raw and real-tasting actually to be eaten. Belgian brands like Godiva and Léonidas were regarded as the last word in pampered bourgeois luxury. (Chantal describes them witheringly as 'glorified cream cakes'.) Only the ultra-traditional houses of Harrods and Charbonnel & Walker could be relied upon to produce anything like a decent praline or truffle. The rest was high-fat, high-sugar, high-turnover industrial choc.

Chantal rents her shop from a charitable organisation called the Joseph Rowntree Trust, distantly connected to the Quaker philanthropy of the Rowntrees of York. It is the kind of place where you can stand for twenty minutes simply gaping at the displays before coming to any kind of decision about what exactly it is you want. The interior glitters with whimsical decorations in pastel and gold, and mirrors with ornate frames.

The atmosphere is sweet-natured, yet covered with a thin dark coating of English irony.

Stepping inside from the grubby thoroughfare of the King's Road, I stood in the doorway for a moment, savouring the colour and cleanness and calm. In the course of my travels I must have patronised two or three dozen chocolate shops, from the scary-chic boutiques of Paris to the rustic chocolate mills of Mexico. Nothing I had seen so far, however, could quite compare with this dazzlingly original sense of style.

As she greeted me at the counter, I noticed Chantal's hands were cool. Chocolatier's hands, cool and graceful and steady.

'Wanna try a Nipple of Venus?' said Chantal.

It is hardly the kind of offer you receive every day. The Nipple was a hand-dipped truffle tasting of the kind of hyper-concentrated Italian expresso coffee that sits in an oily, steaming puddle at the bottom of your cup, with a roasted coffee bean on top. I ate the whole thing at once, crunching the bean for an extra burst of coffee flavour.

'Wanna see my chocolate kitchen?' Parked on the other side of the road, round the corner from the Bluebird, was the famous Rococo van, a three wheeled roll-top number with a 49cc Piaggio moped engine, its bodywork painted in the same Rococo livery of antique blue and white. We climbed in and set off at a cracking pace, buzzing through the traffic on Beaufort Street, beetling over Battersea Bridge and into the south London hinterland where Chantal has her house and makes her chocolate.

In the kitchen at the back, the Rococo team was hard at work. I stood by a white marble table to watch a demonstration of tempering, the process by which *couverture* is heated and rapidly cooled, giving the finished product a deep mahogany sheen. A cauldron of melted chocolate tipped out on to the table top, rolling out in a thick brown tide until the chill of the marble began to slow its progress.

Pinned to the noticeboard was a piece of paper with the scrawled order: 200 LIPS BY THURSDAY.

'Our Red Hot Chilli Lips; we're famous for them. What with Valentine's Day coming up, we've been deluged with orders,' explained Chantal.

After twenty years in the trade Chantal has observed a general change in the British palate, leading us to demand ever more recondite and exquisite examples of items once regarded as basic staples. It has long since happened with oils and vinegars, coffees and teas. Now, she believes, it may be the turn of chocolate.

'It is really rather wonderful, yes, when you give people to taste a proper black chocolate compared with their usual brand of grotty old milk chocolate and you can see their eyes widen and they say: "Wow, there really is such a difference!"'

I asked her about the chocolate-makers she respects. She mentioned Valrhona – partly out of loyalty, I suspect, since she did a stage at Tain l'Hermitage in the early 1980s and still uses Valrhona *couverture* for most of her creations; Bernachon in Lyon, a family business that still makes a small quantity of its chocolate from scratch, roasting and grinding the beans on the premises; Paul de Bondt, a young Dutchman in Pisa whom she regards as one of the very best; and Joel Durand in St-Rémy, the shooting star of French chocolate, still in his early thirties, but already voted among the top ten chocolatiers in France by no less august an authority than the Club des Croqueurs de Chocolat.

'Durand is a great chocolate-maker. He has these amazing ganaches. To me they're so original, they're practically works of art.' Chantal rummaged on her desk for the notes she took last time she was there. 'Here we are. Yes, there were two that I loved: the *bonbon de chocolat aux olives noires de Baux-de-Provence*, with black olives, and the *bonbon de chocolat au lait à la menthe fraîche*. He infuses the fresh spearmint leaves in cream. Incredible stuff.'

Her own specialities are hand-dipped English-style choco-lates filled with fruit and flower fondants, 'the kind of thing Bertie Wooster might send to one of his belles'; truffles made with fresh cream; and a range of *grand cru* bitter chocolate bars with exotic flavourings. On my trips to London I like to buy up a stack of these bars. Some of Chantal's flavour experiments work better than others, though of course it is partly a matter of taste. Chocolate with Maldon sea salt, for example, is a shotgun marriage that almost holds together but finally ends in divorce. Chocolate with lavender is simply too florally bathroomy for my taste. Cardamom is a brainwave, intertwining sinuously with the chocolate's natural notes of fruit and flowers. And the chilli pepper and black pepper bars are sensational – as you almost imagine they might be, when you remember the Aztec taste for savoury, piquant and flowery *cacahuatl*. Ms Coady is in the avant-garde. But like any good innovator worth her Maldon salt, she also has half an eye on the past. Her genial creations are taking us back to where chocolate came from; back to its ancient roots of bitterness and spice.

Back at the shop, a queue had formed. Time to get busy. I stood at the side of the counter and watched Chantal at work in her chocolatier's white gloves, deftly plucking the chocolates from their display and arranging them in boxes.

A local Chelsea woman in her thirties, thin as a rake, dressed in expensive looking frayed jeans and an embroidered leather jacket, was in the process of making a purchase. In her arms she held one small child, while the other ran riot through the shop.

'I'm just getting in my weekly stash,' she explained to me. 'If I run out halfway through the week it's a disaster. I'll have two of your cardamom bars, Chantal, and two of the basic organic plain. Fred, darling, please don't make so much noise. Freddie! We always get through a box of truffles at the weekend – it's my little treat for my husband, he works like such an idiot. What's in it this time, Chantal?'

'Let's see. This week you've got a selection of cardamom and saffron, passion fruit, pink champagne . . . and a couple of single Islay malt. That OK?'

'Fabulous. Put all that in a bag for me, would you, thanks. Oh yeah, I'll also have a lavender bar. And a bag of olives.'

Olives?

'Chantal sells these lovely little choc drop things that look just like green olives.' She picked up the packet from a pannier on the shelf beside her and dangled it in front of me. 'Cute, huh?'

Chelsea Girl left with a big blue and white carrier bag printed with the same dark blue and white design that covers all Chantal's bars and boxes – a French chocolate-mould catalogue from 1906 with all manner of fancy models from fish to birds to eggs and seashells. There was a notable spring in her step, I thought, as she made her way across the shop and pushed through the door. As she set off along the street, kids in tow, she waved at us gaily through the window. Woman plus chocolate equals happiness.

There were ten big white plates on the kitchen table, the black chocolate shiny, genuinely black, like fragments of jet, against the white. Around the table sat half a dozen tasters, some of them restaurateurs and hotel-keepers, all of them friends.

A chocolate tasting is not the easiest thing in the world to organise. To begin with there is the problem of protocol. In what order, for instance, should you arrange the samples? Unsure of myself, I began with the most apparently basic of the chocolate bars – the ones without stated country of origin, *grand cru* or other designation. When it was already too late, I realised it might have been better to take the palate up the scale of cacao percentages, starting with the lowest and mildest, and ending with the mouth-shrivelling astringency of 100 per cent sugar-free Madagascan black.

I seemed to remember that professional tasters drank a glass of cold water between each sample, to cleanse the mouth. Water and chocolate have always been best buddies: I thought of the *Belle Chocolatière* as painted by Jean-Etienne Liotard, and her tray with the glass of water, a glinting prism. One of my tasters, a veteran of olive oil tastings, wondered whether a piece of white bread (crumb, not crust) might not also do well as a cleansing agent. She was right: the bread seemed to mop up the chocolate flavour like a sponge, leaving the palate squeaky clean and ready for the next candidate.

We sat around the table and sucked and slurped on the irregular shards of black chocolate, trying to allow it to melt naturally in the mouth. There is a particular stealthy rhythm to the way chocolate's flavours unfold and unfurl – a much slower rhythm than that of wine, which explodes on the palate soon after it enters the mouth. Chewing chocolate disrupts the gradual build-up of complexity and its even slower decrescendo, a process which in a really fine bitter chocolate can take five or ten minutes from start to finish.

There were moans of pleasure and surprise: how was it possible that chocolate could harbour so many flavours other than that of chocolate? It seemed ridiculous, but the tasters claimed to find violets, cloves, aromas of cigars and fresh toast.

'Definitely cherries,' muttered one under her breath, pencil working in overdrive.

'This one reminds me of the little *chocolatinas* we used to eat as kids after school,' mused a Spanish girl.

We sank collectively into a silence pregnant with concentration and memory, broken only by the snap of breaking chocolate. Some of us closed our eyes, our minds groping for flavours of the past to match those of the present. A degree of mental effort was required to extract these flavour-traces, since sensory memory is one of the least developed areas of the human brain. But we were not averse to criticism where it was necessary, and the least sign of rancidity, of burnt-ness, or the sort of vaguely cheesy under-taste that reveals the cacao has been allowed to undergo the undesirable lactic fermentation, was noted and frowned on. My tasting sheet was soon flecked with dark-brown chocolate crumbs; flicked away with my finger, they only melted into the paper, which, three months later, still gives off a haunting, autumnal aroma.

My first revelation was the 'Manaus' by the venerable firm of Henriet in Biarritz – part of the notable chocolate diaspora in south-west France. Though made from a *forastero* variety in Brazil, hardly a great source of high quality cacao, it had a fine earthy aroma of tobacco and liquorice with a twist of lemon. Valrhona's Grand Couva, from an old plantation on the island of Trinidad, shot immediately into my all-time top ten. It was tropical, sultry, with a nice edge of acidity and a kind of headiness a little reminiscent of wine. Some of these chocolates were acquaintances from way back when, but it was nice to see them again under different circumstances. I had tasted the *criollo* cacao from the Hacienda La Concepción in Barlovento, outside Caracas, at three different points in its life: as the fresh bean, covered in the sweet white juice of the pulp as I stood in the shadow of the tree that produced it; as the fermented bean, toasting itself in the sun of the concrete drying floor, and as a bar of Michel Cluizel's Premier Cru d'Hacienda La Concepción 2000, while walking the gold-paved streets of the 1st arrondissement. Now that I was tasting the chocolate again in the silence and comfort of my own kitchen, it seemed even better than ever. Even as I cursed my overactive imagination, I could have sworn I was picking up the acid-drop flavours of guava and pineapple and mango and the sweet heavy fragrance of tropical flowers. Closing my eyes again, I relaxed and reminded myself of the four hundred different flavour chemicals inherent in a fine chocolate. Who was to say that the chemical components of mango and pineapple and guava weren't to be found among that number? I took another nibble. Behind my eyelids I saw the Caribbean sea, the murmuring cacao woods and the baskets of fruit on the breakfast tables . . .

When I opened my eyes again we had moved on to the *pralinés*. Pierre Marcolini, the revolutionary of Belgian chocolates, has scaled down the typical Belgian *praliné*, a big bomb of sweet smoothness that is generally tricky to eat, into a discreet, thin, austerely presented shape. His chocolates are neater sized and his ganaches are cleaner flavoured than the Belgian norm, and their fillings flirt with fruits and herbs, flowers and spices. His ganache of thyme and orange, which I remembered from the Salon in Paris, sent me into chocolate ecstasy again with its haunting fragrance of thyme giving way to the subtlest possible suggestion of pungent orange oil.

Beside the work of the great Parisian chocolatiers, even Marcolini lacks sparkle. The final part of the tasting took the form of a homage to a trinity of chocolate masters. First came Michel Chaudun and his passionate experimentation, his total dedication, his brilliant use of orange flower, basil and jasmine. Then followed Robert Linxe of La Maison du Chocolat, known in the trade as 'the jeweller' for the ornate and meticulous design of his creations. These are bonbons which, whatever Ricky Martin may say, it is not at all a good idea to shake. But I had been saving the best for last. It was Jean-Paul Hévin, once again, who sent me on a one-way ticket to chocophile heaven. His *pralinés* were simple: plain squares or rectangles, almost ascetic in their lack of decoration, apart from the occasional single ridge or corner by which to identify the different fillings. They were covered in the thinnest chocolate dipping I had ever seen; it cracked delicately under the teeth. Hévin knows how to incorporate the cool, clear, clean flavours of honey, tea and caramel (light and dark), with such restraint that they do not scream at you, but reach you in a stage whisper across the blackout of bitter chocolate.

They are no bigger than the last knuckle of your little finger. Yet they pack a phenomenal punch. Chocolate this good is proof that the better our food is the less we need of it. Inferior chocolates mark out larger portions to be broken off, their manufacturers apparently conscious of the fact that consumers will need to fill their mouths entirely to obtain anything like the same degree of pleasure.

But what about the effects of ingesting such Pantagruelian quantities of pure black chocolate? As the tasting came to a close, I watched my metabolism like a hawk. There was a sensation of fullness, apparently more psychological than physical in origin. The brain flooded with endorphins, perhaps, until it could take no more? Or simply the palate replete with complex, rich and satisfying flavours, exhausted with the effort of processing them on to the hard disc of the mind?

For an hour or two afterwards I wanted nothing to eat, nothing to drink but water. Then all of a sudden, as night fell, I was attacked by a ferocious hunger. First I wanted bread and red wine. Then I dispatched two big bowls of noodle soup with broccoli, Florence fennel, turnip tops and soy sauce, thin beef steak flash-fried in butter, ripe goats' cheese, more wine. My body craved strongly flavoured, powerfully nutritious food. The craving seemed in some way a rebound from the chocolate, as though the wide sensory horizons opened up by the tasting had now to be filled by an experience of other expansive flavours: savoury, meaty, salty, peppery.

But in the still of the night, long after my solitary banquet was over, I found myself seized by the need for more. Returning to the shattered black leftovers on those big white plates, I sat alone at the kitchen table and replayed some of those wild and sensuous flavours in my mind, before slinking dizzily up to bed again.

ARRIVALS

New Zealand and Catalonia –
Towards a new age

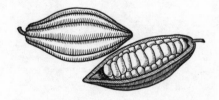

'Everything that man needs for the nourishment of his body and the elevation of his soul is as sacred as himself and should be so regarded.'

(Angelo Pellegrini, *The Unprejudiced Palate*, 1992)

The grapevine is so twentieth century. In our communication-maddened modern world, how we hear about things is through the Internet.

It was late on a Sunday night. I had been at the screen all evening, sifting through the hundreds of choc-related websites in search of appetising trivia. The sites were mostly dreary, drooling, I-love-chocolate rants, poorly written and littered with misspellings. (The World Wide Web has cheerfully abolished the need for such antiquated notions as grammar, spelling, punctuation and capital letters.) I was on the point of switching off and going to bed when up came an address that sounded like somewhere I would like to be: http://www.chocolatetherapy.com.

My mouse raced to the words, and a homepage done up in dark voluptuous colours unfolded in front of me, studded with chocolate shapes you could click on. 'Dare to discover your inner centre! What is your chocolate personality? Find out about yourself; empower yourself through chocolate; it's a life-changing experience. Get centred, know your source; life begins anew, magical transformations take place', burbled a piece of text at the top of the page.

If this was a spoof, it was a devilishly ingenious and thoroughgoing one. The man behind Chocolate Therapy was someone called Murray Langham (Dip. Choc.), 'therapist, counsellor and facilitator'. Through his work in the fields of clinical hypnotherapy and neurolinguistic programming (whatever that might be), together with his immersion in the pre-Christian magical traditions of England, Egypt and Greece, Langham claimed to have developed 'a new way of understanding the self through chocolate as a means for change'. Chocolate Therapy was all about 'healing the body, mind and spirit through liberation. Once self-realisation takes place, it allows you to restore, nourish and rebalance the human psyche.'

It was an ambitious claim. But then chocolate, according to Murray Langham (Dip. Choc.), was much more than a mere food. It was bound up with self-expression, self-esteem, confidence, growth, wisdom, harmony, fulfilment, self-knowledge and other touchstones of the self-help universe. Tapping into its secrets would allow you to 'live your dreams, awaken your spirit, be yourself, discover your hidden talents, unlock your potential, and turn your life around'.

Langham had worked up a series of courses for interested parties, from a one-hour seminar entitled 'You Are What You Love, a Chocolate Indulgence Day' (chocolate buffet lunch included), and the full monty, a two-day residential workshop aimed at 'understanding the chocolate personality'. Whichever you chose, the final aims of this mad melange of secular chocophilia and the mystical mumblings of the New Age remained the same: empowerment, self-realisation and spiritual growth. The guru's role in the process was to help us make the change. Under his guiding hands, we would be transfigured from mere consumers, chomping cow-like on our Dairy Milk, into the higher world of enlightened chocolate beings, serenely conscious of our needs and therefore, Buddha-like, able to control and channel them.

As a theory, chocolate therapy was at the very least intriguing. As a historical phenomenon, I found it gripping. For the ancient Mexicans, as we have seen, cacao and chocolate groaned under the weight of their metaphysical overtones. Yet after the Conquest they largely shed their religious significance, and for the last half-millennium chocolate has been a secular, not a spiritual substance. Ever since my visit to the Playroom, the New Age naming session and Celia's revelations about the ritual use of Flake bars among housewives in their kitchens, however, a question had been nagging me. Was it possible that a change might be under way – a change that was also a historical harking back? Unlikely though it might seem, were we witnessing a revival of interest in the spiritual possibilities of chocolate? And was Chocolate Therapy, with all its baggage of New Age mumbo-jumbo, another piece of proof?

The following morning I hurried to the British Library, the po-mo cathedral of academe on Euston Road. This time, for once, I wouldn't be looking for crispy-paged eighteenth-century medical treatises, nor for agronomical studies of the effect of witches' broom disease on the economy of the Ilhéus region of Brazil. The opus I was after this time was *Chocolate Therapy: Change Your Chocolate, Change Your Life*, by Murray Langham (Dip. Choc.). I filled in an order form and handed it in at the desk, my face betraying a mild flush of embarrassment. There were giggles among the library staff.

It turned out to be a small floppy paperback, not the ponderous tome its title seemed to suggest. I devoured it in minutes. It was nonsense, really, I told myself. Yet more than once its observations came uncannily close to a kind of truth. The author's distinction between a fondness for milk chocolate, on the one hand, and plain on the other, satisfyingly mirrored my own ruminations on the subject of chocolate, nostalgia and human development. As a lover of milk, believed Langham, 'you like to live in the past emotionally; to love that sweet, smooth feeling that is the pure essence of childhood. You're remembering past happiness, a time when things were simple and straightforward.' He might have been talking about my own relationship with Lindt and the brand's nostalgic evocation of summer days in my grandmother's garden. The lover of black chocolate, on the other hand, was 'a connoisseur of the fine things in life, you know what you're talking about and you're a specialist in your field. This can make you dictatorial in your dealings with others. People have to fit into your idea of living, otherwise you'll have no time for them.' Perhaps this was the consequence of my own chocolate self-realisation, I thought wryly: a snobbish intolerance of popular tastes.

But these were just the broad brush-strokes of a much grander theory. The guru attaches meaning to every detail of chocolate use; nothing escapes his piercing vision. The shapes of the chocolates in the box, for instance: each has its secret meaning. ('Circle: I see. Oval: I feel. Square: I build. Rectangle: I think.') And each of the fillings within, though veiled from our view by its robe of chocolate, has something to tell us about our own hidden centres.

> Ginger: You're one of the world's achievers
> Honeycomb crunch: You're a person who isn't afraid to try something new
> Hazelnut: You're a person who works with the wisdom of Mother Earth
> Orange: You're excellent in emergency situations
> Turkish Delight: You're a person on a spiritual quest.

For a person who lives in the northern hemisphere, there is one big problem with Murray Langham (Dip. Choc.). He lives in New Zealand.

Much though I would love to see the land of Kiri Te Kanawa, green-lipped mussels and *The Piano* for myself, a 12,000-mile plane trip was not on my agenda. A 12,000-mile phone call, however, was a different matter. It was nearly midnight here, it would be midday there. Reading the number off the website, I picked up the handset and dialled.

The phone rang with that comfortingly British double ring. Brr brrrrr. Brr brrrrr. I might as well have been calling New Malden as New Zealand, until the chocolate guru answered in a bright squeaky Kiwi accent,

'Hi there, Murray here.'

In my mind's eye I had built up a picture of a charismatic, slightly crazed figure with penetrating guru eyes and lots of wild grey hair. As he spoke, I rapidly redrew my mental images. Take away the aura of echo that surrounded his voice, and Murray sounded like an amiable, normal sort of guy. He sounded like a nice bloke.

'I'm an hour outside Wellington, in a little pretty village. Wellingtonians tend to have their weekend houses here. There are quite a few nice boutique wineries around – mostly heavy reds, some stickies,' he said by way of setting the scene.

'I'm really a chef by trade. Started as an apprentice, working mainly on the baking side. Centrepieces, that sort of thing. I worked in London for a while. I worked at Harrods, Claridges. The therapy bit came later. As my interest in people developed, I started studying. Parallel to that, I started working as a counsellor.'

His road to Damascus came one New Year's Eve, after a few drinks. He and some friends and their children were staying in a beach house at Keri Keri, in a wild coastal landscape of cliffs and sands and great white tumbling waves.

'There were ten or twelve of us up there. After dinner the box of chocolates came out, and the kids started talking about the ones they wanted. And we started fooling around with this crazy idea. What if the kind of chocolate you choose reflects something about you as a person? As time went on, I could see there was something in it. I started saying to clients at the end of a session, "Now, humour me. What's your favourite chocolate

centre?" and working with the responses. I started to see that
people's choices could be defined into a whole load of arche-
types. Like, I know for sure I'm a strawberry person. That means
I really need to be wanted – and in fact I can tell you I'm a
really nice person. Just a little misunderstood.'

The fruit of Langham's early researches was the book I had
devoured in the British Library. Since then there had been a
sequel. His second book, *Hot Chocolate: Unwrap the Flavour of
Your Relationships*, was to his specialist subject what Linda
Goodman's *Love Signs* had been, in its day, to the arts of popular astrology. It was a self-help guide with a difference, a
vision of your love life seen through the gooey prism of
chocolate.

'I've been getting into the Kabbala. All those alchemical
areas, the whole mystical side of things in Europe,' he said. 'I've
been looking into all the old herbals, the old wives' tales,
Culpeper, collecting all the information, thinking about the
power of plants. I've come up with some amazing stuff. The
book's all about how you are in a romantic situation. If you are
an almond person, and your partner is a strawberry person,
how do you get on? Who knows – maybe you'd be happier with
a caramel person? Or maybe there's actually a marshmallow
person inside you struggling to get out?'

Chocolate Therapy is coming soon to a town near you.
But before that, it is going to a village a very long way from
you. Langham's latest project is a chocolate shop in
Greytown, outside Wellington. The location he's got his eye
on is an old house that has been a confectionery shop once
before, in the late nineteenth century. 'It'll be completely
different from any other chocolate shop you've ever seen.
There'll be jewellery, cacao beans dipped in gold and chocolate mandalas on the walls, and cushions reflecting the
themes of the books. We'll have twenty-six chocolate
flavours, and they'll all tie in. We won't be selling the usual

commercial stuff. It's more about letting people get their hands on some really good chocolate.'

This last detail sounds especially promising, for New Zealand is still a little bit starved of really good chocolate. Thanks to the British colonial legacy, Cadbury's milk choc still has the lion's share of the local market. While New Zealand cuisine has leapt ahead into all sorts of pan-Pacific sophistications, there is not much sign so far of a boom in fine Kiwi-made chocolate, nor in the culture of its appreciation.

But the god Ek Chuah moves in mysterious ways, and Murray Langham (Dip. Choc.) believes that the times they are a-changing and the answer is blowing in the chocolate-scented wind. More and more of us are turning on, tuning in and pigging out – but not on the blandly artificial sugar candy the confectionery breadheads want to stuff us with. If there is a true spiritual chocolate to be had, he believes, it is unlikely to be the modern milky factory stuff, but something closer to the bitter black balsam of the ancients, charged with primeval mystery and magic.

'I've seen kids of twelve and thirteen in sweet shops, asking for chocolate with more cacao in it,' he said excitedly. 'People are starting to want real chocolate. They're wanting something more fulfilling. To me the mysticism has been there from the start, but it's on the way back. Call it the subconscious, call it the universal consciousness, call it what you like. I call it the spirit of chocolate, bringing us back to the true path.'

It was an unexpected turn of events, this peculiar amalgam of hardcore gastronomic values and soft-centred spirituality. I put the phone down with a feeling that, strange as it was, I hadn't quite heard the last of it.

And a few weeks later I knew I was right. It was official: after five centuries of separation, chocolate and spirituality were getting back together.

I had come to Barcelona for a long weekend, a soul-soothing present to myself after eighteen long months of travel, talking and eating. Over this year and a half my intake of chocolate had initially soared, only to plummet as I became ever more fastidious and snooty in my tastes, and right now my appetite for the stuff was at an all-time low. I guessed there was decent chocolate to be had in Barcelona, but I had promised myself not to bother with it this time. For a day or two I would put chocolate culture on the back burner, where it could bubble away for a while undisturbed, and take in a bit of ordinary culture instead, like normal people do. I would do the Gaudí trail, and eat paella on the beach.

Chocolate is one of those subjects that, once they have stuck to your life for a while, can prove hard to unstick.

Spring sunshine flooded the city, picking out the yellow in the Catalan flag and the saffron in my paella. After lunch I lost myself in the dark stone canyons of the Gothic quarter, thinking of Picasso and the friendly floozies that unknowingly ignited an artistic revolution. Momentarily free of its sticky obsession, my spirit soared. I was on holiday.

But not for long. In the shadow of the basilica of Santa María del Pi was the kind of scene apparently made to measure for the tourist from some grey and unromantic northern clime. An artisan market had been set up in the pocket-sized square beside the church, with neat awnings that flapped in the breeze. There were stalls selling honey, cheeses, olives, jams, bottled sauces, beeswax candles . . . and there was a stall selling chocolate. I saw truffles and chocolate drops and chunky chocolate bars neatly wrapped in plain brown paper, with a simple design of a cacao tree with pods hanging heavily from its trunk.

A large photograph propped up on the stall showed a village of scarcely believable picturesqueness: a cluster of stone houses on a hill, the spaces between them filled with a froth of spring greenery. The village was the only one in a remote valley in the foothills of the Pyrenees. It had been abandoned since the Civil War, said the woman behind the counter, who had lived there since the early 1980s with a succession of friends and fellow travellers. Three or four of the village houses were now restored, and she had also set up a small modern workshop, which was where her chocolate was made. The brand name, La Vall d'Or, referred to the valley around the village. It was planted entirely with rye, said the woman, and come summer, when the grain was fully ripe and in its splendour, the valley seemed to glow with the colour and warmth of gold.

She was a tiny woman with a serious face, darker in tone than is usual in a Spaniard, and somehow broader: a Latin American face, I would have said. She wore no make-up.

I had been standing at the stall for a while when she darted out from behind it, took my arm and steered me away towards a quiet corner of the square.

'There are things I need to tell you. Things I can't talk openly about. There are things I know that nobody else knows,' she said in a near-whisper. 'But you must come to the village. It is a very quiet place. There we can talk. You'll find it's perfect if you need to read, write, think . . . You can stay as long as you like. Will you come?' She pulled at my sleeve, a five-foot female Ancient Mariner.

There was something alarming about her urgency, not to mention the secrecy she seemed to believe the matter required. I wondered what 'things' she might have to tell me, and why on earth it was to me that she felt obliged to tell them. I said I couldn't be sure when I'd come, but that I hoped it would be soon. And now, thanks very much, but I had to be going.

I was faintly relieved to be free of her presence, but for the rest of that Sunday that woman was on my mind. I couldn't stop thinking about her enigmatic whispered message, and the abandoned village with the chocolate factory in the middle of a golden valley in the Pyrenees. On Monday afternoon, curiosity finally got the better of me. I was waiting for the airport bus in the Plaça de Catalunya when something clicked inside my head. Without thinking very clearly what I was doing, I left the bus stop, crossed the square, took the escalator down to the regional railway station and got on the train instead.

She picked me up from Calaf in her car and we hurtled north towards the village, climbing the sinuous length of the golden valley. She drove without her seatbelt on, straying all over the narrow country road, the conversation leaping from cacao to shamanism to the chocolate industry to her business plans for La Vall d'Or. Disparate subjects, you might think, but they turned out to be all part and parcel of her particular version of the world.

If Antonieta talked, drove and behaved in a turbulent manner, it was, perhaps, only a reflection of her turbulent life.

She was born in Santiago, Chile, and spent her formative years as an avant-garde artist during that *belle époque*, the regime of Salvador Allende. At the heart of her philosophy are two interrelated elements: the origins of cacao among the indigenous peoples of America, and the spiritual wisdom of these peoples. Long before chocolate became part of her life's equation, she knew about cacao. She had seen it in the market-places of Bolivia, Mexico, Colombia and Ecuador, and tasted the drinks the women made from it and the rough, grainy chocolate pastes they ground on their stone *metates*. While she enjoyed the authentic flavour of those rustic products, she felt sure there was something else above and beyond the taste, a primitive force in the raw materials that hadn't been refined out of existence.

She scuttled around in the dark of her house, looking for twelve-volt light bulbs. When she found one, we groped our way up to the kitchen. There was no one else in the village but herself and a Mexican guy who helped her with the practical side of life, which was clearly not her forte. The house was a bohemian mess, clothes draped over the backs of chairs, trestle tables littered with papers scribbled and painted on, clay pots in various stages of completion. Antonieta told me she saw connections between clay and cacao: both were dark brown, malleable masses. Both were powerful presences, firmly anchored to the life-force.

She had been fasting for a week, taking nothing but fruit juice. Perhaps that explained the chaotic, propulsive energy with which she dashed about the kitchen, fixing my dinner. The tiny hurricane finally came to rest for a moment, sitting on a high-backed chair to watch me eat. In her reading glasses, with her hair in a rubber-band bunch from which a few strands escaped to hang down beside each ear, wearing three layers of sloppy sweatshirts, she could have been a radical academic left over from 1968. Her stomach burbled audibly in the silence of the room.

While I ate my supper of wild rice with wild spinach, she began to tell me things.

'OK, you could say I believe in the magical powers of cacao as a plant and chocolate as a substance. Of course the taste is important. But the power goes beyond the palate. Cacao is concentrated energy. Why do you think in a nice restaurant they give you a big plate with just a little food on it, and that little bit of food is enough to satisfy your hunger? Because the food has a concentrated force that goes beyond the material world.

'My chocolate is refined as little as possible. It is more like the chocolate of the indigenous peoples. Because the strength of cacao is preserved through the lack of refinement. What the industry does is remove that strength. The taste and power of cacao is being standardised and weakened, just like with white bread, white sugar and white rice. Food that is really alive does not come from factories. The energy of food manifests itself at the highest level when the food is produced with respect, good taste, expression and love. Which is what I try to do.'

She grabbed a candle, ran down to the workshop and brought back, breathless, a bar of her plain chocolate in its plain brown wrapper.

She broke off a square and handed it to me reverently. I was about to take a bite when she held up a hand.

'Wait. You don't need to taste to feel the power of cacao. Smell it first. Can you feel it here?' She placed an index finger on the bridge of her nose, breathing in deeply.

'It is like a wine; the aroma tells you – yes, this is a good wine. Then, and only then, do you taste with the mouth.'

Given the go-ahead, I took my bite. It was very bitter, rich and densely flavoured. But it was also rough-textured, chewy and granular – a kind of wholefood chocolate, by analogy with wholemeal bread and brown rice. It didn't just melt in the mouth: like the chocolates I had made myself in the cacao lands of Mexico and Venezuela, it had to be worked at energetically with the teeth. It was a proper South American chocolate, only without the overdose of sugar.

Yet the nature of the product was, for its creator, only the surface marker of a much deeper seam of possibilities. The business of chocolate, for Antonieta, was really about the human connection with cacao.

'I don't even like chocolate much. Chocolate for me is a load of nonsense,' she said scornfully. 'Chocolate was invented for royalty, for monks and nuns. Cacao is the true royalty. Cacao is a prince and a wise man. I respect it absolutely. But you see, I owe a great debt to cacao. It was the power of cacao, more than anything, that brought me out of the valley of death.'

Some years earlier, while she was crossing a river bed one rainy night, a flash flood had come rushing down the valley in the darkness. The flood had caught the car in mid-crossing and swept it downstream.

'My two children were drowned. I myself nearly died, but somehow survived,' she said simply.

There was nothing I could say. There was nothing I could do but listen.

'Of course, I was destroyed. I went to Chile for a while, then I came back. What I needed then was a physical outlet for my energies. Part of my mental cure was to do something physical with my hands. I remembered the women in those markets in South America, and I began to make chocolate. There was still no electricity in the village. I worked by candlelight, in silence. I ordered the cacao beans from Ecuador and ground them up in here. I sold the products in the markets in Barcelona. Little by little, I saw the light again.'

While she slowly recovered from her agony of grief, Antonieta became interested in shamanism and the religions of the tribal peoples of the Americas. Always attuned to the ways of the New Age, she now began to attend meetings of the Santo Daime, a Brazilian spiritual movement syncretising Catholic christianity and the shamanic rituals of the Amazon tribes. Under the influence of a hallucinogenic potion made from pounded forest vines, she entered into regular communication with beings she calls the Master Cultivators of Cacao. And it's at this point that the serious mysticism kicks in.

'One time, after taking the ritual drink, I seemed to be sitting with an old man on a train. As the train moved along, he offered me a handful of toasted cacao beans. Seeing him begin to chew them slowly, I did the same. The aroma, the taste, the bitterness of this food, sanctified by the gods of Nature, took me back to the pure origin of the earth and its fruits. That was the moment I realised what my work was to be.

'With cacao I was able to navigate my life again. Cacao taught me to see my reality as I had never seen it before. It gave me the strength to keep on walking in the tunnels of suffering. The Master Cultivators helped me. They told me: cacao is a prince that lives in the aroma. All the properties of the tropical forest are condensed in its seeds. The prince lives in a glass palace in the middle of the wood. The territory of his principality is covered with a golden, humid mist. It is hard to reach the lands of the prince. But the Master Cultivators will show you the way. They can teach you, if your heart is open to their teachings.'

She shifted in her chair, taking a sip of mango nectar.

'What is cacao? It is a sacred seed. It is generosity and abundance. There is so much energy in it – just eating four beans every day is nourishment enough. I want to walk the Way of Saint James eating nothing but cacao. As well as a food, it's a medicine. It increases your mental capacity, cleans the heart, activates the blood. There have been sick people working in my workshop, and I've seen with my own eyes how the aroma has given them new strength. Now is the moment in which cacao presents itself to us in all its manifestations. This is the cacao time.'

We sat in a sudden silence. There was, still, nothing I could say. My brain ached, my stomach too. I am not sure which was proving harder to digest – the mystical revelations of Antonieta, or my wild rice and spinach supper.

I fell asleep on an old mattress in front of the fire. When I awoke, late on Tuesday morning, my hostess had disappeared. There was a note on the kitchen table: she had forgotten to tell me, but she had business in Barcelona. She was opening a shop in the Gothic quarter – a chocolate shop like no other in the world, with the possible exception of Murray Langham (Dip. Choc.)'s future emporium in Greytown. There would be workshops and readings and consciousness-raising sessions: more than a chocolate shop, it would be a kind of cultural centre for cacao. But there was a great deal to do, and she would be gone for three days.

I spent those three days on my own, immersed in a solitude deeper and more complete than I had ever known. For three days I was not only the single inhabitant of the village, but the only human being for the whole length and breadth of the valley. The silence around me was as deep, dark and all-enveloping as a black velvet cloak. I had forgotten what it was like to live without human noise, without traffic, without telephones, television, radio and computers. There were no clocks in the house, and I never knew what time it was: the days panned out into the four primeval building blocks of morning, afternoon, evening and night.

Left to my own devices, I did what anyone would do in my situation. I snooped about the house, reading everything I could lay my hands on, noting, sketching and pondering the imponderable nature of destiny. I flicked through books on Sufism, the Bach Flower Remedies, and the art of chocolate cake-making. In the fridge were unexpected things to find in a bohemian kitchen in a deserted village: twenty litres of thick cream, several enormous packs of good French butter and two bottles of champagne. (For the truffles, I supposed.)

The house was full of examples of Antonieta's art and craft, scattered over the floor and walls. Scribbled drawings of cacao pods with figures emerging from them, as if from wombs, or superimposed on them in radiantly coloured gowns; clay figures of a woman with her hands raised to heaven, perched upon a cacao pod. On her desk in a simple office space, among the mementos of Chiapas, the brochures for shamanic rituals in country houses in various parts of Spain, was a photo of a woman in white Zapotec Indian costume whipping up a bowl of foaming chocolate.

Sitting there at the desk, I read through the Vall d'Or business plans, which were certainly unusual examples of their genre.

'We do not give priority to the economic side. Ours is a

social labour and an act of solidarity, a process of apprenticeship and of personal growth. A Mexican proverb says: Souls do not accept our money, they only use cacao beans to make their purchases.'

Antonieta seemed to reject anything to do with business acumen or financial muscle. Against the brutal pragmatism of her industrial competitors, her lack of financial ambition would be a powerful weapon. Her thoughts about chocolate enacted a wished return to its cultural and social roots. Her ideal was a kind of post-industrialism, predicated on a return to the notion of craft, the importance of barter and the prevalence of spiritual over material profit. It went against every rule in the business book – but by opting out of the race, she seemed even more likely to win it.

Until now, such is the nature of the industry and the mechanics of supply, she had been buying her raw materials from a Dutch cacao grinder. The blend she used, a mix of Ghanaian and Ecuadorean beans, was a good one, but, tainted with corporate bad karma, it wasn't good enough for her. She wrote of wanting to deal directly with indigenous producers in South America, and appeared to have several candidates in mind. One was a landowner in the town of Ceu do Mapia, in the Amazon jungles of Brazil – cradle of *Theobroma cacao* in its pre-cultivated state. Another was in Tapachula, Chiapas, mother of all cacao plantations, where I once stood in the steam-room of the tropical forest and played with hummingbirds.

When I had finished with the house, I roamed around the village. On the hilltop was a Romanesque church with a small square tower. Across the little main street from Antonieta's doorway was the deserted chocolate workshop – carefully known as the *obrador*, to distinguish it from evil factories, but a factory in all but name. On the door was a portrait of the Buddha. I pushed inside and tiptoed among the silent machinery, breathing the pungent smell that permeated everything. It was the fulfilment of a childhood dream, I reminded myself, to be left alone in a chocolate factory; to peer into the enrobing machine – now clogged up inside with solidified melted chocolate; to caress the piles of wrapped bars, to break one open, eat a piece . . . On a shelf in the storeroom were the Cellophane bags of cacao beans Antonieta sells to be eaten raw, each bag with its list of eccentric serving suggestions: 'Begin to walk when the moon begins to grow and stop when the moon is full. Walk in the mountains, eating only cacao beans, drinking only water.'

I took a bag and opened it and crunched a bean in my mouth. It was so horribly astringent it was impossible to swallow. Anything that tasted so vile must surely be doing my spirit some good. It is easy to smile at Antonieta's solemnity where cacao is concerned, and at her furious rejection of corporate values. Yet if there is one clear conclusion to be drawn from the history of chocolate, it's that we have progressively trivialised a substance that deserves to be taken just a little bit more seriously. As a food, chocolate has never been more debased. All this woman is doing, in her passionate and radical way, is to ratchet up its value on the stock market of our souls. If we can never re-establish the ancient sanctities, and if the mystical intensity of New Age chocophilia seems a hard act to follow, a little more respect for a princely plant and a noble product surely might not go amiss.

On the morning of the third day I woke up with a headache and a feeling that I'd overdone it on the silence and solitude. There was still no sign of my hostess and the empty house and village were giving me the creeps. I had things to do in London, people to see, and a plane ticket in my pocket that was probably worthless. The time had come to get out while the going was good and the spring sun still sparkled on the mountains like a scene from some Swiss chocolate wrapper.

I left another note on the kitchen table:

A. Thanks for the chocolate! Hope it all goes well. Love P.

I was conscious as I wrote, scribbling in my keenness to be gone, that I was bidding a bittersweet farewell not just to one woman, but to one of the stranger chapters of my life. I hitched up my backpack, grabbed a few bars from the deserted factory and walked through the waist-high rye to the end of the golden valley.

INDEX